THE BOND
BIBLE

MARILYN COHEN
WITH NICK WATSON

NEW YORK INSTITUTE OF FINANCE

NEW YORK • TORONTO • SYDNEY • TOKYO • SINGAPORE

NEW YORK INSTITUTE OF FINANCE
NYIF and NEW YORK INSTITUTE OF FINANCE are trademarks of
Executive Tax Reports, Inc. used under license by Penguin Putnam Inc.

Library of Congress Cataloging-in-Publication Data

Cohen, Marilyn.
    The bond bible / Marilyn Cohen with Nick Watson.
        p.   cm.
    Includes index.
    ISBN 0-7352-0138-2 (cloth)
    1. Bonds.   I. Watson, Nick.   II. Title.
 HG4651.C692 2000
 332.63'23—dc21   00-026406

Aquisitions Editor: *Ellen Schneid Coleman*
Production Editor: *Sharon L. Gonzalez*
Formatting/Interior Design: *Robyn Beckerman*

Printed in the United States of America

10   9   8   7   6   5

To Chris, my honey bun

Thanks for your encouragement.
Your support is constant as the northern star.

FOREWORD

Visit your nearest bookstore or log on to Amazon.com, and you're likely to be overwhelmed by the dozens of books about stock market investing—and more recently, day trading. But you'll have to look a lot harder to find useful and informative books about investing in the bond market.

That's because the world of bonds has always been remote for a lot of would-be fixed-income investors. Indeed, just try and find out at what price a bond is trading. Unlike stocks, bonds don't have a central exchange or required reporting of bids and offers. So fixed-income investors, big and small, don't know how much dealers are marking up bonds. As a result, they don't know whether they are getting a good price. More often than not, they aren't.

Now there is help. In *The Bond Bible*, Marilyn Cohen finally lifts the veil that has long shrouded the clubby fixed-income world. Cohen succinctly explains all you need to know to be a savvy consumer and a successful bond investor. Most individuals think that they should have bonds in their portfolio, but don't know anything about how to buy them. Consequently, they are sold bonds in the all-too-well-known hard sell. This book puts you in control and teaches you how to buy bonds so that they aren't pushed down your throat.

But make no mistake. This book is not a primer. It's easy enough to learn the A-B-C's of investing in the bond market by logging onto the

Internet and visiting a plethora of fixed income web sites such as The
Bond Market Association's www.investinginbonds.com.

The Bond Bible is for the retail investor who not only wants to take
a more active role in managing his or her portfolio, but also already
knows the investing basics. It's for the baby boomer who has made a lot
of money in the Great Bull Market of the 1990s but thinks it's time to buy
bonds to defend his portfolio against a possible stock market decline. It's
for the retiree who is tired of paying fat broker fees and has decided to
manage her own bond portfolio. And it's for the young investor who
knows enough to invest in bonds to reduce the overall volatility of his
portfolio.

What kinds of information will you learn? For example, most
investors know that Treasury securities are the safest bonds you can buy.
But how many people know that if you want to get extra yield without
additional risk, then you should invest in off-the-run, or older, Treasury
bonds?

Or say you want to finance a large Treasury purchase of $100,000
or more using the repurchase, or repo, market. Cohen lets retail investors
in on several bond broker secrets. How many individual investors know
that you can tell a brokerage firm that you want the repo rate, not the more
expensive broker loan rate that individual investors are usually stuck
with? With that piece of advice, Cohen helps you save between one and
three percentage points on your loan. That's big money.

Another money-saving gem: The bond buyer will learn to ignore the
often-reported current yield, and ask for the yield to worst call. Cohen
recommends focusing on the yield to worst call for callable bonds and
only look at the yield to maturity when you're considering noncallable
bonds.

It is these and other nuggets of knowledge that make *The Bond Bible*
a valuable read and a real service to the retail bond investor. As *Business
Week* magazine's bond reporter, I've had the good fortune of meeting up
with Marilyn Cohen at fixed-income investment conferences through
the years. Without a doubt, she is usually the most dynamic person in the
room. Reading this book is like sitting down and having a cup of coffee

with Marilyn while she tells you what you need to know to wisely invest in bonds.

Perhaps most astonishing is Cohen's ability to make the bond market come alive. She does this by her down-to-earth conversational tone, as well as her informative, often funny, personal stories about toughing it out in the trenches of the bond market for the last 20 years. Now you, as a reader, can join in.

Toddi Gutner
New York City
December 1999

CONTENTS

CHAPTER 6

CHAPTER 7

CHAPTER 8

CHAPTER 9

CHAPTER 10

WHY BONDS?

Bond: A duty, a promise or other obligation by which one is bound
(The American Heritage Dictionary)

The definition of a bond given above is serious and solemn, and it is tempting to regard buying bonds as a dull and stodgy exercise that your grandfather favored as a means of investing his money. This seems especially true today when one considers the stories about those high-flying Internet stocks that incessantly crop up on television and fill the columns in newspapers and magazines.

The idea that bonds provide precious little return in exchange for safety is disputable. It's true that each day brings news of the stock markets in the United States reaching ever more outrageous heights and creating paper millionaires by the thousands. And with the Standard & Poor's 500 index of stocks giving stupendous returns, one might well question the wisdom of putting money in securities that offer lower returns for the sake of safety.

Yet from 1981, we have seen an unprecedented bull run in the U.S. bond market. If in 1981, one had invested in U.S Treasury securities, which were considered the safest bet for an investor, the return on a 25-year Treasury bond would be a whopping 11.21%. Indeed in 1998 alone, the 10-year Treasury note returned in excess of 14%, which is not bad for a "stodgy" investment. These kinds of returns are possible because not only will an investor receive regular coupon payments, but as interest rates decline, the prices of investment-grade bonds (those rated above BBB- by the rating agencies) rise, thereby creating capital gains.

You may also think that bonds are boring. Well, consider the fact that it was overzealous and overleveraged bond trading that bankrupted Orange County and more recently pushed the Long-Term Capital Management hedge fund to the precipice of oblivion.

It is understandable that many people have become obsessed with shares. A multitude of television programs, magazines, news services, and websites devoted to the financial markets and especially the stock markets have sprung up over the past few years.

Furthermore, the bond market seems complicated, an arcane world inhabited by smug, sanctimonious, sharply dressed men, who bandy around words like *defeasance, amortization,* and *collaterized mortgage obligation (CMO).*

Finally, the bond market until recently was opaque to the individual investor, with bonds relatively difficult to buy compared to purchasing stocks. Even if you did go out and buy a bond, you often didn't even know the specifics, which, let's face it, isn't any real way to invest.

TIMES THEY ARE A'CHANGING

The chairman of the Securities and Exchange Commission (SEC), Arthur Levitt, has griped about the bond market's unfairness, and while he himself hasn't done much about it, the marketplace finally has. As I will explain in Chapter 8, individuals can buy bonds at competitive prices over the Internet, and these are the best deals I have ever seen for individual investors.

This begs the question: Should you then put all your money in bonds? No. Bonds are not a stock market surrogate, but a separate asset class, whose characteristics are to provide *yin* when your stocks are in a state of *yang*.

Bonds offer a number of advantages over stocks. They provide a predictable income stream while the return from stocks—although perhaps spectacular over the very long term—can be low or even negative for considerable periods of time. Indeed, stocks went sideways for 16 years between 1966 and 1982, often hitting the 1,000 level of the Dow Jones Industrial Average but never penetrating it, and even dropping way below it.

Bonds also balance your portfolio when the financial world gets out of whack and they are good for meeting large, anticipated long-term expenses such as college fees and weddings. What happened to college funds invested in stocks in the late 1960s for kids expecting to enter college in the late 1970s? Well, it wasn't a pretty sight.

HOW MUCH IN BONDS?

Knowledgeable investors are usually those who allocate their money wisely. You should constantly maintain a certain percentage of bonds in your portfolio, with that percentage depending on your age, risk tolerance, and time horizon until retirement.

One simple way to decide how much of your money should be in bonds is this: The older you are, the closer that percentage of bonds should match your age. If you are 50 years old, then an allocation of 50% bonds and 50% stocks is perfect. If the rise in the value of your stocks pushes the equity side of your portfolio up to 60%, the disciplined investor will take 10% off the table and buy additional bonds to rebalance the portfolio.

As you can see, the older you get, the greater the allocation of bonds you should buy to reduce your risk, until you reach the ripe old age of 100, at which time you probably shouldn't be taking any risks at all.

DEMYSTIFYING THE MYSTIQUE OF BONDS

The process of investing in bonds is different from that of investing in stocks. Evaluating stocks means reading financial statements. Assessing a bond, on the other hand, requires that you carefully scrutinize the bond offering's prospectus, or "red herring" as it is often called by people in the market.

It's there you will find the covenants, the details that can mean mischief or good news for the bondholder. The fine print can make for hard reading with all those unpronounceable words, whose definitions often just add to the general confusion. So in the subsequent chapters I will endeavor to teach you the words that you will need to understand, and I'll avoid throwing jargon at you.

I will also illustrate many of the ideas about investing in bonds and events that have occurred in the bond market over the years with personal anecdotes from more than two decades I've spent in the business.

BONDS DON'T TRADE
IN A VACUUM

It is important to bear in mind throughout this book that reality has a nasty habit of bucking the conventional wisdom. This is because bonds trade on real events, not in a vacuum.

For example, while municipal bonds are considered some of the safest bonds to invest in, suddenly a large municipal bankruptcy such as Orange County's comes along and lays waste to your ideas of a conservative investment approach. I hope you will keep in mind the examples and experiences I give and use these nuggets to help you make money in the bond market above and beyond merely the income from your coupon payments. And help limit any potential losses.

A BRIEF RUN THROUGH
THE CHAPTERS

In the first chapter, "Basically Bonds," I will discuss the income streams from a bond and how the various risks in the market will affect the value of your bond holdings. I will also introduce the all-important Treasury yield curve, the basic tool that sophisticated buyers of bonds use to determine which bonds present the best purchase.

Since the purchase of bonds is primarily to introduce a measure of stability to your portfolio, the first characteristic to know about a bond is how safe it is. In Chapter 2, "The Safe Sector," I will focus on the four safest types of bonds: U.S. Treasuries, federal agency bonds, investment-grade corporate issues, and municipal (or tax-free) bonds.

Chapter 3, "A Little Sexier: More Risk for More Yield," will delve into the world of high-yield bonds, those that are not investment grade and offer a higher yield in return for taking on more risk. I will explain the pitfalls and potential opportunities in investing in these high-yield, or junk, bonds, and show that investors who are willing to apply themselves a little can thrive successfully in this sector.

Bonds not only offer regular coupon payments, but can also rise in value to generate capital gains. Chapter 4, "The Good—and Bad—Bond Gambles," lays out strategies for the more aggressive bond investor who is seeking capital gains on bonds. This chapter will also discuss how you can buy a lot of bonds by only putting down a little money. This is called leverage and can be done by buying the bonds on margin and in the sophisticated repurchase, or repo, market. I will also target the bonds to avoid, such as CMOs, and explain why.

Chapter 5, "The Rating Agencies: Determining Credit Quality," is a guide to the credit rating agencies and to bond insurance. The first and most important point an investor must understand about bond ratings—the scores the agencies put on bonds to designate the quality of their credit—is that these agencies tend to be reactive, not proactive, in response to the changing creditworthiness of any bond issuer. This chapter will show other methods for keeping an eye on the quality of the bond names you own.

"Bond Funds: Weighing the Pros and Cons," Chapter 6, will examine the pros and cons of investing in bond funds and unit trusts—two excellent ways that individuals can buy bonds. There is certainly a place in this world for bond funds. They are great vehicles for small investors and for those wishing to get a taste of the more exotic emerging markets.

On the other hand, paying management fees to invest in Treasury and government agency funds can be a waste of money and may get in the way of an intelligent bond portfolio program. Everyone in the bond food chain needs to be paid, and this chapter will detail how investors pay for putting a bond fund together and covering its day-to-day operations. It will clarify how to minimize those payments and maximize your returns.

The chapter will also review mutual-fund-distributed versus SEC yields, and tell you what to focus on.

I will also discuss the difference between open-end funds and closed-end funds. Although many investors consider the issue of closed-end funds too complicated and not worth the bother, they can be attractive investment vehicles under certain circumstances.

I will begin Chapter 7, "How to Find a Bond Bargain," by giving guidance on how to determine whether a bond is a good buy and, in particular, if the price being asked for that bond is right for that piece of merchandise. In the bond market, two bonds with the same attributes—maturity, coupon, and credit quality—are compared by their yields and their spreads over Treasury securities. The bond that is yielding the most, all other considerations being equal, is the best buy.

However, calculating the yield may become more complicated when the bond in question has a call date, that is, the issuer has the right to buy back the bond from the holder before the bond matures. In this case, an investor should look at the yield to the worst call, and not *The Wall Street Journal*'s listed bond quote, which gives the current yield, a mathematically simple calculation that doesn't take into account the call features.

Chapter 8, "How to Be a Savvy Bond Shopper," will review what I call "little bond lies," the lies that bond salespeople use to entice buyers. This chapter exposes the obvious fibs and provides tips on how one can poke holes in the less obvious lies. Just as the previous chapter dealt with the information needed to recognize a bond bargain, this one will review the information a buyer needs to know about the different stores. I will also discuss the revolution occurring on the Internet with regard to online bond trading.

Chapter 9 is titled "Oddball Bonds: Getting Creative." Wall Street innovations have reached Main Street. Not content with changing industrial America, the nerds are taking on financial America. The pointy-heads on Wall Street have taken bonds and sliced, diced, and cooked them. New bond inventions are everywhere. There are bonds backed by rock stars' royalty payments; there are bonds with put options, bonds with call options, and putable/callable bonds; there's even a premium on the afterlife with death put bonds. Retail investors need to be aware of the pitfalls of moving into this esoteric world. Some of these bonds have value but others are too illiquid for most investors. However, as more and more of these newfangled products are devised, why let Wall Street have all the fun?

Chapter 10, "Managing Your Bond Portfolio," is one of the most important chapters in the book and gives critical lessons that investors must understand when managing a bond portfolio. Structuring your portfolio means determining allocation by kind and quality as well as putting the right percentage of your assets in bond funds. I will give sample portfolios of different sizes.

THERE'S BEEN NO BETTER TIME TO BUY BONDS

There has been a confluence of events that make bonds a more compelling buy than ever before, and by taking advantage of this chance you can balance your portfolio of investments in a professional way and take some of the risk out of investing.

The bond markets in the U.S. are today more numerous, bigger, and deeper than the bond markets of Japan, Germany, or the United Kingdom. There is more information available on the bond markets than ever before to the retail investor (although not yet on the scale of that for the stock markets), and now the advance of technology is allowing the investor finally to buy bonds with the click of a mouse.

CHAPTER 1

BASICALLY BONDS

Are bonds more complicated to understand than stocks? Yes, it's true to say that they are. However, I would also say that bonds are not as complex as some professionals would have you believe, so with the basic concepts safely under your belt, there's no reason why you can't invest successfully in the bond market.

Each of the securities markets has its very own vocabulary and concepts that you need to be familiar with, so in this chapter I will run through the bond basics.

If you are already familiar with the basics of the bond market, then you can probably skip this chapter. However, if you are not, I advise you to read this chapter very carefully and make sure you understand clearly everything that is written.

First, let's take a look at what a bond actually is.

IOU MONEY

A bond is, at its most basic, an IOU. Instead of a piece of paper on which the IOU is written, bonds have something called an *indenture,* which is a legally binding document that lays out the terms and conditions of the loan.

There is the amount of money that you lend to the issuer of the bond, which is called the *principal.* The principal of the majority of bonds is $1,000. In this way, an institution that borrows $1 million in the bond market will usually issue 1,000 bonds, each of which has a face value of $1,000.

Also included in the indenture is the *coupon,* which is simply the stated interest rate that the borrower promises to pay you. Think of coupons as the annual rate of interest expressed as a percentage of the face value of the bond, and this rate is fixed when the bond is first issued. There are some bonds that have floating coupons, but most make fixed semiannual payments.

Take, for example, the AT&T Corporation bond issue 6% due March 15, 2009. The 6% coupon is paid semiannually on $1,000 face value of each bond. This amounts to $60 per year: $30 paid every March 15 and $30 paid every September 15.

What the level of coupon represents is the *cost of money,* which is the interest rate level that an issuer of debt, whether it's the government or a corporation, must offer investors to borrow their money.

The cost of money changes depending on what is happening in the real world. When money is tight and expensive, interest rates are high and issuers of debt will have to pay this going rate. If, on the other hand, there is a lot of money sloshing around the system and banks are flush with cash, interest rates will be low and issuers of bonds can borrow money fairly cheaply.

The indenture also lays out how long the loan will last. The length of time before the bond expires is called the *maturity.* When the bond expires, whether it's after 10, 15, or 20 years, the borrower must pay back the principal. So if you bought one bond with a face value of $1,000, then that is what you get back when the bond expires.

The maturities of fixed-income securities can be anywhere from under a year to as far out as 100 years. The latter have been dubbed century bonds and are normally the preserve of large pension funds. But for the average investor, a bond of 30 years is probably the longest-maturing security he or she will purchase.

Coupon and principal, that's what a bond is made up of.

A SIMPLE YIELD

The *yield* of a bond is the rate of return that you will receive from investing in the bond. The simplest measurement of yield is the *coupon yield,* which is just the same level as the coupon. If you bought a bond with a coupon of 6.70%, then the coupon yield would be 6.70%.

However, this tells you nothing in reality, because after bonds are issued they don't remain locked away in some cupboard but are traded in what is called the *secondary market.* In this secondary market, the price that a person is willing to pay someone else for a particular bond may be more or less than the principal of the bond. In this way a bond may trade at a *premium* to its face value or at a *discount* to its face value.

As I said, most bonds have a face value of $1,000. Now, people in the bond market may tell you that a particular bond's price is 95. What this means is not that the bond is trading at a price of $95, but that it is trading at $950. If a bond is trading at a premium, the price given to you by a broker may be 105. This means that the $1,000 bond is trading at a price of $1,050. You must always add a zero to the bond level given by the market to end up with the actual price where the bond is trading. Why? Because the bond market is a busy place and people in it like to abbreviate things.

Why do bond prices move up and down? It's because of two major risks that are inherent to bonds: interest rate risk and credit risk.

THE RISKS BONDS FACE

One of the principal determinants of a bond's price in the secondary market is *interest rate risk;* that is, the movement of interest rates will positively or negatively impact the price of a bond in the secondary market depending on which direction interest rates are moving. Interest rates change constantly, therefore bond prices change constantly.

(See sidebar: *Why Is It That Bond Owners Lose Money As Market Interest Rates Rise?*)

WHY IS IT THAT BOND OWNERS LOSE MONEY AS MARKET INTEREST RATES RISE?

Think of a seesaw, with a bond's price on one end and its yield on the other. The two ends always move in opposite directions.

| $1,000 Price | 6.25% Yield |

Take the example of a U.S. Treasury 30-year bond issued in 1993. An investor who bought it new paid $1,000 for a security that will pay 6.25% interest, or $62.50, annually for the next 30 years.

That may seem like a decent enough return at the time. But in the bear market of 1994 interest rates zoomed.

Owners of the older T-bond would still be earning 6.25% and if they held the bond to maturity, they would get their full $1,000 back as well.

But if they tried to sell the bond then, buyers naturally would demand that the yield match the market in 1994.

To accomplish that, the bond's price adjusts to the new yield environment. Instead of $1,000, the market price of the bond was about $782, a 22% price decline from what the original investors paid. When factoring in the added return expected by

One of the easiest ways to understand how the relationship between a bond's price and the level of interest rates works is to imagine a seesaw. On one end of the seesaw is the level of interest rates and on the other is the bond's price. If interest rates go down, bond prices move up, and if interest rates go down, bond prices move up. (See sidebar: *Why Is It That Bond Owners Lose Money As Market Interest Rates Rise?*)

The reason for this is not hard to understand. Say you buy a bond that has a face value of $1,000, has a 10-year maturity, and pays you interest of 5% per year. In two years' time, interest rates have risen and the same issuer of that bond is now issuing similar bonds but with an 8% coupon. If you wanted to sell your bond, nobody except the most foolish investor would give you $1,000 for a bond that only pays a coupon of 5%, when he or she could buy a new bond from the same issuer with an 8% coupon. The result is you have to sell your bond for less than the $1,000, at a price that would mathematically work out to the same yield.

"That means I've lost money!" I hear you cry. Exactly. That's why it's called interest rate risk.

To cut down on interest rate risk, you could buy a bond with a shorter maturity than 10 years, because it is less likely that interest rates will turn against you in, say, 6 months than in 10 years. However, if you do this, the amount of interest you will receive will be less.

So now you can see that the longer the maturity of the bond, the more interest it will pay. This is because your money is being tied up for a longer time and the longer you hold the bond, the more time there is for interest rates to change or for something bad to happen to the issuer of the bond, such as bankruptcy.

reinvesting the bond's annual interest earnings, the true yield—called "yield to maturity"—worked out to be about 8.1%, thereby matching the market.

As the seesaw analogy implies, prices rise and fall according to interest rates.

Interest rates have a major bearing on our lives, affecting the amount of money you have to pay back on your credit cards or on your house. If you hold bonds in your portfolio, then the value of your investment depends greatly on the level of interest rates.

What makes U.S. interest rates go up and down? Primarily, it is the state of the economy and sometimes the state of the world's economy. If the U.S. economy is roaring ahead, there is the risk that inflation will pick up. High inflation is bad for bonds because the Federal Reserve has a duty to keep inflation down, so if inflation starts rising it will have to raise interest rates to cool the economy down.

The Federal Reserve is key to the bond market because it sets targets for interest rates. This is why we are so often treated to having every word uttered by the chairman of the Fed, Mr. Alan Greenspan, dissected by the multitude of journalists trying to decipher his views on interest rates.

This is no easy task. Mr. Greenspan once famously quipped, "Since I've become a central banker, I've learned to mumble with great incoherence. If I seem unduly clear to you, you must have misunderstood what I said." Enough said.

Interest rates will always move inversely to the price of high-quality bonds. This brings us nicely to the second major determinant of a bond's price: *credit risk,* which is the risk that you won't receive the coupon payments and principal in full and on time.

In the stock market, there is a wide range of merchandise available to you at different prices. Buying a share in Microsoft will obviously cost you more than buying a share in Starbucks, because it is expected that Microsoft will make more money selling its software than Starbucks will with double espressos.

In the fixed-income markets, some issuers of bonds are more credit-worthy than others. Therefore, the most expensive and lowest-yielding bonds would be those that have no risk of default. Notwithstanding your personal antipathy toward the federal government, the crème de la crème of debt is that issued by the U.S. Treasury

Once you move down the credit chain to the riskier issuers of bonds, such as small companies just starting out in a new business, you will find that these bonds don't move as inversely to changes in interest rates as bonds from investment-grade companies. The prices of bonds from these riskier entities move much more in relation to the financial wherewithal of the issuing institution, because bad financial news will jeopardize whether the issuer will be able to pay the coupons and principal in a timely manner.

When the situation looks iffy, bond prices will go down no matter what interest rates are doing. On the other hand, if the bond issuer has a windfall or quarterly earnings exceed the market's expectations, then the prices of bonds from the company can move up quite dramatically even if interest rates are also moving up.

The total return of a bond investment includes the coupon coupled with the gains or losses in the bond's price, so let's look at a more accurate measure of determining the yield on your bond investment than the coupon yield.

YIELD TO MATURITY: A MORE MATURE MEASUREMENT

As we said, the simplest yield measurement is the coupon yield, which is set when the bond is first issued. However, this assumes that the price of the bond remains at the original price you bought it, and does not take into account fluctuations in the price of the bond in the secondary market. Because the price of a bond will change depending on the level of interest rates, you must take into account whether a bond is trading above par (at a premium) or less than par (at a discount).

The measure that takes into account the coupon and bond's price is called the *current yield* and is calculated by taking the coupon and dividing that by the market price of the bond. The current yield is often quoted in newspapers and by brokers, but even that is far too narrow and useless a measurement for bond investors because you must still take into account the interest you will receive on your coupon payments during the lifetime of the bond.

If you buy a bond that has a maturity of 30 years and you hold the bond for that length of time, you will receive 60 semiannual coupon payments. When you receive that money you have a choice: Spend it or reinvest it. If you opt for the latter, then you can see that the rate of return from the original bond investment will be more than just the current yield.

The yield measurement that factors in all the possible income and losses from a bond during its lifetime is called the *yield to maturity*.

The yield to maturity measures the total amount of money you will earn from a bond investment assuming you hold it to maturity. It includes the interest payments, the interest gained by reinvesting the coupon payments in an investment with a similar rate of return, and the amount of money earned or lost by the change in the price of the bond from your purchase price.

If you take the yield to maturities of Treasury securities with maturities from 3 months out to 30 years and plot them on a graph with the maturities on the bottom and the yield to maturities on the left, you end up with the all-important *Treasury yield curve*. (See historic interest rate charts that follow.)

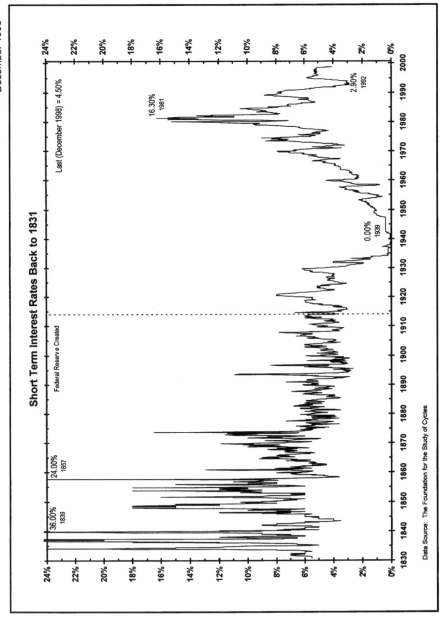

Short Term Interest Rates Back to 1831

December 1998

Last (December 1998) = 4.50%

Federal Reserve Created

36.00%
1839

24.00%
1857

16.30%
1981

0.00%
1939

2.90%
1992

Data Source: The Foundation for the Study of Cycles

Short Term Interest Rates Back to 1831

Highlights

- The yields noted on the chart depict some of the cyclical extremes reached since 1831.

- The highest ever month-end yield was 36% in 1839. The highest month-end yield this century was May 1981 at 16.3%.

- The lowest month-end yield ever was 0.00% in late 1938 and early 1939. In fact, daily data from this period shows several days when yields were actually negative. Furthermore, Ibbottson & Associates calculated the total return of the 1-month Treasury Bill as 0.00% several times during the 1930s and 1940s (see Z-14).

- How can Treasury-Bill rates be negative? It seems impossible by today standards. However, when the economy is perceived to be in a depression, and all prices are going down, the prospect of losing four basis points doesn't look so bad.

- As this chart illustrates, prior to the creation of the Federal Reserve in 1913 (vertical dotted line), short-term interest rates were very volatile. Since then volatility in short-term rates has subsided somewhat.

Some statistics about Short Term Interest Rates (through December, 1998)

Period	Median	Average	Std Dev	+1 Std Dev	-1 Std Dev
Since 1831	5.20%	5.46%	3.59%	9.04%	1.87%
1831 to 1913	5.90%	6.85%	3.67%	10.52%	3.18%
Since 1913	4.00%	4.13%	2.95%	7.08%	1.18%
Since WW II	4.70%	4.83%	3.05%	7.88%	1.77%
Since May 1981	5.70%	6.58%	2.60%	9.18%	3.99%

Data Sources:
The following monthly series have been spliced together:

- 1831 to 1919: six-month commercial paper rates
- 1919 to date: U.S. 3-month Treasury Bills, secondary market average.

This data is available from:
The Foundation For The Study Of Cycles
214 Carnegie Center
Suite 204
Princeton, New Jersey 08540
(610) 995-2120
http://www.cycles.org/~cycles/

For more information see:

- *The History Of Interest Rates, 3rd Ed.* by Sidney Homer & Richard Sylla
- *The Movements of Interest Rates, Bond Yield, and Stock Prices in the United States since 1856* by Frederick R. Macaulay (NBER, 1938)
- The Federal Reserve of St. Louis on the Web at http://www.stls.frb.org/

Chart LTC-2

9

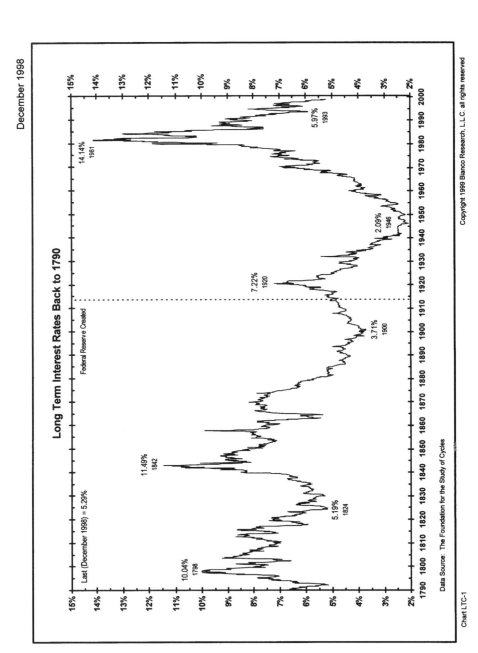

Long Term Interest Rates Back to 1790

Last (December 1998) = 5.29%

Federal Reserve Created

10.04%
1798

5.19%
1824

11.49%
1842

3.71%
1900

7.22%
1920

2.09%
1946

14.14%
1981

5.97%
1993

Data Source: The Foundation for the Study of Cycles

Chart LTC-1

10

Long Term Interest Rates Back to 1790

Highlights

- The yields noted on the chart depict some of the cyclical extremes reached since 1790.

- Long term interest rates, more than any other investment, display a cyclical pattern. That is, their trends often last decades. The shortest trend was a 20 year rise in rates from 1900 to 1920. The longest was a 58 year drop in rates from 1842 to 1900.

- The lowest month-end yield ever was 2.09% in April 1946. The inflation rate, as measured by the year-over-year change in the CPI, was 3.37%. Eleven months later inflation was 19.67% and yields nudged up only 11 basis points to 2.19%.

- The highest month-end yield ever was 14.14% in September 1981. The inflation rate, as measured by the year-over-year change in the CPI, was 10.95%.

- So, it appears that the inflation rate was higher when interest rates were near their all-time lows than when they were near their all-time highs. See chart Z-4 for more details.

Some statistics about Long Term Interest Rates (through December, 1998)

Period	Median	Average	Std Dev	+1 Std Dev	-1 Std Dev
Since 1790	6.01%	6.08%	2.10%	8.19%	3.98%
Since 1919	4.71%	5.40%	2.61%	8.01%	2.79%
Since WW II	5.94%	6.02%	2.87%	8.89%	3.14%
Since Sept. 1981	8.20%	8.60%	2.06%	10.66%	6.54%

Data Sources:
The following monthly series have been spliced together:

- 1790 to 1831: 3% British Consols
- 1831 to 1919: High Grade Long Term Railroad Bonds
- 1919 to date: Long Term Treasuries constant maturity from the Federal Reserve (10-years or more).

This data is available from:
The Foundation For The Study Of Cycles
214 Carnegie Center
Suite 204
Princeton, New Jersey 08540
(610) 995-2120
http://www.cycles.org/~cycles/

For more information see:
- *The History Of Interest Rates, 3rd Ed.* by Sidney Homer & Richard Sylla
- *The Movements of Interest Rates, Bond Yield, and Stock Prices in the United States since 1856* by Frederick R. Macaulay (NBER, 1938)
- The Federal Reserve of St. Louis on the Web at http://www.stls.frb.org/

Chart LTC-1

The CRB BRIDGE Index and Long Term Interest Rates Back to 1790

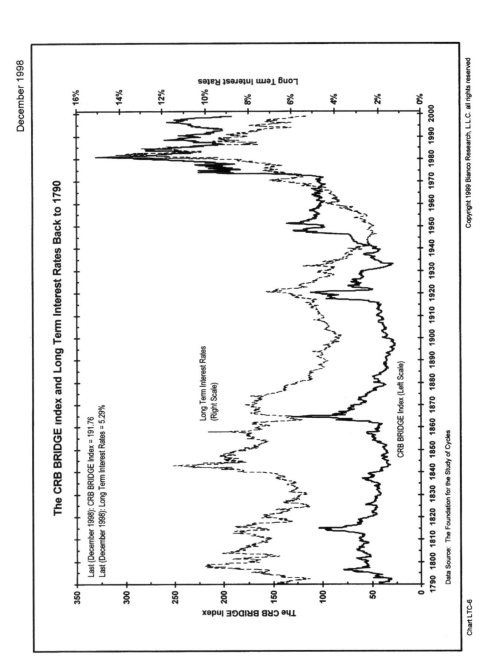

Last (December 1998): CRB BRIDGE Index = 191.76
Last (December 1998): Long Term Interest Rates = 5.29%

Long Term Interest Rates
(Right Scale)

CRB BRIDGE Index (Left Scale)

Long Term Interest Rates

The CRB BRIDGE Index

Data Source: The Foundation for the Study of Cycles

Chart LTC-6

12

The CRB BRIDGE Index and Long Term Interest Rates Back to 1790

Highlights

- During the 1800s, long-term yields and the CRB BRIDGE Index displayed little correlation to each other. However, after the creation of the Federal Reserve in 1913, the CRB BRIDGE Index and long-term interest rates have been highly correlated.

- One would have thought that the CRB BRIDGE Index and long-term interest rates would have been more correlated last century when the U.S. economy was more agrarian. Yet, the opposite is true -- the more our economy moves away from a commodity base, the more the CRB BRIDGE Index and long-term interest rates correlate. We do not have a ready answer for this inconsistency.

Some statistics about Long Term Interest Rates and the CRB BRIDGE Index (December, 1998)

Period	Correlation Between The CRB and LT Rates
Since 1790	33.88%
1790 to 1913	38.65%
Since 1900	78.78%
Since 1971	67.60%

Data Sources:

This chart uses the following monthly series:

This data is available from:
The Foundation For The Study Of Cycles
214 Carnegie Center
Suite 204
Princeton, New Jersey 08540
(610) 995-2120
http://www.cycles.org/~cycles/

The CRB Index
- See Chart LTC-5 for details
Long Term Rates
- See Chart LTC-1 for details

Chart LTC-6

13

The Public's Asset Mix
Households Assets in Stocks and Bonds (As a Percentage of All Assets *Less* Misc. Assets and Non-Corp Equity)

Percentage of All Assets

Equities

Bonds

14

The Public's Asset Mix

Highlights

This chart shows the percentage of household assets in stocks and bonds **less** miscellaneous assets and non-corporate equities (i.e., sole proprietorship). We excluded these categories so that we can show households investment mix in marketable securities.

This chart is direct stock ownership **plus** holdings in "intermediaries" (i.e., mutual funds, pension funds). We did this by assuming that household ownership in these intermediaries was similar to the entire industry and allocated each into either stocks or bonds. For instance, household holdings in mutual funds are divided by the total weighting of stocks and bonds in all mutual funds (see chart FoF-3). We are assuming households own these intermediaries in the same weightings that are found in the entire industry. We felt this was reasonable as household is the largest segment of these intermediaries.

The percentage in stocks reached its all time peak in Q1 1999. Bonds reached their second lowest percentage in Q1 1999. Only Q1 1973 was lower.

Data Sources:
Federal Reserve Board
- Z.1-Flow of Funds Accounts of the United States. These data are released during the second week of March, June, September, and December.

They can be found at:
- http://www.bog.frb.fed.us/releases/Z1/

Chart FOF-7

15

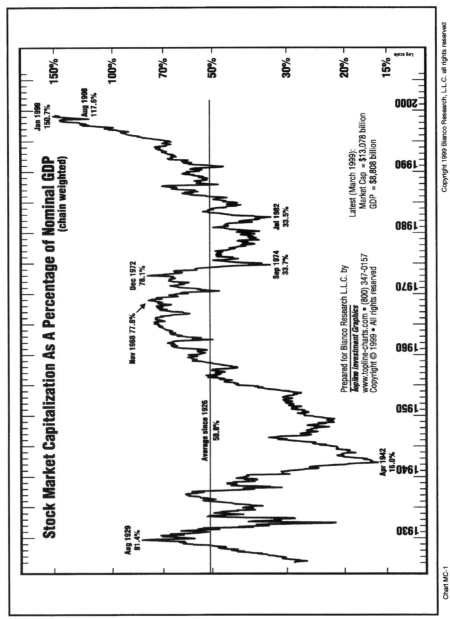

Stock Market Capitalization As A Percentage of Nominal GDP
(chain weighted)

Jan 1999
150.7%

Aug 1998
117.6%

Dec 1972
78.1%

Nov 1968 77.8%

Sep 1974
33.7%

Jan 1982
33.5%

Average since 1926
50.8%

Aug 1929
81.4%

Apr 1942
16.0%

Prepared for Bianco Research L.L.C. by
Topline Investment Graphics
www.topline-charts.com • (800) 347-0157
Copyright © 1999 • All rights reserved

Latest (March 1999):
Market Cap = $13,078 billion
GDP = $8,808 billion

150%
100%
70%
50%
30%
20%
15%

Log scale

2000
1990
1980
1970
1960
1950
1940
1930

Chart MC-1

Stock Market Capitalization as a Percentage of Nominal GDP

Highlights

- Our definition of stock market capitalization is the voting shares of all publicly traded common stocks. No ADRs, closed-end funds or preferred stocks are included in this calculation.

- Currently the capitalization of stocks is about $12.86 trillion versus nominal GDP of $8.7 trillion. This put the ratio at 148%.

- The last time this ratio was below its long term average of 50.1% was November 1990. The August 1929 peak of 81.4% was exceeded in September 1995 and the first time this ratio crossed 100% was November 1996.

- Some argue that the trend toward going public puts an upward bias in this ratio. They point out that in 1929 there were a little more than 500 companies in this calculation versus over 8,500 now. However, the capitalization of the S&P 500 alone is now above $10 trillion putting the S&P 500 ratio to nominal GDP at 120% -- well above the 1929 peak.

- Chain-weighted GDP back to 1959 has been incorporated into this.

Sources

Ibbotson And Associates
225 North Michigan Avenue
Chicago IL 60601-7676
Phone (312) 616-1620
Fax (312) 616-0404
- http://www.ibbotson.com/

Factset Research Systems Inc.
One Greenwich Plaza
Greenwich CT 06830
Phone (203) 863-1500
Fax (203) 863-1501
- http://factset.com/

Commerce Department
Publishes the Gross Domestic Product Statistics.
http://www.stat-usa.gov/

Chart MC-1

THE CURVES OF THE BOND MARKET

A good understanding of the Treasury yield curve is the foundation for any good bond investor and trader. The Treasury yield curve is a graphic summary of the interest rate levels for every Treasury security with maturities from 3 months out to 30 years, and shows you what kind of rate of return you should expect for investing your money for a particular length of time.

The shape of the Treasury yield curve changes constantly because expectations of interest rates fluctuate from day to day. This is not hard to see why: Investors base their interest rate forecasts on predictions about the future state of the economy, the level of inflation, and the level of the U.S. dollar, none of which could be considered a stationary target.

The normal shape of the curve is sloping upwards. This shows that the longer the maturity of the bond, the more yield you will receive from the bond.

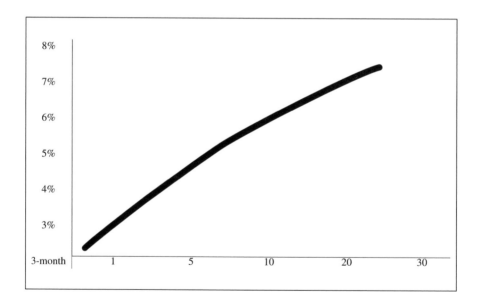

However, this shape may change depending on what the market and investors like you expect interest rates to do. For example, the curve may become inverted, where the yield to maturity on the 3-month Treasury bill is higher than that for the 30-year Treasury bond.

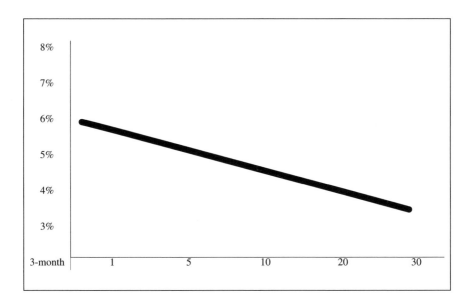

This happens when the market expects inflation and short-term interest rates to rise, and so investors take money from long-term securities and plow it into short-term securities. This is also called a negatively sloped yield curve.

If or when the economy does start to slow down, then bond prices may start to rally and interest rates will decline. The inflection point where the negatively sloped yield curve changes to a normal shape can produce some of the most dynamic bond rallies and the greatest opportunities for bond investors. But pinpointing that exact transition point is a lot easier said than done.

You might think that just by looking at the yield curve you could tell where the economy is going. Unfortunately, this is as about as reliable as reading the accounts of what Mr. Greenspan and his cohorts at the Fed supposedly said. The shape of the yield curve shows the market's expectations of where the economy is headed, but while the market may be able to make an educated bet, it remains just that: a bet.

For every economist who says interest rates are going higher, you can probably find one who expects them to fall. After all, an economist is often harshly described as someone who will tell you tomorrow why his predictions of yesterday didn't come true today.

We will refer to this yield curve constantly throughout this book, almost ad nauseam, because it forms the baseline for all bond investing. Not only does it tell you what kind of return you will get for investing in various Treasury securities, but all bonds are priced relative to Treasury securities. As such, the yield curve will tell the rate of return you should expect for everything and anything that is not a Treasury security.

Because Treasury securities are considered the safest bonds to own, all other bonds, whether issued by government agencies, municipalities, or companies, are priced relative to Treasury securities.

For example, if a Treasury security with a maturity of 5 years is yielding 5%, then a similar security from a corporation would be priced at a number of basis points (1 basis point is 1/100th of a percentage point) above this to reward you for taking on extra risk.

If you are going to tiptoe out of Treasury securities into riskier credits, then you need to ensure that you will get a significantly higher rate of return for your trouble, because you don't have the safety and security of the U.S. government behind the loan. You cannot assess this risk accurately without a baseline, and that baseline is the Treasury yield curve.

CHAPTER 2

THE SAFE SECTOR

The bond market is several times larger than the stock market. This has its advantages and disadvantages: You are really spoilt for choice in what you can buy, but at the same time the sheer range of options can be a little daunting.

The easiest way to distinguish between issuers of bonds is by their creditworthiness, or how likely it is that the issuer will repay the interest and principal on the bond in full and on time.

As I said in the previous chapter, the U.S. government holds the torch for being the least likely bond issuer to default on its obligations, so let's start with debt securities from Uncle Sam.

U.S. TREASURIES

In addition to being free of credit risk, Treasury securities (called bills, notes, and bonds, depending on the maturity) have a number of other advantages over bonds from other sources.

Treasury securities are very liquid, which means that it's easy for a holder of these bonds to buy and sell them. At the beginning of 1999, the amount of public debt stood at over $5-1/2 trillion, and it is this size combined with the fact that the Treasury market is one of the world's largest

21

bond markets with enormous depth and numerous participants that makes these securities so liquid.

Unfortunately, the complexity of the financial markets means not all Treasury securities have the same liquidity. When the Treasury issues a new batch, or offering, of Treasury securities with a 5-year maturity, they replace the old 5-year Treasury securities as the most frequently traded issue.

The new ones are called the *on-the-run* Treasury securities, while the old ones become the *off-the-run* Treasury securities. Because the on-the-run Treasury securities are traded more frequently, they are more liquid and usually demand a slight premium over the older issues, which means a lower yield. However, sometimes this difference can reach unusually wide levels.

Normally the difference in yield between the two types of Treasury securities with the same maturity is one or two basis points (a basis point is 1/100th of a percentage point). But in August 1998 this difference reached as much as six basis points, so that the yield on the new 5-year Treasury securities was 6.06% and the yield on the old 5-year was 6.12%.

The reasons given for this wide discrepancy were many and complex, but you should be aware that external factors do have a habit of throwing a curve ball, creating dangers but at the same time opportunities for the smart investor. (See sidebar: *Off-the-Run Madness.*)

Treasury securities also have what is known as excellent "call protection," which means that the Treasury cannot call, or buy back, the bonds before they mature.

Call risk in a bond is an important determinant of its price. Suppose a company called Cohen.com issued a 10-year bond in 1995 with a 10% coupon. Under the terms of the bond issue, it states that Cohen.com has the right to buy back some or all of these bonds after 5 years.

Why would Cohen.com want to do that? Well, since 1995, the Internet has taken off and the company now has fantastic earnings and so is not such a great credit risk as it once was. Together with an overall fall in interest rates, Cohen.com could now issue those same bonds with only an 8% coupon. The result: The company calls the bond and reissues them with a lower coupon, leaving the investor holding either cash or the new bonds that pay less.

With Treasury securities, the federal government has no right to call noncallable bonds before maturity, thereby eliminating any uncertainty for the investor.

Concerning taxes, Treasury securities are subject to taxes at the federal level but are exempt from state and city taxes. This is important if you live in a state with high levels of income tax such as California, New York, or Massachusetts.

Another advantage of Treasury securities is that they are held in "book-entry form." This means that instead of actual pieces of paper to lose, the bonds you buy will be held directly in the *TreasuryDirect* system operated by the Bureau of Public Debt, or in the book-entry system of financial institutions or brokers.

So how do you go about buying Treasury securities? In comparison to other forms of investing, buying Treasury securities is relatively simple. And with the advent of the Internet, it's become easier still.

Assuming you have a computer and access to the Internet, just go to the Bureau of Public Debt's website at www.publicdebt.treas.gov and from there you can open an account and take part in the periodic auctions the Federal Reserve conducts on behalf of the government. To open an account you need an account name, an address, a social security number, and an account with a bank or other institution so the necessary payments from your investment can be automatically wired to you.

As well as being very simple, the *TreasuryDirect* system eliminates transaction costs that you might incur if buying Treasury securities through a broker, and it also means that you will get the same yield as the institutions receive.

Treasury bills, notes, and bonds are issued by the Treasury through competitive and noncompetitive bidding at more than 150 auctions held throughout the year. Information about these auctions can be found on the website. The Treasury announces the exact auction dates about 7 to 10 days before each auction, but every February, May, August, and November, it will give a 3-month calendar listing tentative dates for the auction.

OFF-THE-RUN MADNESS

Is it important to be aware of what the institutions are doing in the Treasury market? Yes, absolutely. The most recently auctioned Treasury note or bond is known as the "on-the-run" issue; it is actively traded, easily leveraged, and liquid to borrow and sell short.

By virtue of their borrowing power, the institutional heavyweights can often squeeze extra basis points out of trades that you and I never could. Speculators and hedge funds can put up only a few cents for every dollar of Treasuries they buy through the overnight repo market.

During tumultuous times in the market such as the October 1987 stock market crash and the near collapse of the Long-Term Capital Management hedge fund in 1998, Treasuries rose spectacularly on a flight to quality. In plain English, if the financial situation is unstable, investors sell any speculative positions they own and buy, buy, and buy more Treasuries from one to 30 years in maturity. The worse the financial markets get, the more Treasuries will appreciate.

And guess what? This recipe works.

"There must be a catch?" I hear you ask. Indeed there is: There can be a wide yield difference between the on-the-run Treasuries and the off-the-runs. In fact, the crisis of 1998 generated the largest differences in

To participate in one of these auctions, you need to fill in and send off a simple form called a noncompetitive tender. This can be done over the Internet, by phone, or by mail. The Treasury auctions involve registered financial institutions bidding for the Treasury securities at a certain yield. Once all the bids are submitted, an average yield is calculated that you and the institutions will pay for these securities.

Since Treasury securities have a face value of $1,000, the minimum investment in Treasury securities is $1,000.

The process of buying Treasury securities is a relatively painless process compared with other types of bonds, and it's fairly easy to build up your own portfolio of Treasury securities with different maturities.

If you decide to sell your Treasury securities before they mature, *TreasuryDirect* will take care of that too. Through its *Sell Direct* service, for a nominal fee the service will obtain quotes from a number of brokers and sell your securities at the highest price offered.

Treasury securities come in a variety of maturities, although the government has cut the number of these recently because as the deficit declines not as much debt needs to be issued. According to The Bond Market Association, the amount of new debt the Treasury issued in 1998 fell 9% versus 1997 to $2 trillion.

The shortest-dated security is the Treasury bill. The maturities for T-bills are 13, 26, and 52 weeks. The 3-month and 6-month securities are auctioned every Monday, so it's always easy to buy these securities. Because the time span before redemption is so short for these securities, they do not pay interest in the form of a coupon but are sold at a discount to par. If you purchase T-bills in the secondary market this means a bill with a face value of $1,000 is sold at, say, $900, but at redemption you get back the full $1,000. The interest is therefore $100.

T-bills are the safest of the safe. Not only is there no credit risk, but because the maturity is so short they are also effectively free of interest rate risk. They are extremely liquid and banks, funds, and money managers treat T-bills as cash.

yields between the on-the-run 30-year Treasury and the off-the-runs that I've ever seen.

The reason had nothing to do with credit quality and everything to do with liquidity. For the first time in my memory there was little to no liquidity in the off-the-run issues. When the institutions sold in panic, dealers only wanted the most liquid issues so investors who owned off-the-runs saw the price of their holdings rise less dramatically. Sure, the subsequent healing process narrowed the yields between the on-the-runs and the off-the-runs, but this took months. I think one of the reasons was credit lines and leverage dramatically decreased and the big players got somewhat reduced in terms of both money and egos.

For individuals, buying off-the-run Treasuries represented that rarest of times: a chance to make money at the expense of the big guys. The off-the-run issues were worth 10 to 13 basis points more on a yield basis with no strings attached (assuming you were an investor and not a speculator).

The financial columnists were agog, and investors, long used to getting the short end of the stick, were searching for the missing catch. Gloriously, this time there was none.

Next down the timeline are Treasury notes, which have maturities of between 2 and 10 years. Because of the longer maturities, the notes have more interest rate risk associated with them and so their prices fluctuate more than T-bill prices. Therefore, there is more opportunity for a rise in the note's price, resulting in capital gains, but alas more opportunity for a fall in the price, leading to capital loss.

Treasury bonds are those with maturities of 30 years. The government has phased out 15- and 20-year bonds.

Finally, there are securities known as zero-coupon Treasury securities. These are also called "strips." The name strips is derived from the process of creating a zero-coupon security. In Chapter 1, I explained that a bond consists of two revenue streams: the coupon payments and the principal. Therefore a strip is where the income streams have been separated to create two securities.

It doesn't actually matter which part of the strip an investor holds—the principal or the coupon part—because, as with T-bills, the holder of a zero-coupon Treasury security will receive no coupon payments. Instead the zero-coupon Treasury security is priced at a large discount to par, which means when the principal is returned at par, the difference between the original price you paid and what is returned will include the coupon payments as well as the interest on interest.

There are drawbacks associated with zero-coupon Treasury securities. For the individual investor, buying a zero-coupon Treasury security can be a tricky business, because the differences in prices can vary greatly between brokers. Therefore, it's essential to shop around to get the best price.

The tax issues associated with zero-coupon Treasury securities are also important because although you don't receive interest payments on the security, you are nevertheless taxed as if you did. Therefore, zero-coupon Treasury securities are good investments for tax-deferred accounts such as Individual Retirement Accounts (IRAs).

The high degree of volatility—or the susceptibility of the security to price swings because of changes in interest rates—of zero-coupon Treasury securities can be a drawback or a benefit if you decide to sell the security before it matures. The rule is that the lower the coupon of a bond, the higher its volatility. Zero-coupon Treasury securities have no coupon at all, ergo they are the most volatile. In fact, long-term zero-coupon Treasury securities are about 20 to 25% more volatile than normal-coupon Treasury securities.

So what are the most attractive Treasury securities? Well, of course, this depends on your risk criteria and portfolio needs, but historically speaking, intermediate-term Treasury securities maturing between 7 and 12 years pay a large percentage of the 30-year bonds' return without the market volatility.

With all these advantages you might be thinking, Why don't I just plow all my money into Treasury securities and forget about them? In any investment there are trade-offs and the very advantages of Treasury securities create their own disadvantages. Because the market is so efficient, there is little chance of any Treasury security being mispriced. And because they are the safest bet, they pay out the least. Therefore, to get more bang for your buck, you should look down the credit rung and think about buying . . .

FEDERAL AGENCY BONDS

The amount of debt issued by the federal agencies is huge. According to The Bond Market Association it totaled $6 trillion in 1998.

Bonds issued by the federal agencies such as the *Federal Home Loan Mortgage Corporation (Fannie Mae)* and the *Federal Home Loan Banks (FHLBs)* are backed by either an explicit guarantee from the government or at the very least a moral guarantee. As a result, they are usually thought of as having little or no credit risk and pay only a marginal level of interest above Treasury securities.

But history teaches us caution if nothing else and there have been several occasions when the reliability of these agencies has been called into question.

For example, between 1982 and 1984, the farming industry in the U.S. was in deep financial distress, which caused many farm failures. Many of these farms had borrowed from the *Federal Farm Credit Banks,* and they began defaulting on these loans. The number of defaults reached

AGENCY CURVE BALL

After hearing the constant mantra throughout my career about the safety and security of government agency bonds, it became second nature to believe that our respected government, by way of our equally respected Treasury, would never allow an agency to default on its notes or bonds. After all, several bond books used the phrase *an implicit guarantee of the U.S. government* in their definitions of this debt.

Well, life rarely conforms to a simple definition, and this is never truer than in the financial markets.

During the 1980s farm crisis, there was actual talk about a default on bonds issued by the Federal Farm Credit Banks (FFCB). All you had to do was turn on the evening news and watch one family farm after another being foreclosed on. Farmers had borrowed a lot of money from the FFCB and expanded their farms. Unfortunately, interest rates on their loans shot up at the same time prices for their crops declined—a surefire recipe for disaster.

Historically, agency paper trades at a wider spread over Treasuries and so gives a higher yield. The spread varies, but a rule of thumb is that agency bonds yield 35 to 40 basis points over the comparable maturing Treasury.

But this farm crisis was spelled with a capital "C" and the financial markets

such a level that many people began questioning whether the agency would ultimately fail. In the end, the agency was saved by a combination of new management and a fortuitous turnaround in the farming industry. (See sidebar: *Agency Curve Ball.*)

Most federal agency paper is callable, which means that there is a certain amount of call risk you must factor into your calculations of whether to buy a government agency paper. In an environment of declining interest rates, the agencies buy back a lot of the debt they issued previously at higher rates.

However, because of the high denominations involved, the market for federal debt tends to be dominated by the institutions. Most retail buying is confined to the debt from Fannie Mae, the FHLBs, and the Federal Farm Credit Banks, so let's concentrate on those.

Fannie Mae

Fannie Mae was established in 1938 by the federal government to help expand the amount of money available to mortgage lenders during the Depression. In 1968 it became a private, shareholder company. Its stock is listed on the New York Stock Exchange (NYSE) under the ticker symbol FNM, and it is now a component of the S&P 500 index.

Fannie Mae is one of the world's largest issuers of debt securities, and with a decline in the amount of new Treasury securities being issued, Fannie Mae has stepped into the gap and initiated what it calls Benchmark issues as a substitute. As of the end of 1998, Fannie Mae's debt totaled $843 billion.

While it remains to be seen whether this agency debt can fully act as a Treasury security substitute, the agency's debt is very liquid and does offer an additional yield over Treasury securities.

Federal Home Loan Banks

There are 12 regional Federal Home Loan Banks and they are controlled by the federal government but nominally owned by the nation's savings and loans (S&L) institutions. The purpose behind these banks is to lend money to the S&Ls when they experience financial difficulties, which (as most of

smelled ruin. Fear overcame greed and the selling and spread widening turned chaotic.

At the time of the crisis, I was a bond broker and did a lot of highly leveraged transactions for wealthy investors, meaning customers put up only $15,000 to control $1 million of bonds. (There were a number of tax advantages associated with this, but these tax loopholes have been long closed.) The preferred instrument for this play was FFCB notes.

As the farm belt news worsened in the winter of 1985, the price of the bonds tanked. Sure, they were government agencies. And, sure, there was a "quasi guarantee," but when the sentiment in the bond market changed, all rational thought went out the window. Spreads widened to 175 basis points, which was unheard of and unprecedented.

This caused unspeakable pain for my clients on leverage. Because bond investors only had to put up 1.5% (or $15,000) to buy on margin instead of the 50% needed for stocks, the plunge in bond prices meant margin calls came every other day. Double whammy: Prices eroded and the leverage magnified the effect.

The moral of this: Investors must learn to expect the unexpected. Even the perception of the FFCB repudiating its debt was enough to push an already panicked market over the edge.

So what happened to my leveraged clients? Those who held on received their tax benefits but lost money, because their cost of financing far exceeded their interest. Those who bought into the panic, meaning they waited until the prices hit near rock bottom and held onto the paper during the recovery, made out like bandits.

you remember) happened to a terrifying degree in the 1980s.

The FHLBs had about $277 billion of debt outstanding at the end of 1998, much of it in fixed-rate securities that can be called. Bonds are underwritten by investment firms and dealer banks or as direct placements. The minimum denomination for the FHLBs' debt varies from $10,000 to $500,000 or more depending on the complexity and associated risks of the bond.

Federal Farm Credit Banks

The Federal Farm Credit System also is controlled by the federal government, but it is nominally owned by the 37 different farm banks that make up the organization. The System includes the Federal Land Banks, the Bank for Cooperatives, and the Federal Intermediate Credit Banks.

The purpose of the Federal Farm Credit Banks is to make loans to farmers and cooperatives, and today the System provides more than $61 billion in loans to more than a half million borrowers. The banks have the implied backing of the federal government.

For individual investors, the minimum required investment for the System's short-term debt is $50,000, but the longer-term paper needs only a $1,000 minimum investment.

Unlike with Treasury securities, there is no way for this debt to be purchased directly from any of the agencies, so that requires brokers, which of course means fees, fees, and more fees.

GINNIE MAES

Mortgage pass-through securities issued by the *Government National Mortgage Association (GNMA),* a division of the Department of Housing and Urban Development, are known as *Ginnie Maes*. Although they are sometimes classed as federal agency debt, I have separated them from the previous section because these securities are a class all to themselves.

Ginnie Maes are not issued by the GNMA itself, but the institution acts as an insurer for the securities. A Ginnie Mae is created by pooling mortgages insured by the Federal Housing Administration and the Veterans Administration. Investment bankers take these mortgages and securitize them, and then turn them into a bond. For that service, the bank gets a 1/2–percentage-point servicing fee, meaning a Ginnie Mae with an 8-1/2% coupon is backed by a 9.00% mortgage.

After the securitization process, the bonds are sold to either institutions or individual investors or both. The mortgage payers keep paying their mortgages and that 9.00% is passed through to the servicer, who in turn pays the bondholder 8-1/2%. If you are a bondholder, you receive interest and principal payments monthly so the number of mortgages in the pool gets smaller and smaller as time goes on.

Ginnie Maes are popular with investors because they are guaranteed against default by the federal government, yet can yield about 100 to 125 basis points more than Treasury securities, and unlike other bonds, interest on them is paid monthly.

Ginnie Maes, however, have two disadvantages: The interest on them is subject to state income taxes, and their maturity is unpredictable because homeowners often refinance their mortgages if interest rates fall.

Ginnie Maes tend to perform best as an investment vehicle when the interest rate environment is serene. If interest rates are falling, people will prepay their mortgages and you'll be stuck holding cash at a time when interest rates are low and it would be difficult to find a similarly yielding instrument unless you're prepared to buy a bond from a less creditworthy issuer.

If interest rates rise, you're still at a disadvantage. Prepayments will slow so you'll have to hold your Ginnie Mae for longer than you thought, and at a time when people are issuing debt at juicier interest rates.

For people who must pay state income taxes, the advantage of a Ginnie Mae over a Treasury security is almost wiped out by these two disadvantages. But if you don't pay state income taxes (as in Texas and Washington) or you invest through a tax-deferred IRA or 401(K), Ginnie Maes outyield Treasury securities.

As you can see, Ginnie Maes are very complex instruments so investing in them should be studied thoroughly. If they do appear to make financial sense, you must follow these four simple rules.

First, you must know as much as possible about the Ginnie Maes you are about to buy. You should know the original face amount of the pool you are taking a piece of, what part of the country the mortgages are located in, and if the pool has been in existence for some time, what the history of prepayments has been. Location matters because people in Florida, for example, move less frequently and so prepay more slowly than do people who have mortgages in California.

Second, avoid trading Ginnie Maes. Only buy one if you are reasonably sure that you (or your heirs) will hold it until the last principal payment has been paid, either 15 or 30 years after issuance.

Third, before you buy a Ginnie Mae, get at least two quotes from different brokers. This is especially important if you're forced to sell the Ginnie Mae. The difference between where you can sell versus buy Ginnie Maes can be wider than a mile for retail bond investors. A difference of two to four points is common. Four points on $25,000 means you're paying $1,000 for the privilege of buying a bond, no mean sum. If you don't have two brokerage accounts, try haggling.

Fourth, it doesn't make sense to invest large amounts in any one pool, because you will lose geographic diversification. If you have a large amount of money invested in several pools, the mortgages covered by your investment will span a larger number of areas than a small investment would. Since mortgages in the Midwest tend to be paid off slower than those mortgages on the East and West coasts, if prepayments do pick up, the slower rate of the Midwest will offset those of the coasts.

After reading this, you might think Ginnie Maes aren't worth the effort, but at times of serene interest rates, Ginnie Maes offer a safe and secure investment at a nice spread over Treasury securities. Later we will discuss alternatives such as Ginnie Mae mutual funds as well as the off-shoots of Ginnie Maes such as Collateralized Mortgage Obligations (CMOs).

MUNICIPAL BONDS

Municipal bonds are bonds issued by states, counties, and other divisions of states to finance the building and servicing of public services and facilities, such as airports and roads. The distinguishing feature of municipal bonds is their tax treatment.

Whole books are devoted to the tax aspect of bonds, but basically there are two types of taxation: the capital gains that result from selling a bond at a greater price than you bought it for, and the tax on interest income generated from the bond. The tax advantage of municipal bonds applies to the interest income.

As I mentioned before, the amount of Treasury securities being issued is falling. The number of municipal bonds too is falling after peaking in 1993 at about $1.5 trillion, and this decrease should accelerate.

The refunding of some issues can artificially swell the supply of municipal bonds. Suppose a town floats a $50-million issue in 1996 to finance a bridge. Interest rates drop in the next few years and the town wants to refinance this debt at these lower rates. However, the issue isn't callable yet so the town floats a second issue and sets aside the proceeds in an escrow account funded with government securities to pay off the first issue as soon as it can be retired. Now there are $100 million of bonds outstanding—but not for long because the original $50 million will be called away at the first opportunity as written in the bond indenture.

Muller Data, a division of Thompson Financial specializing in municipal bond data, estimates half of the total outstanding municipal bonds, some $645 billion, will mature by the year 2009.

This fall could be offset by the authorities replacing the maturing bonds, but I don't see this happening for a number of reasons. Voters are

1987 MUNI CRISIS

I have learned more about investing during crises than when things are going well. Not only should you learn to avoid past mistakes, but you should also be able to spot opportunities when things are going badly for others.

In 1986, Congress yet again began fiddling with the tax code. On January 1, 1987, it decided to increase the capital gains tax from 20 to 28%. So in December 1986, many investors thought it might be time to hightail it out of some of their stocks, book their profits, and save the 8% capital gains differential.

The brokerage industry convinced retail investors to "park" their proceeds in long-term tax-free municipal bond funds in order to pay the capital gains tax on April 15. But the fickle finger of fate let those investors down big. Beginning in January 1987, the bond market went into a tailspin—interest rates rose relentlessly until the October 1987 crash. The ugly bear market slaughtered bond investors, and I mean all bond investors.

The investors who "parked" their money in long-term municipal bond funds learned that when you decide to park funds, you should make sure there's a braking mechanism—in 1987 there wasn't.

The relentless rise in rates was a disaster for bond funds, and those unfortunates who owned muni funds

more reluctant than they were to approve boondoggles, and with the privatization of everything from hospitals to power and other utilities, future debt financing is moving from the municipal market into the taxable market.

This lack of supply of municipal bonds comes against a backdrop of increasing demand from baby boomers who are retiring and buying these securities for income in their retired years. Municipals will no longer be for our coupon-clipping parents. Baby boomers will become the coupon-clipping parents.

Since 1983, yields on municipal bonds have ranged from 70 to 105% of yields on Treasury securities. If you are in the 28% tax bracket, a municipal bond that yields 80% as much as a Treasury security is attractive, and if you are in the top federal and state tax brackets—effectively, in excess of 45%—municipal bonds look even more attractive.

The tide hasn't turned yet, but successful investing is about anticipating future trends. If you need liquidity, buy a municipal bond fund with a low expense ratio, which I'll cover in Chapter 6. If you don't need the liquidity, buy high-quality bonds directly and hold them to maturity.

Again, call risk is important here. If the volume of municipal bonds does continue to fall, then in all likelihood you will see a shift of the supply/demand curve. Protect yourself from this by focusing on noncallable municipal bonds.

However, the municipal bond market is a difficult place for the individual investor because of its opaqueness. Investors rarely know if the price being paid is fair and "on the market."

There is the Municipal Securities Rulemaking Board, an orga-

all headed for the exit door at the same time. The result was that in most cases municipal yields traded on top of, or exceeded, Treasury yields.

There was a fire sale all right. Muni bonds of the best credit quality were yielding 100 to 110% over Treasuries. This has happened at only one other time in my career, during the meltdown of the bond market in September and October 1998.

I learned an important lesson from this: "When they're crying, you should be buying." So anytime there's a muni sale like those in 1987 and 1998, buy the best-quality munis that yield the same or more than Treasuries.

nization set up to police the activities in the municipal bond market, but as with most self-regulating organizations, its actions are limited and, to be honest, I don't think it has done anything terribly effective to benefit the individual investor.

It appears that every sector of the bond market has its potential problems and municipal bonds are no exception. But over the years I have discovered it always pays to purchase the highest-rated municipal bonds available. After all, most investors in the municipal bond market are seeking a safe predictable tax-free income stream with little risk or volatility. (See sidebar: *1987 Muni Crisis.*)

The lack of transparency and information available to the individual investor about the municipal bond market also means that commission from brokers tends to be high, running to as much as four points per bond ($40 per $1,000 bond). We will discuss how to avoid some of these problems in this market in Chapters 7 and 8.

CORPORATE BONDS

A corporate bond is essentially a loan to a corporation by an investor. Buying corporate bonds is more complicated than buying Treasury securities because there are so many more variables involved.

The price of a Treasury bond is basically determined by the coupon and maturity, but the price of a corporate bond also depends on the bond's seniority, its credit rating, the covenants, call features, liquidity, and event risk. And those are just the basics.

Treasury securities all have the same credit strength, but those issued by corporations can take many different forms, including senior notes, subordinated debentures, and convertible bonds. There are important differences between these securities and they also form a hierarchy in terms of what is paid back first in the event that the company goes bankrupt, so it is important to exactly understand what you are buying and where you stand in the food chain.

Corporate bonds also offer a number of different features. New structures are emerging all the time as underwriters get cleverer and cleverer. Some of the more common ones are bonds with put options, where the buyer has the right to sell back the bond at par before the redemption date. Treasury securities are fixed-rate bonds in that the coupon is set at issuance, but some corporate bonds are sold with floating rates, where the coupon is reset periodically above a benchmark such as the London Interbank Offer Rate, or LIBOR.

An investment-grade corporate bond is one that is issued by a corporation with a credit rating above Baa3 by Moody's and BBB- by Standard & Poor's. (I will look at rating agencies in more depth in Chapter 5.) Bonds issued by corporations with a lower credit rating are called high-yield, or junk, bonds, and are for those investors who are willing to take a bigger risk for meatier returns. I'll discuss these bonds in Chapter 3.

If you were quizzed on the number of corporate names that can issue AAA-rated bonds, what would you answer? One hundred? Eighty? Fifty? Well, the answer is a paltry 18 names.

According to a survey conducted by S&P, as of May 31, 1999, the pool of U.S. industrial bonds breaks down as follows:

Rating	Number of Corporate Names
AAA	18
AA	55
A	218
BBB	346

The corporate bond market is growing dramatically, primarily as a result of the steady fall in interest rates and the relative strength (and therefore credit quality) of U.S. companies in this unprecedented period of economic expansion. Alas, there has not been an equivalent increase in the number of investment-grade names because corporations have been all too ready to take on more debt and splurge this money on acquisitions.

By far the largest holders of corporate bonds are the life insurance industry and pension funds. For the individual, though, the complexity as well as the fact that corporate bonds are fully taxable at all levels—federal, state, and local—means that they demand more attention. By the end of Chapter 8, you should be able to spot what is a good buy and what is not.

CHAPTER 3

A LITTLE SEXIER: MORE RISK FOR MORE YIELD

It may be tempting to think that a simple way of getting more bang for your buck would be to buy top-quality corporate bonds instead of Treasury securities. After all, General Electric is hardly likely to go bankrupt and you will get as much as 30 to 60 basis points more yield than with a similarly maturing Treasury security.

Unfortunately, it's not that simple.

A common misunderstanding among many people is that there are a lot of high-quality investment-grade bonds out there. There aren't.

The relatively meager number of corporate issues you have to choose from falls further when you consider that first dibs go to the investment-grade mutual funds, investment-grade closed and open-end funds, and the money managers. Once all these institutions and professionals are finished picking what they want, how many bonds are really left for the little guy? Not a lot.

With the corporate bond universe so slim for the retail investor, if you really want to boldly go into the world of corporate debt, then you will have to consider moving further down the chain in terms of credit quality and into the world of high-yield debt. In that case, you will have to know and understand the company's bonds just as if you were buying the stock.

The lack of choice at the top-end of the bond market may force you into an area you perhaps thought you would never touch with a 10-foot barge pole. But if you do your homework, you may end up actually thanking these institutions: You can pick some real gems out of the rubble while substantially increasing your yield.

HIGH YIELD OR JUST OLD JUNK?

There's an old bond market saying, "When I own them or my clients own them, they're high-yield bonds. When somebody else owns them, they're junk bonds."

There are many professionals in the high-yield bond market who get quite upset if you keep referring to their area of expertise as "junk." This is because this sector of the market today is a far cry from the scandalous days of Michael Milken and Drexel Burnham Lambert in the 1980s. Yet negative connotations persist and, in any case, it's a lot easier to say "junk" than "high-yield."

Certainly there is a lot of junk out there, but how many of you know that, until 1998, Time Warner was rated in this category? Admittedly if you've had to wait several hours in your apartment waiting for the cable guy to show up, you might agree with all the nuances that the label "junk" carries. But let's face it, a household name like Time Warner doesn't really belong in the same class as Cohen.com, a company that doesn't have products, assets, revenues, or a clue.

A BRIEF HISTORY OF THE JUNK, I MEAN, HIGH-YIELD BOND MARKET

Mike Milken, for all his faults, can be credited with legitimizing the whole concept of high-yield bonds as an asset class. He increased the depth of the market and the underwriting of the bonds, but unfortunately not to a degree that could save his or the market's skin when things went horribly wrong.

There have always been bonds that were definitely in the speculative category. But what changed in the early 1980s was that American corporations underwent a massive amount of restructuring and the term *leveraged buyout* became part of the everyday lexicon.

How did the companies leverage themselves to do these buyouts? They issued high-yield bonds. Some of these were good deals, but inevitably some were bad. And when the economy took a turn for the worse in 1989, the massive debt these corporations had taken on began to take its toll and it became a sellers' market. This reached crisis point when Drexel, the principal player in this market, went under, and regardless of whether you were holding the good guys or the bad guys, you couldn't sell your junk bond for love or money.

While this proved an ignominious end for the career of Milken in the securities industry (he went to jail), it planted the seeds for today's high-yield bond market.

The brains behind the high-yield department at Drexel began looking elsewhere for jobs on Wall Street and found themselves at the major and minor Wall Street firms such as Merrill Lynch, Jeffreys, and Donaldson, Lufkin & Jenrette. These firms have since become very interested and proficient in high-yield bond underwriting and analysis, allowing this part of the bond market to grow at an astonishing rate.

From these humble (some would say disreputable) beginnings, the U.S. high-yield bond market in 1999 was worth around $465 billion. Underpinning this rapid rise to legitimacy has been the economy.

DEFAULT RATES AND THE ECONOMY

High-yield bonds are classed purely by credit risk: the risk that a debt holder won't receive the interest payments and principal in full and on time. This is, therefore, intrinsically tied to the default rate: the rate at which corporations are not able to pay the interest or principal on their obligations. The defaulted debt index is a market-weighted index of the monthly return on issues that have defaulted on their interest payments.

When the U.S. economy is on a tear, the default rate is usually low because corporations are earning money and are paying their bills.

Edward Altman of New York University calculated a default rate of 1.6% on high-yield bonds in 1998, which is only slightly higher than a median default rate of 1.5% recorded over the preceding 27 years. The rate of 1.6% is darned good if you consider that the default rate was over 10% during the Milken debacle in 1990.

U.S. companies have been the beneficiaries of a booming economy fueled by high levels of consumption since the mid-1990s. Order books are overflowing, earnings are plentiful, and cash is on hand to pay the bondholders their interest and principal.

However, there are those companies that have poor debt service coverage and only have enough money on hand to cover interest payments one time. Should the economy start to skid and the consumer tighten his or her belt, the ability of these companies to make timely interest payments will deteriorate and they may have to resort to a bank credit line.

There is another scenario where a company may be in a bad sector of the economy even though the economy as a whole is humming along. This is what happened in the supermarket sector in the late 1990s. The economy grew in 1998 and 1999, yet we saw supermarkets such as Bruno's fail. Competition from Sams Club, Costco, and other warehouse-oriented supermarkets eroded profits and left companies like Bruno's and Penn Traffic in the junk heap.

So how do you know if we've entered a new era of lower default rates? There is a lot of research and heated debate about this, and there are two schools of thought on this matter.

There is the apocalyptic vision that we will eventually return to the high levels of default seen between 1982 and 1990. Martin Fridson, a senior analyst at Merrill Lynch, colorfully refers to this as the "Dog-Returneth-to-Its-Vomit" school, which is taken from the proverb, "As the dog returneth to its vomit, so the fool returneth to his folly."

Basically, subscribers to this view believe investors have forgotten the lessons from the past and the hubris of today, which will inevitably lead us to a return of the dark days of double-digit default rates we saw during the Milken reign.

Then there are the optimists who believe the large default rates seen in 1990 were an aberration and we are bound for a "Return to Normalcy." This optimistic school of thought argues that defaults will fluctuate around the low average levels seen during the 1970s.

This is no mere academic debate. If you're stuck holding high-yield paper when everyone else is fleeing for the exits, it is very unlikely as a lowly individual investor that you will find a buyer. Conversely, if the optimists are right and we have entered a new era of low default rates, you could be missing out on some very fruitful investments.

Not wishing to appear as one who sits on the fence, my gut feeling is we'll probably remain somewhere in between. Don't be complacent; keep an eye on the macroeconomic picture and what is happening around the company whose bonds you hold. But at the same time, technology, a deeper market, and a feeling that at least some lessons have been learned from the past make the high-yield market a credible place to invest some of your money.

Public pension funds as well as foreigners are now tiptoeing into the high-yield bond market, and as the number of investors continues to grow with the size of the market, so much the better for everyone involved.

HOW TO TELL THE JUNK FROM THE HIGH YIELD

This is what it all boils down to. I wish I had an easy answer but I don't. Instead it involves hard work and, needless to say, an element of luck. Experience helps, but even the professionals get fooled. Plenty of experienced high-yield money managers after painstaking analysis have seen some of their investments get crushed; the companies may not actually default, but at the very least they become severely distressed.

The most important point is never put all your eggs in one basket, but diversify across rating categories and sectors.

Also try to look at this as a fun exercise. There is no better feeling than to find a company, do research on it, make a bet on it, and be proven right. You'll make a tidy profit, too.

Because this part of the market can prove so tricky, the individual investor who has relatively little money to place in the junk bond market might find bond funds a better way to invest. We will discuss such funds in Chapter 6.

While the stock market looks at earnings, the industry standard in the high-yield bond market is earnings before interest, tax, depreciation, and amortization (EBITDA). Since you can't fight city hall, this is what you need to look at when you are considering a high-yield investment.

Analysts in the high-yield market study EBITDA because they want to scrutinize as many variables as possible to see how much money is left to make the interest payments to bondholders. This information is available from brokerage research reports and documents available on the Internet. You can also call the company and request its current financial reports.

As I mentioned before, when the economy sours and the bottom line of businesses deteriorates, how much money a company has to cover its interest payments is crucial. If a company has, for example, six times interest coverage, then it is more likely to be able to ride out the bad times than a company that can cover interest only two times before resorting to a bank revolving credit line or a restructuring of the debt payments.

During the Drexel era, I'd read bond prospectuses. Some would say, in not so many words, "We have no idea how we're going to pay the bondholders, but golly gee we'll really try." For a prudent investor, this is just not good enough.

High-yield analysts also look at EBITDA minus capital expenditures. Why does capital expenditure count? If a company is extremely capital intensive, such as the new telecommunications firms, then it must use a lot of its revenues on this part of the business to keep itself a viable venture. Therefore, you must consider how much the company's capital expenditures are on an annualized basis to determine what it needs to keep itself an ongoing business. Service industries are less capital intensive than the old smokestack industries. Find out whether at the end of the day the company is left with any free cash flow of significance. If the answer is yes, then you are probably onto something. The analysts' financial reviews contain this information.

However, EBITDA isn't the final word. In the 1980s, some of the companies that highly leveraged themselves to finance the build-out of their operations looked on paper to be prime candidates to become debt welchers. But what some people didn't see, including myself, was that technology was going to revolutionize what they were doing.

I remember in the 1980s giving speeches using Turner Broadcasting as an example of a company that had a mountain of debt. How, I asked, was Mr. Turner ever going to pay everybody back? But he did it, because he was the right guy, at the right time, with the right product.

The equivalent in 1999 is the "business plan" bonds from the new telecommunications companies. The bonds are known as such because the only assets the companies have are business plans or perhaps just a blueprint to lift off a few satellites and create a whole new telecommunications concern. Perhaps the business plan is a great idea, but an entire infrastructure needs to be created. Risky? You bet. But if it works, it will be payday!

It all depends on how risky you want to get. Interest coverage is important, but then again so is a good business plan.

NOT ALL COMPANIES START OUT WITH EQUITY

Most of the public at large thinks that if there are bonds out there, then there must be accompanying public equity to boot. Not true. An important point to remember is that not all companies start out with equity. Some start with debt instead, and these can be good investments.

The big issue here is disclosure. Admittedly, as an investor you won't get the day-to-day news like you would with a stock that's publicly traded. Also, there are no real-time continuous prices for corporate bonds and access to prices for the individual investor is limited. Instead, many high-yield investors monitor stock prices of the companies in their portfolios. High-yield debt is commonly regarded as a close cousin of equity: When stock prices rise, often so does the debt.

Although there is not as much disclosure, private companies that issue bonds are required by law to file with the Securities and Exchange Commission (SEC) financial statements (the 10K and 10Q), which contain the information a person needs to make a prudent investment decision.

Paradoxically, this lack of information can also be a good thing. Some of those companies are thinly traded and not well known, and as a result can be mispriced or just picked up on the cheap because of the risk premium. Often small issues are overlooked by large investors because of the lack of liquidity, and this may give small investors a real edge.

Companies that begin with debt typically either are private or have been bought out by venture capitalists such as Kohlberg, Kravis & Roberts. These buyout specialists buy up small companies or those that are struggling, build up the earnings, and then issue shares through an initial public offering (IPO). They then use some of the funds from the IPO to pay down a portion of the debt and hopefully move closer to investment grade.

Moving toward investment grade is important for young and struggling companies. With better interest coverage and a decline in the cost of capital, the company will reduce the spread it has to pay over Treasury securities to borrow money from the bond market, an important step in becoming a well-greased financial engine.

During the late 1990s, the number of companies without public equity issuing debt increased, primarily as a result of the booming market and the better reception that these issues were receiving in the bond market. Issuing debt is not necessarily cheaper, but it allows companies to raise larger sums of money than an IPO would.

Wall Street is always looking for improving credit quality and therefore you should too. If you can find some of these companies, buy the bonds when they're junk and hold onto them through this growth period; you will be a bondholder of a company that is becoming less in jeopardy of not being able to make the interest payments. The bond price will also start to appreciate.

Ultimately, most companies don't actually make it over that bump from high yield to investment grade, but many do move up the credit quality scale.

Although you should remain vigilant about the credit quality of a company whose bonds you own, a downgrade from a rating agency does not necessarily mean they're going down the tubes.

Just like life, companies have ups and downs. A firm may get downgraded because it had a couple of bad quarters, the senior management was changed, or it strayed from its business plan. Don't panic. You have to ride out the good times with the bad. But a constant analysis of the situation is imperative. (See sidebar: *You Can Do It Yourself.*)

A PECKING ORDER

In the worst-case scenario when you do happen to pick a company that because of either bad luck or bad management does go bankrupt, then there is a pecking order as to who gets paid off first.

Needless to say it's usually the banks that get the first crack at the assets. Bank loans are at the top of the list of obligations that get paid off in the event of a bankruptcy, followed by the senior bonds, senior subordinated bonds, and down through the list to preferred stock and common equity. By that time there's usually nothing left for equity holders anyway.

So which bonds should you buy? Luckily, I don't have that much experience with companies going bankrupt. I have experienced two cases of bankruptcy in 22 years. One was Integrated Resources, which appeared to be doing well but very suddenly went bankrupt in the 1980s. It turned out that the company was experiencing some problems in its business, which it didn't disclose to the analysts on Wall Street and were never picked up on by the auditors. There's really no way to insulate yourself from these types of occurrences. The second bankruptcy was Marvel Holdings, which I'll discuss a little later.

When buying high-yield bonds, I prefer to buy the senior or senior subordinated bonds that pay coupon interest. I would stick to those because they are usually the largest issues and the most liquid, so if you're forced to sell, you have more of a chance of finding a buyer. Examples include Chattem Inc.'s 8-7/8% Senior Subordinated Notes due April 1, 2008, and Big 5 Corp.'s 10-7/8% Senior Notes due November 15, 2007.

There are investment banks and hedge funds that trade the bank debt of corporations, but this is not something to which an individual has access.

DIFFERENT TYPES OF
HIGH-YIELD BONDS

As well as different credit qualities of bonds, there are many different structures of bonds.

Because of the nature of the companies that inhabit the high-yield world, many companies are just starting out and don't have the immediate cash flow to make the interest payments.

The market has tried to accommodate this, and the investment banks have designed a number of bonds such as deferred interest bonds, zero-coupon bonds, and step-up coupon bonds. The deferred interest bonds allow the issuer to put off the interest payments to a later date, the zero-coupon bonds (as we discussed in Chapter 2) have no interest payments but are instead sold at a deep discount to par, and step-up bonds have coupons that begin low and rise over the life of the bond.

A zero-coupon bond is probably the riskiest of all situations. Unlike step-up bonds, zero-coupon bonds pay no interest until the maturity date and you are betting that the company will be able to make the principal payment, which would include the interest payments during the life of the bond, on maturity.

In the late 1990s the market was flooded by these types of bonds from the telecommunication companies that were just starting to build out their networks and didn't yet have the cash flow to pay out interest.

One advantage of these types of bonds is that there is no reinvestment risk for the investor. Reinvestment risk is the uncertainty over what

Watching consumer-spending patterns is very important for profitable investing. During prosperous years, we consumers trade up our cars, homes, furnishings, jewelry, clothes, and sometimes spouses.

What about the lean years? Most baby boomers have no recollection of these. Sometimes it's the obvious products and services that can provide steady sales, earnings, and stability during these times. If you're looking for these features in consumer-related companies, stay away from apparel of any type—too trendy and volatile. Instead, look for products and companies you use and can relate to. Two that come to mind are Chattem and Michaels Stores. Both companies are low technology. Chattem provides goods on a mass merchandise basis. Michaels has a niche market.

I first came across Chattem when I noticed my husband powdering his feet with Gold Bond Powder. From what I understand, athletic people always worry about keeping their feet dry and comfortable. Together with radio and TV commercials about Gold Bond Powder, it made me wonder who made the product, how was it distributed, and what else did the company sell? A quick look at the can told me that Chattem was the company.

the level of interest rates will be when you reinvest the proceeds of the coupon payments. Will interest rates be higher or lower at the time you invest these proceeds from the bond? You don't know. With zero-coupon bonds that uncertainty is taken out of your hands because it is computed into the initial price of the bond.

On the flip side, these types of bonds are very volatile and highly sensitive to company news and changes in the level of interest rates. If interest rates move against you, the price of the bond will move sharply down and selling the bond before maturity will result in a significant loss. If the company that issued the high-yield bond gets into financial difficulties, the price of your bond will rapidly erode.

Of course, if you pick the right company you could have a big payday. The yield on these bonds is often about 400 to 500 basis points over Treasury securities. However, before buying a bond read the business plan very, very carefully.

The market became so saturated in the late 1990s with these zero-coupon bonds that the issuers of such bonds moved into over-funded bonds. These bonds are in essence a halfway point between the zero-coupon bonds and conventional cash-pay bonds.

From the issuer's standpoint, an overfunded bond is similar to a zero-coupon bond. The company pays no interest for the initial life of the bond (say, five years) out of its operating cash flow and then begins to pay coupons at a predetermined rate.

For the investor, however, there is no period without coupon payments. This is because the company will place some of the proceeds of the bond issue (the overfunded part) in an escrow account, from which investors will be paid semiannual payments equivalent to regular coupon payments plus interest generated from the escrow account.

The main problem with these bonds is that an investor is making the same bet on a high-yield company that lacks cash flow, but may not receive the same level of payback that a normal zero-coupon bond would give. As an individual investor, if you're willing to risk investing in such a company, you would be wise to make sure you

Chattem is a publicly traded company whose shares are listed on NASDAQ. It makes and manufactures all kinds of toiletries and cosmetics including Gold Bond, Icy Hot, Bullfrog suntan lotion, Cornsilk makeup, and Ban deodorant. My kind of company!

In good, bad, or indifferent economies people still need deodorant, makeup, and foot powder. Chattem sells its products through large and small drug and grocery stores. Over the years, management has been truthful, hard working, and honest. The stock and bonds have done well and I continue to give them my full support.

Michaels Stores has been another success story. Every year at Halloween and Valentine's Day, I bake many cakes, cookies, and candies for my nieces at college. After my baking marathon, I festoon the delicacies with, say, decorative spiders, ghosts, and bloody teeth or Valentine doodads bought along with festive napkins at my local Michaels Store.

What I noticed though was that I needed to buy my things many weeks before I needed them. Michaels has great stuff, but I had to get there early or my basket wouldn't be full of the best decorations.

I later found out Michaels is a NASDAQ-listed company and has bonds outstanding. It also operates a specialty chain of home decorations, arts, crafts, and picture frame stores called Aaron Brothers.

There was a time when these stores weren't properly tended but no longer. The management is on the ball and my bonds have been steady coupon payers with no headaches.

Yes, you can find high-yield bond ideas yourself. Just keep your eyes open to the simple everyday goods and services, and then study the companies that produce them.

will receive a maximum amount of reward for your endeavors. As such, zero-coupon bonds can be more profitable than overfunded bonds.

There are also pay-in-kind high-yield bonds, commonly referred to as PIKs. These are very risky investments because, instead of receiving coupon payments in cash, you get additional bonds. Companies that issue such bonds are normally the most cash strapped and have balance sheets that are leveraged to the hilt.

READ THE FINE PRINT
BEFORE YOU BUY

High-yield bonds generally have multiple call dates. It makes perfect sense that if management accomplishes its goals and business improves, then revenues will roll in, cash flow becomes more plentiful, and interest coverage improves.

High-yield bonds are usually structured so that if the business does improve as planned, the issuing company may be able to call its bonds on a prescribed date and reissue new ones at a lower coupon rate. Therefore, one of the ten commandments of investing in high-yield bonds is to find out all the call dates and figure out the yield to worst call date. (I'll cover this in more detail in Chapter 7.)

Another major detail of high-yield bonds is called a "claw-back" provision. Simply stated, claw-backs allow a predetermined amount of bonds to be called if the company does an equity financing.

This feature is a double-edged sword for the investor.

The good news is that the equity financing pays down some of the debt, and that's why your bonds are taken away. You may be paid a premium for this claw-back provision. Another plus is that less of a debt burden means more cash flow, which usually begets better interest coverage.

The bad news is obvious: You must relinquish some of your juicy bonds and find a new home for the proceeds. According to the research done by Merrill Lynch, the percentage of high-yield bonds that are subject to these claw-back provisions is between 20 and 39%.

Another detail to keep on your radar screen when buying high-yield bonds is the change-of-control provision. There's no mystery in this one. If the company whose bonds you own is taken over or merged with another, this may "trip" the change-of-control provision.

This is the one case where the bondholder has the option of whether to hold onto the bonds or to "put" them back to the company. The price an investor will receive if he puts them back to the company is normally 101, which means that you will get $1,010 for every bond with a face value of $1,000. Naturally this means that you will have to obtain information about the acquiring company and its financial wherewithal, but often the acquirer is a better-quality company with deeper pockets.

I have had this happy occurrence happen a number of times. A few examples include when Sears purchased Orchard Supply, a company specializing in products for do-it-yourself homeowners. Overnight my Orchard Supply high-yield bonds became investment grade. The same happened with Bally Grand Casino when Hilton Hotels purchased it—*voilà,* overnight another high yield to investment grade transformation.

Unfortunately, sometimes the high-yield frog is kissed not by a beautiful investment-grade prince but by another amphibian. (See sidebar: *Kissed by a Frog.*)

The bottom line is that you must be aware of these details before you buy the bonds. The details may be written in small type, but their consequences can be larger than life for your investment.

HOW TO PICK A BOND

When is junk truly cheap and when is it expensive? Well, that depends on when you're talking about. Obviously, during the Milken and Drexel debacle, high-yield bonds that were really junk had spreads over Treasury securities that ballooned out to about 1,000 basis points.

On the other hand 1998 was a time when these bonds were really in demand. The Merrill Lynch High Yield Index for a 10-year high-yield bond narrowed to a record low 278 basis points over a Treasury security with a similar maturity. Investors just weren't getting compensated in yield for the risk they were taking.

On average, though, the norm is between 400 to 500 basis points over Treasury securities, generous compensation for the risk you are taking.

Remember, the tighter the spread to Treasury securities, the less of a bargain the bond is. This is important because high-yield spreads to Treasury securities are a dynamic target. You want to buy a high-yield bond when the spread over Treasury securities is wide, and sell the bond when the spread has narrowed.

I would advise you to use the Peter Lynch way of investing in this part of the bond market. Mr. Lynch, a former fund manager at Fidelity Investments, recommends that you pick names of companies that you are familiar with as well as businesses you understand.

For example, if you have a mobile phone from Nextel, a fre-

KISSED BY A FROG

In 1998, my clients owned Dawson Production's bonds with a 9.375% coupon and a maturity date of February 1, 2007. Dawson was a production company in the oil and gas industry, plugging wells, maintaining wells, providing vacuum services, and so on. In the summer of 1998, Key Energy Group announced it would purchase Dawson for $14.00 per share and assume its debt. The Dawson bonds had a poison put that allowed for the redemption of the bonds at 101 if a takeover were to occur.

Those of us familiar with Key Energy's highly leveraged balance sheet and aggressive management in a deteriorating industry knew this match was made anywhere but in heaven so we gleefully put our bonds back to Key Energy (a lower-quality credit) and rode off into the sunset.

quent issuer in the high-yield bond market, and are happy with the product, then you can logically assume that other people feel the same as you. This leads you to conclude that it is a well-run business and one that could be worth investing in.

Find out whether the company has publicly traded shares. This is important because you get all the news that everybody else receives immediately—earnings, changes on the board, analyst upgrades or downgrades—and you won't have to wait until the 10K or 10Q is generated. If you are privy to the same information that is available to the analysts and institutions, it creates a more level playing field.

> The Dawson bonds that remained took on the credit quality of Key Energy, which was a downgrade from Dawson as a standalone entity.
>
> So how do the bonds look today? The size of the original bond issue was $140 million, but those who elected to keep the bonds hold only 1,046,000 of them. As long as Key Energy stays in business and makes its interest payments, the bondholders will likely be okay. However, if they try to sell the bonds, finding a counterparty will be no easy task. With a little over 1 million bonds left, there will be little to no liquidity or buyers for these bonds and so they'll probably have to hold on until the maturity date.

A word of caution, though: Even with all the relevant financial information at your fingertips, don't assume that means there is a level playing field between you and the institutions.

Alas, the institutions will always have the edge over the little guy, despite noises made by the SEC. Herb Greenberg, a columnist for the financial website *TheStreet.com,* wrote an interesting article in January 1999 about this matter.

How, he asked, was it possible that an analyst at the investment bank Salomon Smith Barney could put out a report to institutional brokers at seven o'clock in the morning about how Tel-Save had "announced" several "new key strategic incentives" when Tel-Save didn't publicly announce any such thing until about three o'clock in the afternoon?

The incentives included a renegotiated agreement with America Online that would result in AOL buying $55 million worth of Tel-Save stock at $19 per share.

How did the analyst know? Did the fact that Salomon Smith Barney is Tel-Save's investment banker have anything to do with it? You decide.

As Greenberg said in the article, "While it's not unusual for a company to give analysts guidance about corporate events, it's not considered kosher to get the equivalent of a full-blown news release before the rest of the Street."

The SEC strictly prohibits companies from disclosing nonpublic information material selectively to favored investors or analysts, but in reality this kind of thing happens all the time. It's an ugly truth that we all have to live with.

As an individual bond investor you are also not privy to the conference calls and the visits to the firms themselves, but that makes you no worse off than if you were a stock investor.

Fortunately, companies such as Broadcast.com are trying to change the tide of the information flow by broadcasting over the Internet the company/analyst conference calls.

Basically there are two kinds of high-yield investors. There are those investors who are really looking for the ultimate score, buying into a start-up company and getting a lot of yield and an increase in the price of the bond as it moves up the credit quality scale.

Then there are those investors who are just looking for a significantly higher yield over Treasury securities, but don't want to cast their fate to the wind by buying a start-up company that may or may not succeed.

If you go with a company that has three or four times interest coverage, there is a reasonable cushion if the company experiences a couple of bad quarters because of a downturn in the economy or if the industry itself goes through hard times.

There are also those companies that are living right on the edge and don't even have the ability to generate a dollar in net pretax cash flow to pay your dollar of interest. If you invest in such a company, you should make sure you are getting a significantly higher spread over Treasury securities, because the ability to make the timely interest payments is impaired.

If you are somebody with a lot of money to invest and need that higher income stream, then I would advise putting together a portfolio of high-yield investments diversified by industry group and names within that group. Buy some consumer companies (Chattem, Big 5 Sporting Goods), cyclicals (WCI Steel, Del Webb), utilities (AES Corp.), and theaters (AMC Entertainment).

If an investment goes belly up, but it represents only 2% of your portfolio, then all is not lost.

WHEN THINGS GO BAD

One of the biggest pitfalls of being an investor is that you can do all your homework and still end up picking a loser. I was an investor in Marvel Holdings. Thinking reasonably that kids will always want to read comic books, it seemed a good bet at the time.

Unfortunately, the management at Marvel proved less than competent. Management overpaid for two acquisitions and never recognized the problems they had created. They did not have their arms around the company's problems and ultimately the bondholders were left holding the bag.

Now that is by no means true of all high-yield companies, but unfortunately it has happened and will certainly happen again.

Timing in the financial markets is everything and deciding when to head for the exits during bad times is a difficult choice. The high-yield market doesn't make this any easier for you. Because of its relative newness, it doesn't have the depth of the stock market and so getting out isn't always possible. As an individual investor you have the worst of both worlds. The institutions are always first in when things are on the up, and they're first out when things are on the down.

If a company does experience problems for whatever reason and bond prices start falling, the lemming mentality takes over and everyone usually heads for the exit at the same time. You as the small guy will be at the back of the queue. If it makes you feel a little better, often the institutions can't get out either. Because of this, it's essential that the money you allocate to the high-yield bond market should be money that you won't need in an emergency. It's obvious that if you have cash needs when the

BRANDED INCOMPETENT

When I have new positions to buy
and am in the process of selecting
bonds, I tend to study companies
whose products and management
goals are readily understandable. No
business plan bonds for my clients—
I prefer tangible products and
achievable results.

In 1997, I was reading my usual Wall
Street research reports when I came
across Commemorative Brands,
which made me reminisce about my
high school days. I had visions of
young 16- and 17-year-olds standing
in the high school quad in the late
1960s. Cheerleaders were wearing
their boyfriends' class rings on a
chain and swivel. I saw class keys,
pins, and high school jewelry of all
types—all the merchandise that
Commemorative Brands manufactures and sells today.

Talk about a built-in market. There
is a huge range of types of commemorative, achievement, and event jewelry, cards, diplomas, and paper
products for sports teams, schools,
and organizations.

So I dug in and learned that this pri-
vately held firm (owned by Castle
Harlan Partners II Limited Partner-
ship in New York) had publicly
traded bonds.

All kinds of exciting things were happening with the company: the integra-
tion of a ring operation in Austin,
Texas, targets for cost savings, geo-

high-yield market is suffering, you
may have to sell at an inopportune
time at a vastly reduced price. Your
high-yield bond portfolio will not
be your most liquid investment.

I hope that technology and
the Internet will gradually help the
individual, but it's unlikely that
there will ever be a truly level playing field so you will just have to
live with this inequity. Understand
it and work within the parameters.

When a company does expe-
rience problems, if it's a company I
have studied as closely as possible,
if it has a management I have some
confidence in, and if there is a logical reason for the downturn, then I
give it more time.

Think of it as you would a
stock. If Cisco has two bad quarters, does that mean it will never
improve? No, of course not. The
same is true of companies that
issue high-yield bonds. It's just that
they are living nearer the edge and
a couple of bad quarters matter
more because of their leveraged
balance sheets.

For cyclical companies,
should you buy when everyone else
is selling? You hear a lot about the
contrarian approach and the key is
undoubtedly finding the bottom or

identifying the top of the market. This is no mean feat and many people have lost their shirts getting it wrong. If you are an experienced high-yield investor, then this approach is a possibility. If you are reading this book, then you're probably not an experienced enough bond investor to do this.

Don't always trust the analysts; they can get too close to management and be blindsided as easily as you and I. You can get a good idea of what I'm talking about if you listen to a company's conference call following an earnings release. There is often a lot of cheery banter between some analysts and the management that sounds a mite too friendly to me.

This is what happened with Marvel. There were analysts on the conference calls who knew the chief executive officer very well, yet they along with everyone else weren't kept up to date with the problems that management was experiencing. It's important that the average investor realize that the professionals can also get kicked in the teeth because they too are not told the truth or because bad news is withheld.

Probably one of the most depressing times to be an investor graphic growth opportunities. The management painted a bright picture.

By 1998, however, the financial goals and plans were not materializing and the management was having difficulty controlling expenses. The problems were hitting the prices of the bonds. Between July and November 1998, the bonds fell to 70 cents on the dollar from 101 cents. And then came the news that the CFO had departed the company.

I nursed this position along for months but after much thought I decided it was time to say *sayonara* and sell my bonds and those held by my clients at a loss. In my view management had lost all credibility.

Have things gotten better since then? Not really. The president and CEO have been replaced by a specialist in turning companies around. The company's credit facility from the banks has been amended many times and is tied to an equity infusion, which means the owners of the company must put money into the company in return for nonpublicly-traded shares.

The deadline for the equity infusion was the end of March 1999, but this deadline was extended to the end of May and then extended again to the end of June. Finally, by year end an equity infusion materialized.

The company did not make all of its January 15, 2000, coupon payment. Boy, how management wrecked a perfectly good business. What a shame!

The moral of this is to give management a time horizon to fix the problems. Don't buy their excuses unless
the excuses make sense and in some
cases you can verify them. It's better
to take a loss than sit through a
bankruptcy.

is when you watch management ruin a perfectly good business. Unfortunately, this happens all too often. In business as in sports there are a lot of egos out there and you must be sure that what the management is doing is in the company's interest, not the management's. (See sidebar: *Branded Incompetent.*)

A classic example of this is the takeover. What better way to impress the next door neighbors than to buy their house. Unfortunately, the reality is that most mergers just don't work. It is an exceedingly tricky business integrating two companies and I often get the impression that management doesn't even take the time to work out the details of how to carry this through successfully until after they've signed on the dotted line. By then, of course, the damage is done and it's too late.

SUCCESS WITH HIGH-YIELD BONDS

Management does everything it promised it would, the bonds are upgraded to investment grade, bond prices soar, and the spread over Treasury securities narrows. That's the Promised Land.

A less ambitious goal is one where the company stays in business, it makes the interest payments in a timely manner, you get your principal back on either the call date or the maturity date, and you generate the rate of return that you locked in. That's a successful high-yield investment.

As more and more investors realize they can't live on the paltry yields generated by the money markets, certificates of deposit, or Treasury securities, I expect the high-yield bond market to become a bigger and better place for all types of investors, including the individual investor.

CHAPTER 4

THE GOOD—
AND BAD—BOND
GAMBLES

Just as some investors in the stock market put money into stocks not for the dividend payments but with the hope that the share price will rise, some bond investors aren't satisfied with clipping the coupons but also seek capital gains, or a rise in the price of their bond investments.

If you make a bet on the price of a bond rising or falling, you are basically making a wager on interest rate movements. Put simply, if interest rates rise, the price of a Treasury security will fall; if interest rates fall, the price of the Treasury will rise.

For example, say the economy is racing along at a good clip and inflation is creeping up, then you could bet that the Federal Reserve will raise interest rates to try to cool down this overheating economy. Alternatively, the situation could be that interest rates are high and the economy is slowing down, and you could wager that the Fed will lower rates to give the economy some slack to grow.

There is also a time when you can bet that a financial crisis, such as the collapse in the Long-Term Capital Management in 1998, will cause a flight-to-quality and push up the prices of Treasury securities and high-grade corporate bonds.

If you are one of those investors who want more than just the coupon payments but also capital gains, then you are by very nature being an aggressive investor.

The biggest danger, of course, is that you are wrong and you will be forced to sell the securities at a lower price than you bought them, thus incurring capital losses. At the very least, you would have to hold onto the bond you selected and wait for the next economic cycle or the crisis to pass.

Financial institutions gamble a lot of money every day on the movement in bond prices. The number of individual investors who seek primarily capital gains on their bond investments is probably very small. However, this number is likely to grow with time. We've seen a bull market in bonds spanning the 1980s and 1990s, and a lot of individual investors have received a significant rate of return on their bond investments through capital appreciation, which is very tempting.

There are, of course, good gambles on bonds and bad gambles on bonds, so in this chapter I will try to spell out the ones that are perhaps worth a wager and ones that you should very definitely avoid.

Each of these entails a risk; it's just that some are more risky than others.

THE BEST GAMBLES

The best bond gambles are those that involve Treasury securities because there is no credit risk involved in the equation, the government being considered a perfect creditor.

It's important to note that a bond's annualized return is generally calculated by using three fundamentals: coupon payments, price appreciation or depreciation, and interest on the coupon payments, which is called compound interest. The further an investor goes out on the yield curve (the longer the maturity of the bond), the greater potential for appreciation or depreciation of the bond investment. That's why most coupon-clipping retail investors generally purchase short to intermediate bonds, while it is the hedge funds and institutions looking for double-digit total returns that speculate in the 20- to 30-year maturities.

If you believe interest rates are on their way down and bond prices on their way up, then you can potentially make money. For example, you could buy $500,000 worth of Treasury bonds with a 5.25% coupon due February 15, 2029. At a price of 95 cents on the dollar, the yield to maturity in 1999 would be 5.60%.

The question is, how sensitive is the price movement of this Treasury security to interest rates? The answer is, very sensitive. This bond's *duration,* or sensitivity to interest rates, is 15 years. Duration is a complicated calculation to do yourself, but your broker or the online brokerage from which you bought the Treasury security will be able to tell you the duration.

In plain English, duration of 15 years means that a move of one percentage point (100 basis points) in interest rates would generate a move of approximately 15 points in the bond price. If rates decline from 5.60% to 4.60%, the 15-point rise in the price of the bond would generate a gain of approximately $75,000. Conversely, if rates move in the other direction up to 6.60%, then you will lose $75,000.

The example above involves an ordinary coupon-paying Treasury security. If you wanted to increase the stakes, instead of buying coupon-paying Treasuries, you could buy zero-coupon Treasury securities on an unleveraged basis.

Unleveraged means that for every dollar you put up, you get one dollar of investment. Basically, you pay all the cash upfront for the security.

If interest rates do move, you'll get the most bang for your buck with a zero-coupon Treasury bond.

As we explained in Chapter 2, zero-coupon bonds are those that don't pay semiannual coupons but instead are priced at a discount to par. You receive the interest and principal at maturity.

The reason you will get the most from a change in interest rates with zero-coupon Treasury securities is because they are the most volatile of U.S. government securities. This means that the price of the security responds in a more exaggerated way to the interest rate environment than does a comparable coupon-paying Treasury security.

Zero-coupon Treasury securities are more volatile to the tune of anywhere between 20 and 25%, the amount depending upon the bond's maturity. Therefore, if you buy a 30-year zero-coupon Treasury security and simultaneously buy a 30-year coupon-paying Treasury security, should interest rates fall by 100 basis points, the price of the zero-coupon Treasury security will rise significantly more than that of the coupon Treasury security. There's built-in leverage in the zero-coupon bond because there are no interest payments.

You could also buy a zero-coupon Treasury STRIP (see Chapter 2) such as those that mature on February 15, 2029. If the STRIP has a price of 18.50 (or $185 per $1,000 face value), it yields 5.82%, while the corresponding regular coupon 30-year Treasury security yields just 5.60%. By putting up $499,500, you'll be able to purchase $2.7 million face value of these zero-coupon STRIPs. If interest rates decline one percentage point, the bond price would rise from 18.50 to 24.686 to give a gain of $167,022 in a six-month period. With a duration of 29.81 years, these long-term STRIPs are the riskiest bet because the volatility is so much higher than that of the short-term STRIPs.

Since the advent of zero-coupon Treasury securities in the early 1980s, if investors feel the economy is going into a recession or they think interest rates are too high historically for what is a low inflationary environment, they will buy zero-coupon Treasury securities with different maturities. (See sidebar: *Just Because You've Never Heard of It Doesn't Mean It's Not So.*)

BUYING BONDS USING
THE REPO MARKET

If we go back to the original example using the 5.25% Treasury bond due in 2029, it involves putting up $500,000. Now, few of us have that kind of money lying around waiting to be invested. However, by leveraging yourself you can control $500,000 of bonds and the chance to make $75,000 by putting up only $50,000 and financing the remaining balance.

The word *leverage* has rather an ominous ring to it. After all, that was one of the ways Long-Term Capital Management got itself into such a pickle when its credit lines started being pulled and it had to liquidate its positions at a loss.

However, both types of investor—institutional and individual—play the Treasury market using leverage. If it's done with care and a complete understanding of what one is doing, buying on leverage can sound a lot riskier than it actually is.

When people talk about a "carry trade" it means they are buying Treasury securities on margin and financing it in the overnight repurchase, or repo, market. If you are right in your interest rate prediction, your bond trade can generate a positive carry. This simply means that the income you receive from your Treasury position exceeds the interest rate on the loan. If you earn 5.25% and are paying 5.00%, then you will have a positive carry.

Because institutions tend to have a better credit standing than you or I, they can buy Treasury securities on very exaggerated margins, meaning they put down a small amount of money in order to control a lot of bonds. With so much money at stake, even the smallest move in the price of a bond can reap huge windfalls for the institution.

A retail investor can typically buy Treasury securities on 10% margins for 30-year Treasury bonds, and 2 to 3% for 5-year Treasury notes. This means that if you put down $100,000, you could control $1 million worth of 30-year Treasury bonds. Even if the price of the bond moves only a half point, then on that leverage you can make money, coupled with the chance of a positive carry. But if rates turn against you, the position will prove to be a loser—temporarily if you hold onto the bonds and the market turns in your favor, or permanently if you decide to sell out the position immediately.

It is a relatively easy process for an individual investor to buy bonds on margin. All you have to do is call a full-service brokerage, such as Merrill Lynch, Bear Stearns, or Goldman Sachs, and tell them you want to leverage Treasury securities using the *repo market.*

Follow this rule: Always ask the broker to use the repo market to finance your Treasury purchases. Whatever you do, don't finance your Treasury purchases in the same way that you finance your stock purchases.

JUST BECAUSE YOU'VE NEVER HEARD OF IT DOESN'T MEAN IT'S NOT SO

My experience of writing for *Forbes* magazine has had many high points and a few low ones.

In 1997, I wrote a column on zero-coupon bonds from Exxon Shipping and General Motors Acceptance Corporation. The bonds had a special feature: no tax on the imputed interest as with zero-coupon Treasury bonds.

One of the points I made was that with these long-term issues due in 2012 and 2015 you have a potential interest rate play if yields decline. After all, these zeroes will appreciate 20 to 25% more than their coupon-brethren will if rates decline. A fantastic capital gains play.

The column went on to explain the other virtues of these tax-deferred zeroes. I know the Exxons well because I have personally owned them since the early 1980s. I have never ever received a 1099 for the imputed interest.

Well, to put it politely, after I wrote this, all hell broke loose. I received e-mails, air mails, and yelling males. Brokers called me a liar. Accountants told their clients there was no such thing as a tax-deferred zero-coupon bond.

I spent the next few days faxing descriptions of the bonds from the

Stocks are financed at the broker loan rate, which is the rate of interest that a brokerage firm borrows from the bank plus a nice little markup. For instance, if you have a retail account at Merrill Lynch and the broker loan rate stands at 5%, depending on your loan they can mark it up anywhere between one and three percentage points. This means that you could be paying about 8% on your loan.

That margin rate is for stocks, which are not only totally different securities from bonds but also most certainly don't have the same credit quality as the U.S. government. So why pay a rate of 8%?

The repo rate paid to finance Treasury securities represents the interest rate charged for the borrowed cash. Most brokerage firms use an open-ended repo that expires daily and is automatically renewed at the next day's rate.

Most of these firms—such as Merrill Lynch, Bear Stearns, and Oppenheimer—have the ability to allow retail investors to finance Treasury securities at a much lower rate in the repo market. But you have to ask for it. Don't be shy, it's your money we're talking about here.

WHAT IS THE REPO MARKET?

The repo market is a $2.5 trillion market for overnight loans that finance holdings of government debt. It's a pretty complex beast, but having a reasonable working knowledge about it is enough to use it effectively.

Primary dealers of Treasury securities—those that can put in competitive bids at Treasury auctions—have what's called a *matched repo book.*

The primary dealer brings money in from institutions like the state of California that want to invest significant amounts of funds for a short period of time, but need access to these funds at short notice. That's one side of the ledger.

On the other side of the ledger are other institutions such as hedge funds that want to finance the purchase of Treasury securities in the overnight market. Basically someone like Merrill Lynch acts as the middle guy.

For example, the state of California phones Merrill Lynch and says it wants to invest $100 million but will need to access this money quickly. Merrill Lynch will pay the state of California approximately the federal funds rate as interest, which for the purpose of this example I'll put at 4.50%.

Then a hedge fund phones Merrill Lynch and says it wants to buy $100 million of Treasury securities on leverage. Merrill Lynch will charge the hedge fund a rate that is slightly over the federal funds rate.

Merrill Lynch is probably making 3/8 to 1/2 percentage point on matching these two sides up, which, considering the amounts of money we're talking about, works out to quite a tidy profit. The collateral that the

information vendor Bloomberg, the CUSIP numbers, and the front sheet of the original 1982 prospectus to these naysayers.

Brokers who either didn't believe me or didn't bother to try to find these bonds told inquiring clients that these bonds weren't appropriate for them. They also used the occasion to switch these customers into "something more appropriate." Appropriate my #?@, these are investment-grade bonds that anyone can hold or trade for potential capital gains.

Just because you've never heard of a specific type of bond doesn't mean it doesn't exist.

state of California is given for its $100 million is the Treasury securities. Usually the loan is collateralized at 103 to 105 cents for every dollar. This overcollateralization provides a safety net and some wiggle room in case bond prices decline. If prices decline a lot, the state of California will ask and receive additional collateral for its $100 million loan.

This is also the reason that brokerages such as Merrill Lynch don't automatically offer this service to people like you and me, because it needs to involve large amounts of money to make it a worthwhile exercise for the brokerage firm.

With individual investors, they would much rather you finance your purchases of Treasury securities at the higher broker loan rate. It's less paper work for them and certainly more profitable.

To ram the point home, I'll say this once again: *You have to ask for the repo rate. Don't wait for them to offer it.*

The minimum amounts that a brokerage will allow you to finance Treasury securities in this way varies; some will do it for as little as $100,000, while others won't do it for less than $5 million.

But if you want to speculate properly in the Treasury market, you have to do it in the repo market because your cost of carry will be reduced significantly.

To leverage Treasury securities you need to set up a separate repo account at the brokerage firm. You will have to fill out a repo account form, which is a little bit more complicated than a regular brokerage account form, but it's not that onerous.

Considering this account will allow you to control $1 million worth of bonds by only putting down $100,000, you'll be surprised at the ease with which you can set up one of these accounts.

However, although the amount of money you can control is substantial, the risk involved is not so great that you can lose $1 million. This is because if you can't make a margin call when interest rates move against you, the brokerage firm will sell out your position in the Treasury market. Basically it is using your Treasury bonds as collateral on the loan.

There is some risk here, but it is certainly not as risky as selling short an option on a stock, which can involve unlimited downside risk.

It's not hard for you to get into the repo market, but you have to ask and you have to be asking the right people. Discount brokers won't do this, only full-service brokers.

If you think we're at a peak in yields and prices are going to go up, buying Treasury securities using the repo market is most definitely an example of a good bond gamble.

With regard to the tax implications of buying Treasury securities on margin, the coupon income is fully taxable for federal income tax purposes and exempt from state income tax. Consequently, the margin interest or repo interest expense is only a deduction for federal tax purposes, not for state purposes.

To summarize, if you want to get more bang for your buck than you get with Treasury securities:

- Buy zero-coupon Treasury securities.
- To up the ante, buy Treasury securities on leverage.
- To leverage your position, use the repo market, *never* the broker loan rate.

TARGET TERM TRUSTS

If you don't feel up to buying zero-coupon Treasury securities yourself, there are mutual funds out there that specialize in buying these securities. The fund managers buy zero-coupon Treasury securities of a variety of maturities and they put them in what's called a "target term trust." In this way, the zero-coupon Treasury securities will mature in steps in 2010, 2011, and so on.

If you want to be a market timer and don't have the will or the time to do it yourself through a broker, then using these target term trusts is a good way to speculate on an interest rate move. We will discuss these funds further in Chapter 6.

The problem with target term trusts is that you will pay management fees for something you can do fairly easily yourself. The target term trusts do enjoy economies of scale by buying bigger positions than you could purchase by yourself, but on balance I think you're better off buying the individual bonds.

FEDERAL AGENCY AND CORPORATE BONDS

If you want to get a little more risky in your interest rate bets, then you could try buying federal agency and investment-grade corporate bonds instead of Treasury securities.

Beginning in 1998, the amount of debt the government issues has declined dramatically as the deficit has fallen. The federal agencies, notably Fannie Mae, Freddie Mac, and the Federal Home Loan Banks, started to issue large, liquid issues of bonds that they have dubbed "bench-mark issues" or the like. These issues are anywhere upwards of $2 billion in size.

What they are trying to do, but by no means completely succeeding in doing as yet, is to create issues that would function as a substitute for Treasury securities. Unfortunately despite government guarantees, these issues still don't have the perfect credit quality of Treasury securities and the spreads that they are priced over Treasury securities are still subject to widening and tightening.

Alternatively, you could invest in investment-grade corporate bonds, which will give you a good ride for your money if interest rates decline. You should try to buy the most liquid issues. Interest rates have steadily fallen since the 1980s and U.S. corporations have been taking advantage of these low interest rates in this country by buying back their existing debt and refunding it at the much lower interest rates. In early 1999, AT&T broke the record for the largest single corporate bond issue with an $8 billion bond offering.

You can finance your purchases of federal agency bonds in the repo market, but there's no repo market for corporate bonds. Sorry.

Lastly, if you are buying bonds on margin, please do shop around for the best rates because they can differ wildly. On a $500,000 debit balance,

Charles Schwab once quoted me a rate of 50 basis points over the broker loan rate, which was a net 7.5%, while Merrill Lynch wanted a net 8.4%. There are different rates for larger debit balances and rates do vary widely from one brokerage firm to another, so do your homework.

MUNICIPAL BONDS

Trying to generate capital gains using municipal bonds is an okay bond gamble if you think interest rates will decline. You can buy zero-coupon municipal bonds or 30-year municipal bonds and you will get capital appreciation if interest rates decline, but not as much as with Treasury bonds and investment-grade corporate bonds.

Another problem with municipal bonds is that they are not as liquid as either Treasury securities or some investment-grade bonds, which is important if you ever need to get out of a bad position quickly or want to sell quickly to take your profits.

Also, don't buy municipal bonds on margin. Remember, the beauty of municipal bonds is that the coupon payments are exempt from federal taxes and sometimes state and local taxes, too. Therefore, you can't write off the margin expense like you could when buying a Treasury security or corporate bond, because then you would be having it both ways. It would be nice, but unfortunately it's not allowed.

I've heard many people argue that taxable municipals are a bond bargain, but I'm not so sure. For one thing, municipalities for many years ran their finances using smoke and mirrors. Although I think that most municipal authorities are better at running their finances than they used to be, the idea of buying a taxable bond without full access to the financial information a company is required by law to release and without the reward from buying a high-yield bond from a private company is a gamble that I would avoid. I think this is more an institutional market than one that an individual investor should get involved with. Certainly taxable municipal bond yields more closely match corporate bond yields, but you would be flying by the seat of your pants—and your broker probably won't know any more than you would.

Finally, municipal bonds and corporate bonds, unlike Treasury securities, often have call features, something we discussed in Chapter 2. This is a problem if you are using municipal and corporate bonds for a bet on a decline in interest rates. Should interest rates decline enough, the municipal authority or corporation in question may decide to call the bonds, leaving you holding cash in a declining interest rate environment.

Should you just stick to noncallable bonds? Noncallable bonds do generate greater capital gains than callable bonds, but because there's no free lunch in the markets, noncallable bonds yield anywhere from 5 to 10 basis points less than comparable callable issues.

It is possible to make considerable capital gains from municipal bonds, and I run a number of portfolios that are chock-full of municipal bonds, which have appreciated in price significantly because of the decline in interest rates we've seen over the past few years. However, the individuals who bought these municipal bonds weren't making an interest rate bet, rather they were just locking in a high tax-free yield.

NONDOLLAR BONDS

If you keep up with international events and have an understanding of the currency markets, this is a very interesting bond gamble although it can be a risky one.

Assuming you buy the sovereign debt of a country, such as Bunds from Germany and Gilts from Great Britain, or good-quality U.S. corporate bonds that are denominated in a foreign currency, the currency is the key to everything and it will either make or break your investment.

This can be a fairly dangerous bond gamble because you are adding currency risk to the interest rate risk. If you buy corporate debt in another currency, you're also bringing in credit risk. Quite a combination of risk and perhaps a recipe for disaster.

You could even buy the bonds on margin and take your bond gamble to new realms of riskiness. Not a good idea unless you are an extremely sophisticated investor or just rich enough to not care.

The absolute worst debacle I've been involved in was with nondollar bonds. In the 1980s, there was a new fad where corporations did currency swaps and issued Australian- and New Zealand–dollar bonds. The problem was that at that time the market for the currencies being used was small in relationship to the amount of currency needed to back the issuance of the new debt. As a result, once the huge amount of bond issuance was over, the Australian dollar fell seven cents in one night.

Beware of following fads. The craze may contain the seeds of its own destruction.

If you are determined to dabble in this market, stick to the government debt of countries with deep capital markets. I would also look for a country that either is on a tear with interest rates on an upward trend or has an appreciating currency. Alternatively, invest in a country where a new government has come in to sort out the mess in which the previous administration left the economy. This way you're limiting the downside risk because hopefully most of the bad news has already happened. It's difficult to pinpoint the economic bottom. A good example of this could be Japan.

Every full-service brokerage has an international desk that will sell you nondollar-denominated bonds. Investment banks help governments and companies bring their bond issues to market, and when the bonds are issued, the bank normally keeps some of them in inventory.

It's not usually something the brokerages will offer you, but most will be glad to give you a piece of their inventory if you ask. The minimum investment is usually anywhere between $25,000 and $100,000, depending on which brokerage you use.

It's normally hard for individual investors to get into a new issue unless it is one of the regular government funding auctions.

There are exceptions. In 1999, Salomon Smith Barney lead managed a new bond issue for Japan, which was targeted to retail investors as well as institutions. It was a dollar-denominated note in which the performance was tied to the depreciation of the Japanese yen versus the U.S. dollar.

After almost 10 years, investors are beginning to wonder when the Japanese will finally get their act together. I'm not sure we've reached the bottom yet (I didn't participate in Salomon's bond issue), but as of the close of the century, there are some signs of a recovery in the country.

If the Japanese economy did turn around, the yen would most likely appreciate against the dollar.

The Japanese government issued so much new debt in 1999 to try to kick-start the faltering economy. As I write, the Japanese government has just passed a mammoth simulative budget worth around $700 billion, which involves a lot of public work spending that will be financed by more deficit spending bonds. The budget is aimed at pulling the economy out of its worst recession since World War II.

Expect Wall Street to come up with many more derivative products like the yen "put" bond mentioned above. Retail investors are getting much more sophisticated, and these products that were primarily the domain of institutions have now gone Main Street. I will discuss this further in Chapter 9.

Finally, there are many mutual funds that cater to investors interested in nondollar-denominated bonds. The majority of these have done poorly over the later part of the 1990s, as the dollar has been the king of currencies. But we know that no kingdom lasts forever and nondollar-denominated bonds will undoubtedly have their time in the sun again. Working out correctly when this time will arrive and buying in at the bottom is the risk you have to take.

ASSET-BACKED BONDS

Asset-backed bonds involve the securitization of payments from loans, such as those from credit cards and cars. The banks package these loans and sell them on to investors in the form of bonds.

I must admit here that I've never actually bought an asset-backed bond, and I don't intend to anytime soon. Although asset-backed bonds certainly haven't received the same level of negative press that collaterized mortgage obligations (see below) are getting, I think this type of investment is still basically an institutional market.

That's not to say this asset class won't eventually go Main Street. Traditional asset-based bonds involve the securitization of loans that enjoy relatively predictable amounts of cash at predictable times. However, over the past few years Wall Street has been securitizing more esoteric forms of payments such as revenues from record sales from household names like pop singer David Bowie.

Although securitizing royalty payments may give the bonds a more popular appeal, whether this is a good thing remains to be seen. These bonds are very complicated to analyze properly. During September and October 1998 when Long-Term Capital Management was close to collapse, asset-backed bonds suffered hugely. If this happened to the institutions that have all those rocket scientists working for them, what do think would happen to you?

CMOs—JUST SAY NO

The worst, and I mean positively the worst, bond play you can make is to get involved in collaterized mortgage obligations (CMOs). If a broker phones you and tries to sell you this garbage, firmly tell her no, and if she persists, just hang up.

A CMO is a derivative security that is backed with underlying mortgage pools as collateral. The collateral can be multi-family housing mortgages, commercial property or nonconforming mortgages, plus a laundry list of others. However, what makes CMOs different from those vanilla mortgage pools such as Ginnie Maes (backed by VA and FHA mortgages), which can be good investments, is that the mortgages are chopped, spliced, and diced into different tranches. A CMO tranche is a structure with payment objectives for specific investors. Needless to say, the institutions get the best tranches and the garbage that's left—yes, you've guessed it—gets sold to people like you and me. Right from the get-go, you're onto a loser.

In fact, sometimes the investment bank will create specific CMO tranches for institutional investors. The institutions will tell the banks they want mortgages that will pay so much for so long, and they create a CMO to order. What's left over the bank will sell to lesser-quality institutions and the real toxic waste goes to the retail investors.

Try asking your broker for a CMO with a certain coupon and maturity date. That noise you hear in the background whenever you call the broker to find where that CMO is will be the sound of her dragging her feet. CMOs are a product that is sold to individual investors, not bought.

With interest rates falling, brokers will once again try to push these instruments onto unsuspecting investors. This is a bit contemptible because it was only in 1994 that CMOs blew up, leaving everyone with something nastier than egg on their faces.

The brokers, no doubt, are betting on the market's famously short memory.

What happens is that the brokerage firms left holding the less-than-sterling tranches of these CMOs have a sales meeting in the morning. The managers tell the salespeople, "Okay, we have $15 million of these CMOs today. Here are the selling points. Go out and get rid of them."

Armed (and very dangerous) with these "selling points," they find all the little people they do business with and sell the CMOs to them.

What's the sales pitch? To entice you, the broker will tell you that this investment has impeccable credit quality. Indeed it probably does with Ginnie Mae, Fannie Mae, and Freddie Mac pass-throughs. However, that's where the good points end.

The broker will also tell you this investment will earn so many basis points over those boring old Treasury securities. What she won't say is that large interest rate shifts such as those in 1993 (when rates went down) or those in 1994 (when rates rose) can cause horrible things to happen to the CMO's duration, cash flow, and market value.

The average life? Don't believe what the broker tells you because she's only guessing. She can't predict it with any degree of certainty.

Even sophisticated institutional money managers can be fooled by CMOs. I know of several who in 1993 purchased long-term Freddie Mac bonds maturing in 23 years that were supposed to be insensitive to interest rate moves. In fact, the sales pitch was that the CMO yielded 1.5 percentage points more than Treasury bills with return of capital in 6 to 9 months.

What happened was a disaster. It took well over 3 years until the entire principal was returned.

Couldn't the CMOs have been sold? Certainly, but at a huge loss and with great difficulty.

Brokers probably tell you the truth about what the prepayment assumptions are—that you will get so much interest every month, and so much principal—but that's just the problem, they're only assumptions. The behavior of the underlying mortgage may not even come close to past experience and you may end up with a long-term, low-yielding, and illiquid security.

The language used with CMOs should give you an idea of for whom these products are really designed. The tranches include targeted amortization classes (TACs), planned amortization classes (PACs), inverse floaters, interest-only tranches, principal-only tranches, and residuals. Only institutions could come up with these names and only institutions have the staff, training, time, and ability to analyze these instruments properly.

I must tell you that I have angered many of the powers that be with this line. My article on this subject in *Forbes* magazine in 1997 caused quite a stir. Many third- and fourth-rated brokerage firms complained. They were upset, perhaps understandably, that I was killing their lucrative business in selling something nobody with the proper facts would touch if it were the last investment on earth.

The Bond Market Association even had the temerity to send me a nasty letter and telephoned to chastise me. My reply to the lady who called was that I am nothing but a flea on the backside of the bond market so why are you getting so upset unless there is something to my arguments. The complaints were not coming from Bear Stearns, Merrill Lynch, or Salomon Smith Barney, but from the third-rate brokerages fearful that I was killing a nice way to get rid of garbage.

This is not a bad bond gamble; this is the worst bond gamble. Be warned.

BOND FUTURES

Today, there are many individual investors who speculate in the futures market using interest rate futures, *speculate* being the operative word here. You can make money faster than a speeding bullet or you can blow up like a nuclear holocaust.

Futures began in the commodity markets, but have since branched out into the currency, stock, and bond markets.

A future is basically a forward contract but with a few distinguishing characteristics. A forward contract is a contract drawn up

THE GREAT SPECULATOR

I have to admit that I'm a terrible trader. Buying and holding an investment is my style. But once in a blue moon I am filled with the burning desire to throw caution to the wind and try to make some serious bucks.

I was a bond broker before I became a fixed-income money manager. One day, a colleague of mine at the brokerage began to extol the virtues of selling options on futures because the bond market was "certain" to fall in price.

I can't remember the specifics of the trade—perhaps I've blocked them out—only the outline of the suicide mission I agreed to participate in, which was selling naked options. If you sell options naked, or uncovered, you are exposing yourself to unlimited risk.

So I sold options on the interest rate futures, betting that bond prices would decline. I figured my maximum exposure was between $10,000 and $15,000, with the potential to make $30,000.

Boy, was I wrong! Drinking kerosene would have been more pleasurable. Everything went wrong at once. At 11 that night, I received a panicky call from a broker in Japan who was yelling that U.S. Treasury prices were rallying hard in Asian trading. My position was going against me and I had a loss on paper of $30,000. I was scared, but my guess was that

between two parties that says party A can buy a product from party B at a given price.

Futures, however, are standardized. They are used only for certain products, ranging from meats to metals, for certain delivery dates, and for certain amounts of the product. This standardization allows the futures to be traded on an exchange, an important point if you wish to get out of the position.

Unlike with a forward contract, you must put up margin money to purchase a futures contract. This is not a down payment but a show of good faith, to demonstrate that you have the ability to make the payment when the time comes. If the market starts moving against you, you will get a margin call from your broker in the blink of an eye. This is why dabbling in futures can cost you more than an arm and a leg.

The futures market is a speculative market. Most participants have no interest in the underlying commodity. Can you imagine one of those Armani-clad guys on the exchange floor taking delivery of 3,000 bushels of wheat?

No, these speculators are there because of the opportunity to make money, pure and simple.

Although futures for Treasury bills, notes, and bonds are called interest rate futures, the futures express the value of the underlying instruments, not the interest rates themselves. If interest rates fall, the price of the futures will rise, just like the prices of the underlying bond securities will rise.

Therefore, if you think interest rates will fall, you should buy futures. If you believe rates are on their way up, you should sell futures.

Futures offer you a way of leveraging yourself in the Treasury market. You aren't literally borrowing money, but you are, in effect, borrowing short to lend long.

Let's give you an example. Suppose you think interest rates are destined to fall, so you buy one March contract on the Chicago Board of Trade exchange. Each contract represents $100,000 face amount of long-dated Treasury securities. The price for this future is 111-14/32 and you put down $2,700 as a margin payment. You are now controlling $100,000 worth of Treasury securities with only a very small margin payment.

If you're right and interest rates do decline, then the price of your bond contracts will go up. If

things would improve by the morning because trading in Treasuries in Asia is very thin and one large trade can exaggerate any move.

Wrong again.

Another two hours passed and the broker called me again to inform me that I'm now down $200,000! While this wouldn't bankrupt me, it would certainly put a serious dent in my personal finances.

I decided not to cover the position because I was sure (I'm reminded of that phrase, a fool and his money are easily parted) the market would eventually go my way. I didn't sleep a wink all night. How could I? My net worth was evaporating.

I was at my office at 4:30 the next morning in a very agitated state. Luckily, the government released the producer price index numbers at 8:30 A.M. (EST) and the numbers were awful, causing bond prices to tank.

In the end, I got out losing less than $10,000 and vowed never to sell naked options again. To this day I have kept my promise.

If you insist on opening yourself up to unlimited risk, make sure that you have either nerves of steel or a whole lot of money to lose. My advice would be to leave this to the professionals, who are gambling with other people's money.

you're wrong, however, get out as fast as possible. Remember, because you're controlling so much money, only a slight move in the wrong direction will mean the size of your losses will be substantial. There's no bottom here; the size of your losses will grow exponentially with each move against you.

In reality, of course, the broker will be on the phone the moment there's a move against your position, asking for more money. If you can't make the margin call, the position will be closed for you.

Despite the risks, there are a lot of individuals who use the futures market. (Remember Hillary Rodham Clinton and her sizable profits in the cattle futures market?) Surprisingly, for the risk involved, it's a simple procedure to open up a commodities account with a broker.

In fact, the Internet has even reached the futures market, and there are several websites that offer investors the ability and information to take part in the futures market online. I will discuss this further in Chapter 8.

A final word on the futures market, which may highlight the cutthroat nature of this market. For every long in the futures market, there is a short. For every cent you make, someone is down a cent. You'll be up against a lot of very sharp and savvy people who don't like to lose.

Speculating in the futures market can be a bad gamble unless you have a sizable chunk of capital, are knowledgeable, and are very quick witted.

FUTURES OPTIONS ON BONDS

No doubt by now you've heard of stock options, those wonderful little things that managers at companies are given as a reward for cutting jobs and helping to raise the stock price.

These options give the holder the right to buy the related stock at a given price, regardless of the market value of that stock. The amount an option can be worth is staggering, considering it could, for example, give you the right to buy a share of America Online at 5 cents when it's currently trading at $140. If you have 100,000 of these options, whew . . .

The above is an example of an incentive option, something given to employees of the company. But there are also futures options, which are traded on futures exchanges.

A futures option takes its name from the futures contract that under-lies it. What the option does is give the holder the ability to buy (a call option) or sell (a put option) the underlying security at a given price (strike price) by a certain time.

Like an option on a stock, you are making a bet that interest rates or the price of the Treasury security will be at a certain level within a certain time. Basically with a stock option you are making a bet that the price of the stock is going up or down. With an interest rate option you are mak-ing a bet that interest rates will go up or down.

For example, you could buy an option that would give you right to buy the March future on the long Treasury at a given price.

If, as in the example above, the futures contract is trading at 111-14/32 and the option's strike price is 110-12/32, then your option is, using the industry lingo, *in the money.* This is because you can buy the underlying future at a cheaper price than it is currently trading at in the market. If, however, the option's strike price is 112-18/32, then you are *out of the money.*

The risk of losing money in this game is limited, because if the underlying future never reaches the strike price by the expiration date of the option, then you would stand to lose only the price of the option and the commission you paid for the option.

For example, say you buy five June Treasury bond call options with a strike price of 112. The options were trading at 1-57/65 each or $9,453 for the lot. If the price of the June T-bond future never reaches above 112, the most you lose is $9,453.

However, if the option does become in the money, then you have the choice of exercising it and buying the futures contract, or selling the option at a profit. (See sidebar: *The Great Speculator.*)

Although the options market on bonds is a more sophisticated mar-ket than it was a few years ago, it has still not been embraced by individ-ual investors to the same extent as options for stock have. I think it will happen, so if you want to get a head start on the Joneses next door, then a look at these might be worthwhile.

Buying options on futures is becoming increasingly easy for individ-ual investors. Full-service brokerages will all offer this to you on request and the ubiquitous Internet is getting in on the act, too. However, leave the selling of options to the pros, because this involves unlimited risk.

TO GAMBLE OR NOT TO GAMBLE

Buying bonds to create capital gains is basically a sound way to increase the value of your portfolio, just as if you were to buy growth stocks.

The worst move you can make is to buy CMOs and the least risky is to buy Treasury bills. In between, on a descending scale of riskiness there is buying Treasury securities using the repo market, and buying foreign-currency bonds, options, and finally futures. A pyramid can illustrate degrees of risk.

You know how much you can afford to lose, so invest accordingly.

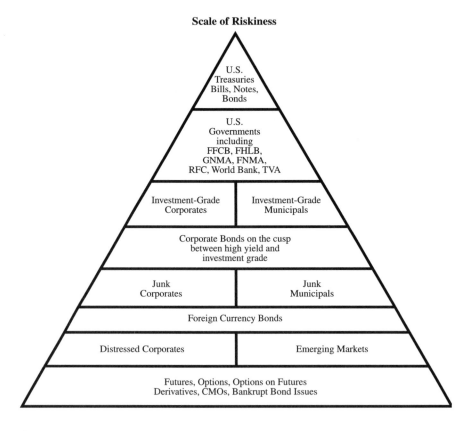

Scale of Riskiness

U.S. Treasuries Bills, Notes, Bonds

U.S. Governments including FFCB, FHLB, GNMA, FNMA, RFC, World Bank, TVA

Investment-Grade Corporates | Investment-Grade Municipals

Corporate Bonds on the cusp between high yield and investment grade

Junk Corporates | Junk Municipals

Foreign Currency Bonds

Distressed Corporates | Emerging Markets

Futures, Options, Options on Futures Derivatives, CMOs, Bankrupt Bond Issues

CHAPTER 5

THE RATING AGENCIES: DETERMINING CREDIT QUALITY

If you've invested in bonds before, you've probably heard of the rating agencies. There are four main rating agencies: Duff & Phelps, Fitch/IBCA, Moody's Investors Service, and Standard & Poor's. There are many others that cover particular countries and sectors.

Of those four listed above, by far the best known and largest are Moody's and S&P. As a retail investor, you will likely encounter these two the most.

Both of these rating agencies were set up this century: Moody's in 1900 and S&P in 1970, the result of a merger between Poor's Publishing Company and Standard Statistics Company.

The rating agencies' function is to take a debt issue and assign a rating to it that indicates in a somewhat simplistic way the likelihood that the issuer of the said security will default on it.

It must be noted that the agencies' ratings are not a recommendation to buy or sell any particular debt issue. The rating is merely a third-party assessment of the risk that the issuer will default on the debt issue.

Moody's and S&P are full-service agencies in that they rate all types of debt obligations from commercial paper to asset-backed securities, and they rate all types of issuers, from high-yield corporations to foreign governments.

The ratings agencies are overseen by the Securities and Exchange Commission (SEC), which dictates that the agency must carry out a rating process that is credible and sound in its methodology. The SEC also stipulates that there must be no conflicts of interest between the rating agency and the organization it is rating.

Let's take a look at how the agencies arrive at their ratings.

HOW RATINGS ARE DETERMINED

Don't underestimate how much work goes into rating a debt issue. It involves the analysis of many quantitative and qualitative factors of the past and present in order to give a credible prediction of the future. No mean feat.

The rating agencies look at four elements called the four Cs: capacity, character, collateral, and covenants.

Capacity is the ability of the issuer of the debt to repay the interest and principal in a timely fashion. This involves looking at all those statistics that we described in Chapter 3 and more: the financial statements filed with the SEC, EBITDA, business plans, and so on.

Character is, as you might expect, a more subjective look at the issuer of the security. This involves looking at the history of the management, its past success at sticking to the stated business plan, its honesty toward the investment community, and the transparency of its operations, among other things.

Some companies are known for their prudent fiscal management, others for recklessness. The rating agencies have longer memories than the market's notoriously short one.

The agencies also look at collateral, meaning the assets that are being used to back the debt.

Finally, there are the *covenants*. The covenants are the terms and conditions under which the debt was issued, and some can be more restrictive than others. Included in the covenants are where the issue ranks on the scale of who gets paid back first in the case of default—

senior or subordinated bonds—and also what call provisions there may or may not be.

KNOWING YOUR ABCs

The symbols the rating agencies employ to indicate what category each debt obligation falls into differ only slightly. The accompanying box looks at the various rankings of Moody's and S&P, with the highest quality at the top and the lowest at the bottom.

Moody's	S&P
Aaa	AAA
Aa	AA
A	A
Baa	BBB
Ba	BB
B	B
Caa	CCC
Ca	CC
C	D
(Moody's uses numerical modifiers to show the standing within a specific category. A 1 indicates the higher end of the rating category, 2 midrange, 3 lower-end category rating.)	(S&P uses [+] or minus [-] signs as modifiers that show the standing within the rating category.)

As you can see from the table, the categories track each other fairly well until you get down to the speculative categories.

I'm consistently hard on the rating agencies, yet I do use their ratings as a guideline. Am I a hypocrite? Probably, to a degree.

The agencies are paid big money by bond issuers and often their ratings are right on target. However, it's their mistakes that I, and everyone else for that matter, focus on. Why? Because mistakes can mean downgrades, which usually mean a fall in the bond's price, which translates into paper losses, which then turn into realized losses.

Investors use the standardized ratings to attach acceptable yields to the bonds of the issuers. Standardized ratings allow individual and institutional investors to compare the risk of one corporate or municipal bond with another.

Although I've probably talked about the Orange County municipal bankruptcy to death in this book, it is a prime example of a misstep that turned into a blunder.

Just months before Orange County declared bankruptcy, it issued millions of dollars of new bonds. Yes, the rating agencies gave the issue good marks. Yet a few weeks later, the county declared bankruptcy. How could this wealthy county manage to pull the wool over the eyes of very experienced rating services? I don't know the answer other than to

The investment-grade rankings run from Aaa/AAA down to Baa/BBB-, after which the rankings are considered noninvestment grade.

One problem that the agencies face with these rankings is that in order to be at all meaningful, they can't be too complicated. Therefore, while two bonds may have identical ratings, one may still be less likely to default than the other one.

WHAT DOES THIS MEAN TO YOU?

What we have discussed so far may seem rather academic, but unfortunately you cannot ignore these ratings as much as you might like. This is because the ratings do have at least some effect on the prices of the bonds that you either hold or may wish to buy.

To pretend that once a bond is rated it will always have the same ranking is naïve. These ratings are updated periodically (although perhaps not as often as some people would like) and if circumstances have changed since the last rating for the better or for the worse, the bond is upgraded or downgraded correspondingly.

Numerous studies have concluded that a change in ratings has no impact on the price of the bond because the market, being an efficient arbiter of the credit quality of an issuer, has already priced in any change by the agencies.

However, there are times when a rating agency unexpectedly changes a rating, causing the market to sit up and take notice. The rating agencies are by no means perfect, but then neither is the market.

The biggest change in price caused by any announcement by the ratings agency would probably come if a debt issue moves above or below the line separating investment grade and high yield. This is because there are many funds that are prevented from buying high-yield debt so they can buy such an issue only when it reaches investment grade.

Also, many fund managers measure the success of their portfolios against a benchmark index such as Lehman's Corporate Bond Index. To do this effectively, the managers must hold all the issues that are included in the index. So when a debt issue is added to the index after it is upgraded to investment-grade status, there is sometimes a big rush by many fund managers to purchase this issue, thus driving up the price.

say that in my opinion vital information must have been omitted, hidden, or never addressed by the various parties.

You couldn't blame the investors for buying the bonds, which were far from perceived as being a risky investment. They weren't stretching for yield when they purchased pre-bankrupt Orange County bonds, because the county was doing well and the bonds were truly investment grade.

The ghost of Orange County lingers and it still leaves a nasty taste in many investors' mouths. So what can we learn from this? Some individual investors in California learned that investing in investment-grade bonds is perhaps not as safe as they had assumed; others put the experience down to a fluke occurrence. Alas, I for one have seen dozens of flukey bond events occur over the years, some we can duck while others come out of nowhere and smash us in the teeth.

I guess the one thing I've learned is not to expect any apology from the rating agencies.

PROBLEMS WITH THE AGENCIES

Much criticism has been leveled at the rating agencies, especially since the economic crisis in the Far East in 1997 and 1998, which showed the agencies to be asleep at the wheel.

To be fair, the market was caught unaware as much as the agencies, so it would be a bit harsh to blame the agencies for not warning us sooner when they are often dismissed as an anachronism.

Nevertheless, a quick look at some of the problems associated with the rating agencies will at least give you some idea of why you should use the ratings from agencies only as one small element in your investment strategy. (See sidebar: *Remembered for Their Mistakes.*)

The most common criticism is that the agencies are reactive, that the announcement of a change in a rating comes after the market has already factored in such a change.

There is some truth to this. The most pointed criticism has come in the wake of the financial crisis that literally swept though the Far East like a tsunami wave toward the end of 1997.

While the institutional investors were busy dumping emerging market equities and debt, the rating agencies were only just waking up from their torpor. When they finally did act, it was a case of much too little much too late.

One particularly embarrassing example occurred in December 1997 when one of the rating agencies announced that South Korea was still investment grade even though the press had already revealed that the country's central bank had effectively run out of foreign currency.

These were big bond issues, not just some small issue from an obscure municipality. The rating agencies really let investors down. There was a lot of criticism then, but unfortunately this seems to have died down and it looks suspiciously like business as usual. The rating agencies never really seem to change, which is very frustrating for investors.

An interesting aside here is that the analyst at one of the major rating agencies in charge of South Korea left shortly after the debacle to join an investment bank. From this lofty perspective, he began to rail against the agencies for missing the boat, which, as one of his former colleagues acidly noted, was a tad hypocritical.

There are numerous other examples of belatedness. In 1994, the rating agencies conferred an investment-grade rating on a new Orange County municipal bond, only to watch the county declare bankruptcy a few weeks later. How could this happen? The analyst must have been completely out to lunch, dinner, and breakfast the following day. (See sidebar: *A Safe Haven in Pre-Refunded Bonds.*)

It seems when the agencies are wrong, they are grotesquely wrong. When they stumble, it's usually off a very steep precipice, taking all the little and big investors down with them. To know that you are unlikely to be alone when a catastrophe occurs may or may not give you some comfort.

One argument as to why the agencies get things wrong is that they are paid for the work they do by the people they rate. Before 1970, the agencies undertook the work of rating public debt offerings for free, but with the number of debt issues increasing exponentially, the agencies had to expand dramatically and were forced into charging for their services.

Does that mean they are dishonest or whorish about their work? Certainly not, but I can't imagine how you can maintain total objectivity under that type of pressure day in and day out. On many occasions an issuer will scream bloody murder about an agency's rating, arguing it is much too low. (Of course, they never argue when the rating is higher than expected.)

This kind of pressure on the analysts would seem to indicate that even at the most subliminal level there is the propensity for an analyst to be a bit more lenient on an issuer than if there were no money involved. There is too much of a human factor involved in these ratings that can skew the results.

There is also the problem associated with unsolicited ratings undertaken by agencies such as Moody's. Many investors feel a rating done without the permission of the said issuer cannot be complete because the agency does not have access to all the information it requires for paid ratings.

A SAFE HAVEN IN PRE-REFUNDED BONDS

During my entire career in the bond market, I have always preached the gospel of purchasing pre-refunded municipal bonds as the safest haven in the market. When all hell is breaking loose, these pre-refunded municipal bonds are the one safe place to be. This is because the money the municipal authority needs to pay the interest and principal of the pre-refunded bonds is held in an escrow account at a bank and invested in supersafe Treasury securities and government agency bonds.

When Orange County went bankrupt—undoubtedly the biggest crisis to hit the municipal bond market in decades—I held in my client accounts millions of dollars' worth of tax-free bonds issued by various Orange County municipalities. The names on these bonds ranged from small cities like Yorba Linda to large ones like Anaheim, the home of Disneyland.

When news of the Orange County treasurer's financial shenanigans that precipitated the bankruptcy hit the newswires, my heart stopped and my mouth went dry in fear.

The problems with Orange County went way beyond what anyone thought possible and it became apparent that this misguided soul had been tapping county funds and the funds of many small communities in the county that had been left in his care to play his high-wire financial games.

This practice even came under investigation by the Department of Justice after some issuers claimed that Moody's was abusing its market power by issuing unsolicited ratings to force the issuers to pay for services instead, something Moody's strenuously denied at the time.

At the very least, you should be aware that an unsolicited rating might not be as complete as one that was paid for by the issuer.

KEEPING TRACK OF CREDIT

If you can't totally rely on the rating agencies' ratings, what can you do to keep track of the credit quality of the bonds you hold in your portfolio?

Don't worry, you don't have to fly by the seat of your pants, always reacting to events rather than anticipating them.

The simplest way to at least keep in step with the market is to stick to bonds that have public equity.

As I said in Chapter 3, companies that have outstanding equity as well as bonds are well covered by the financial news media and by the investment community. There is no shortage of analysts out there. Obviously some are better than others, but you can always find one who is willing to give his or her time to explaining the issues confronting a company whether it be in newspapers or magazines, on television, via the Internet, or even over the phone.

You can extrapolate the information the analysts give about the stock and apply it to the bonds.

Getting continuous quotes is also more of a problem with bonds than with stocks. However, if the issuer of the bond also has equity and the stock price is plummeting, that could mean something is afoot that the marketplace knows about, but which the rating agencies have either failed to see or not had time to react to. As we mentioned before, the rating agencies are too often reactive and, in such cases, of little use to you. By the time they get around to confirming what is happening, you've already lost your shirt.

For municipal bonds, unfortunately there is of course no equity, so these bonds present more of a challenge because often you have to go on blind faith, which is not the best way to invest.

What if the escrow accounts had not been properly set up and funded? What if the money that should have been held and escrowed with Treasury securities in the banks had found its way back into the county's general fund, the one that suffered all the losses?

During a market panic touched off by news of fraud, you can't take anything for granted, so I began the painful process of checking out each and every bond. I had to call every city treasurer or finance director of each municipal issue I was holding to get the name and a contact person at each escrow bank and a contact person at the bond underwriter to verify or negate my worst fears.

But my fears weren't justified because it turned out that all the bonds were properly escrowed. Curiously, though, the market action in the bonds reflected my misplaced fears. While nobody actually traded any of these escrowed bonds in the first few days after the news broke, the bids reflected discounts of 20 to 25%. In a couple of weeks, however, the prices on the pre-refunded bonds recovered to normal levels.

The owners of regular Orange County bonds were not so lucky. Even though the bond brokers tried to reassure buyers that Orange County would return to financial health, these bonds lost as much as half their value.

INSURANCE IS NO SURE THING

Years ago, municipal bond investors were under the misconception that insurance meant price protection in the event of anything going wrong. Alas, history has taught them a few lessons to the wise.

Since the 1980s more and more municipal bonds have come to market with insurance. The reason is simple: Investors want it. And not just the little guy buying $20,000 of municipals, but the big municipal bond funds, too.

We all want protection from the unknown. If you've learned anything from this book, it is that you have to expect the unexpected and, yes, periodically a hole appears in your safety net and you land with a nasty bump. This is especially painful when you have taken steps, such as buying insured bonds, and you still get kicked.

Concerning municipal bond insurance, you should know that it does not necessarily preserve the tax-exempt status of these bonds, the main reason why anyone buys municipal bonds. The bankruptcy of the Allegheny Health hospital that we mention in this chapter brought this unwelcome truth home to many investors.

Tenet Healthcare Corp., a for-profit healthcare corporation, purchased eight of Allegheny Health's hospitals

Don't think defaults on municipal bonds are uncommon. We all heard about the bankruptcy of Orange County because it was so huge, but there are hundreds of defaults every year that involve much smaller sums of money. If you happen to have the bad luck to be involved in one of them, it's most decidedly a big deal to you.

In the case of municipal bonds, I would suggest you stick to very large, very good quality issues from a big state with a large population (it's probably taxed to the hilt) with large GDP growth. Stay away from those esoteric taxable municipal bonds.

A recent default that went largely unreported was 1998's default by Allegheny Health hospitals. The amount involved was considerable and some of those bonds issued were even insured, which brings me to my next point.

INSURING AGAINST THE UNINSURABLE

If you needed proof that states and municipalities can be just as reckless with money as any corporation, you need look no further than the issue of municipal bond insurance against the risk of default.

For municipal bonds there are insurance consortiums that insure bonds against default. The primary consortiums are MBIA, AMBAC, FSA, and FGIC. If you want to know more about these institutions (such as what those acronyms stand for), you can go to their respective websites at www.mbia.com, www.ambac.com, www.fsa.com, and www.fgic.com.

What these organizations do is that in return for a fee from the municipality, they will guarantee that the investors receive their timely interest and principal payments.

as part of the bankruptcy reorganization. So now the IRS must decide and rule on whether the bonds of these eight hospitals remain tax-exempt or become taxable because their parent, Tenet Healthcare, is a for-profit organization.

When Allegheny defaulted on its bonds, the uninsured bond issues plummeted in price while those that were insured by MBIA did just fine. Yet now the holders of the insured bonds are having to deal with the potential tax implications of these bonds, the ruling on which will have a huge impact on their price.

There's no such thing as a sure bet in bonds. Expect the unexpected.

An important point here is that in the event of a default of an insured issue, you don't get all your money back at once. The insurer will make the relevant interest and principal payments instead of the municipality.

If a bond is insured, it will reduce your yield anywhere from 10 to 15 basis points. The money to pay for the insurance has to come from somewhere. However, you have the extra guarantee that if the little hospital bond issue you hold should go down the tubes, you'll still in theory get your interest payments on time and the principal on the maturity date.

While this sounds nice and dandy, the main problem I have with this insurance gig is that the process has not been tried and tested to any great degree. The consortiums have never been tested to the max when there have been several large, simultaneous defaults.

Also the sums involved can be considerable. MBIA's loss from the exposure to Allegheny Health is estimated at $170 million. Although this was the largest-ever loss by a bond insurer, it represented only one of four major such events in the industry's 25-year history.

Each time a default has occurred, the insurance organizations went ahead and made the payments successfully.

The outlook for these consortiums looks rosy as long as the economy is in good shape. Indeed, by most accounts there is no current evidence of systemic risk in the industry.

The insurers are also taking steps to insulate themselves from any potential large losses. The consortiums are increasing the size of their loss reserves and, more important, over the past few years they have diversified into businesses other than bond insurance.

A quick look at the insurers' websites shows the range of services they now offer: investment management, services for municipalities, and insurance products other than bond guarantees. FGIC is the insurer that has invested most heavily in areas outside of its core operations.

Merrill Lynch estimates that industry profits from outside of the financial guarantee area increased to 12% in 1998 from 10% in 1997.

When all is said and done, rather than go down this bond insurance route, I personally prefer just to buy an excellent-quality general obligation bond or an excellent-quality municipal bond that has been prerefunded with money that is sitting in an escrow account. But insured municipal bonds that have a decent underlying credit rating are fine investments for your portfolio. (See sidebar: *Insurance Is No Sure Thing.*)

A SIGNPOST ON THE INVESTMENT ROAD

You have to adopt a healthy touch of skepticism when you deal with these ratings from the various agencies. Take them with a generous grain of salt but don't overlook their research. Each rating agency has an impressive website offering market outlook, research, rating methodology for various industry groups, and in-depth industry overviews. They also share research on many sectors including corporate, municipal, and emerging market debt. Press releases are an additional precious freebie that gives you first-hand reports in a timely manner. You can log on to their websites at www.standardandpoors.com, www.moodys.com, and www.fitchibca.com.

The most important tool at your disposal in managing a bond portfolio is the Treasury yield curve. If the yield curve is your road map to your ideal bond portfolio, then the agencies' ratings are signposts along the way telling you that you are going in the right direction.

Don't rely on the ratings alone, just use them.

If after all this your skepticism toward the rating agencies extends to such a degree that you wouldn't ask them for the time of day, then stick to Treasury securities, excellent-rated corporate bonds, and good-quality general obligation municipal bonds.

CHAPTER 6

BOND FUNDS: WEIGHING THE PROS AND CONS

Surprising as it may seem today with the focus so much on the stock market, in the early 1980s there were actually many more bond funds than there were stock funds. Now here we are in the new millennium and the situation has reversed: There are many more stock funds than bond funds.

The real growth has been in equities and not with bonds, but bond funds still offer many good features for the individual investor. Needless to say, though, they also have bad features, so choosing whether bond funds are for you rather than buying individual bonds involves weighing the various pros and cons of each investment method.

While I can't say, "Yes, you should buy bond funds," or vice versa, I will give you the necessary information so that at the very least you can make an informed decision about which is the right way for you to go.

There are numerous different bond funds run by hundreds of different management companies. Management companies, such as Fidelity Investments or Charles Schwab, normally have a family of stock and bond funds from which you can choose.

The structure behind bond funds is that the management company acts as an investment advisor, lending its expertise to managing the variety of funds within the family.

The assets of these funds are held by a custodian, a third party such as a bank, which means that if the management company runs into trouble, it can't raid the assets you paid for to bail itself out.

BOND FUND VOCABULARY

Let's look at some of the terms you must be familiar with when investing in bond funds.

Bond funds, just like those for stocks, differ in their type as well as which sectors of the bond market they are involved in. There are *open-end* bond funds, *closed-end* bond funds, and *unit trusts.*

These funds have various characteristics that differentiate them from each other (which will be explained in more detail later in this chapter), but in general investing in a fund means that instead of going out and buying the bonds yourself, a manager takes money from investors and buys a portfolio of the type of bonds that are laid down in the fund's prospectus. So if it is a municipal bond fund, the manager will build up a portfolio of municipal bonds.

As an investor in the fund, you will be given shares in the fund. These shares can be bought or sold on a daily basis. Therefore, if your bond fund is performing well, you can expect your shares in that fund to rise, and if the bond fund is doing badly, the shares will likely fall.

The price of your shares is the *net asset value* (NAV). The NAV is calculated at least once a day (the timing depends on whether it is an open-end or closed-end fund) by taking the value of all the assets in the fund, dividing that by the number of outstanding shares in the fund, and then subtracting the expenses of the fund.

Just like any shareholder, you will receive dividend payments from the bond fund. You can either receive the dividends in cash or have them reinvested in the fund. The dividend payments make up the bulk of your income from the bond fund and form the basis for working out the *yield* of the fund.

The yield is one variable that allows you to compare the performance of various bond funds. However, it's a tricky beast and, sorry, you must be aware there are various yield calculations.

Let's say you are looking through *The Wall Street Journal* and notice an overlooked fund called Cohen.com's Internet Bond Fund. To find out whether it's worth investing in, you call up the fund management company and find out that the fund's yield is 5%. However, look a little closer at the fund tables in the newspaper and you will see that the bond fund's shares pay out 8% a year in income dividends.

Why the discrepancy of three percentage points? The smaller number is the *SEC yield* and the larger number is the *distributed yield.* The SEC yield is the result of a ruling by the securities watchdog Securities and Exchange Commission. This rule forced the funds to use a formula designed to prevent them from paying out artificially high dividends to entice investors and to give one measurement that allows a reasonable comparison of performances to be made.

The SEC yield measure takes the yield to maturity of the bonds in the fund over the past 30 days, adjusts this figure to take into account expenses charged by the management company of the fund, and finally annualizes the figure.

Obviously, the inclusion of the expenses is one reason why the SEC yield and the distributed yield differ, but another major factor is that the SEC's calculation takes into account bonds that are trading at a premium.

To pay out large dividends, a fund could stock up on high-coupon bonds. These bonds have higher current yields than the all-important yield to maturity. In Chapter 1, I discussed the various types of yield measurements for bonds. The current yield is the coupon of the bond divided by the price at which the bond is trading. However, to take into account all the various sources of money you will earn from a bond investment assuming you hold it to maturity—interest payments, the interest gained by reinvesting the coupon payments, and the amount of money earned or lost by the change in the price of the bond from your purchase price—you must look at the yield to maturity.

Let's take the example of a fund that buys the 13.75% Treasury security that matures in 2004. The bond is trading at 137 ($1,370 per $1,000 face value), so by dividing 13.75 by 137 the current yield comes to 10%—a healthy yield. But what happens when the bond matures in 2004? Well, the fund would have a loss of 37 points because the bond is trading at 137 but all that is returned is the principal, or 100. The yield to maturity takes this into account and gives a lower, and more realistic, yield figure of 5.55%.

So should you stick to the SEC yield? Well, being the pessimist that I am, I actually find this figure still a little too optimistic because it doesn't take into account inflation. If inflation is running at 2% per year, it is eroding the value of your bond fund. If you get a 5% yield from the fund each year, the purchasing power of that income you receive in dividends is now worth 2% less than it was a year ago. It gets worse if you take into account income taxes, too.

I don't want to be too much of a party pooper, but it's best to take into account all these variables before you get too excited and book that summer holiday in Hawaii in anticipation of a payout that just won't materialize.

However, all is not lost, because if you hold the shares in the bond fund for a long period of time, the best measure of performance is *total return.*

The SEC yield of the Cohen.com's Internet Bond Fund, as we said before, is 5%. That means for every $1,000 you invest, you get dividend payments of $50 per year.

However, if you decide to reinvest that money in the bond fund, you will get compound interest. Also, the NAV, or the price of the shares, of the fund may increase, giving you a larger total return.

Before I wrap up this vocabulary lesson on the fund industry, you must be aware of two more terms: *load* and *no-load funds.*

Regardless of whether you invest in a load or no-load fund, every management company charges a management fee to invest your funds. This fee can be anywhere from 20 basis points for an index fund to 100 basis points (1%) for an emerging market fund. This management fee is fair enough; the fund manager needs to be paid after all.

However, there are sometimes extra expenses called loads. Load funds are those that as an individual investor you have to pay a sales commission of between 2 and 5-1/2%. I've even heard of some funds with a load of 8%.

WRONG FUND, WRONG TIME

There are numerous references to the years 1993 and 1994 in this book, principally because they encapsulated two years of extremes: 1993 gave us extremely low interest rates whereas 1994 gave us very high interest rates.

In 1994, a newly divorced woman was referred to me. It turned out that following her divorce in 1993, she went to her bank. The helpful bank manager told her the virtues of the bank's bond funds, as certificates of deposit were at sub 3% yields and bond fund yields were significantly higher.

Because she had never made a single investment decision in her life and only knew how to deposit money and use her checkbook, she was easily persuaded and liked the sound that her GNMA bond fund was sold as government-guaranteed.

Unfortunately, no one ever explained to her the concepts of interest rate risk, prepayment risk, and fluctuating net asset values. She was also sold a municipal bond fund, never mind the fact that the woman had no idea of what her tax bracket was. She also paid a large load even though she didn't know what a load was.

The New Year brought nothing but bad interest rate tidings. By the time the woman arrived on my doorstep, she had incurred large losses. Her GNMA fund was down over $20,000

That money generally comes out of the money you put up front. So if you are a small investor and put in $10,000 and your fund is charging 4%, then $400 is going out of your account and in reality you're only investing $9,600 in the fund.

Competitive pressure within the fund industry has changed the way some funds charge their load. Some now don't do it all up-front, but instead take the money out over the course of three or five years. There are other funds where the loads come out of the back end, or if you hold onto the shares in the fund for a length of time, say five years, the management company waives the fee altogether.

Especially with interest rates lower than during the 1980s, these management fees and loads can make a heck of a difference to your total return from the fund, so it's vital you shop around before you decide which fund to invest in.

This does beg the question of why anyone with an ounce of sanity would buy a fund with a load when there is a host of no-load funds from which to choose. Well, I think people buy load funds because they are sold them. (See sidebar: *Wrong Fund, Wrong Time.*)

For example, a broker may call his client and say, "Hi, Mr. Schwartz. I see you've got $20,000 sitting in your account. How would you like to earn safe secure income via Ginnie Maes? The minimum amount to buy a Ginnie Mae is $25,000 but I can put you into a Ginnie Mae fund so you can take advantage of these safe, government-guaranteed securities."

Brokers must always disclose the amount of commission and fees they charge, but there are a lot of people who don't understand bonds and funds, and end up paying exorbitant rates because they simply don't know any better.

How much is too high a management fee? That depends on what kind of bond fund you invest in. For example, a Treasury bond fund where the management fee is 35 basis points when short and intermediate Treasury securities are only yielding a little above 5% is an outrage, especially when you add in the unlikelihood of generating much of a total return. Also, as I discussed before, you can invest in Treasury securities relatively easily yourself.

For high-yield bond funds, a management company may charge you 1% or 100 basis points. This may

and her long-term municipal bond fund was down over $10,000.

Although she had been assured that she could get her money out whenever she needed it, the bank omitted to tell her or she didn't understand that the amount would perhaps not be the original amount.

This type of thing went on a lot in 1993 and was well documented by the *Los Angeles Times*. There were numerous stories about little old and young ladies (and men) investing in bond funds that were not suitable for them. They lost significant amounts of money and the banks had numerous lawsuits.

So what happened to the woman? She sold her bond funds and took her losses, and I then managed an individual bond portfolio for her. She eventually left me because I was constantly lecturing her that she was spending her principal and would blow through her divorce settlement shortly at her rate of spending.

If she had held onto her bond funds until 1995 as interest rates began to fall, she could have come out unscathed. Alas, she had incurred too many losses on the funds to wait out the bad years. She was most definitely sold the wrong funds at the wrong time.

seem a lot, but I think they provide a lot of added value because to invest in these bonds yourself would require you to study the companies, interest coverage, and all the other things we discussed in Chapter 3. Instead, you are paying a fund manager with all his or her experience to do this analytical work for you and, just as important, to keep up with the performance of the particular companies in the fund. I think you get a lot of value here for a fee of 1%.

BOND FUNDS VERSUS INDIVIDUAL BONDS

As a very general statement, you can usually do better if you buy the individual bonds yourself, principally because no matter what bond fund you buy, you will have to pay a management fee.

Individual bonds also give you a finite maturity, so you can be sure that at a particular date in the future you will be paid back your principal in full by the issuer of the bond (assuming, of course, that the issuer hasn't gone bankrupt).

Bond funds, because they are a portfolio of bonds, only offer you an average maturity. Should a bond in the portfolio mature or be called by the issuer, then the manager of the fund will take the proceeds and invest them in another security.

So how do you know the manager is buying the right bonds? Well, actually you just have to trust that she knows what she's doing.

If you decide to invest in bond funds, it is important that you read the prospectus for the fund very carefully and see what the investment guidelines are for the fund. A lot of bond fund managers have gotten themselves into tremendous problems because they said they were offering an investment-grade bond fund or a high-yield bond fund, but ended up tweaking the portfolio by putting in emerging market and/or derivatives to increase the return of the fund.

When the economic crisis hit East Asia in the late 1990s, some investors in investment-grade bond funds were surprised to find that there was emerging-market debt buried in the funds. There are bond funds that are called high-yield bond funds yet you can see smatterings of about 3% to 4% of the funds' assets that are invested in emerging-market debt. That's fine as long as emerging-market debt is one of the categories that the bond fund allows.

Similarly, many bond funds suffered from the derivative debacle that occurred in the bear market of 1994. Interest rates rose and a lot of the derivatives that the brokerage firms had sliced and diced and sold to states, money managers, and hedge funds did not react like their computer models said they would. As a result, the prices of the derivatives plummeted, which in turn caused liquidity in the market to dry up. This is one of things that took Kidder Peabody and Orange County down, and helped Procter & Gamble to generate something like $200 million in losses.

So when you look at the prospectuses of the bond funds, you have to make sure that (1) over the years the fund managers have stuck to the investment rules of the fund and (2) what they said they were going to buy was in fact what they actually bought.

Investors sometimes express concern over the possibility that some management companies might stuff the bond fund with junk issues that their investment banking arms underwrote and couldn't get rid of.

This certainly happened in the 1980s when fund management companies thought they could get away with murder, and often did. The infamous Drexel Burnham was guilty of doing this with some of the less-than-stellar junk bond issues it underwrote.

However, I would stress that the SEC and the competitive nature of the bond fund industry have resulted in a lot more openness so something like this rarely happens anymore, if at all.

The advantages of investing in a bond fund include instant diversification. When you build up a portfolio of bonds yourself, you must be sure to diversify among credits and sectors so that if one area collapses, you won't see your whole portfolio go down the tubes.

A fund by its very nature comprises many bond issues that you would be hard pressed to emulate, even if you were exceptionally wealthy.

Also, a fund can generally buy more of the bonds than you could as an individual so the fund enjoys economies of scale and can buy the bonds at a better price.

Finally, decisions over reinvestment can be easily taken care of by just reinvesting your dividends back into the fund. Thus, the time-consuming analysis can be left to the professionals.

So you can see that one method of investing is not better or worse than the other. It depends on your circumstances. Basically, if you answer yes to one of the questions below, I would advise you to at least consider investing in bond funds:

- Are you looking to invest between $1,000 and $50,000?

- Are you very much a part-time investor and take no pleasure from the investment process?

- Do you wish to invest in the more esoteric parts of the bond market?

DECISIONS, DECISIONS

You can probably see that shoveling your money into a bond fund is far from being a no-brainer. In fact, you have almost as many decisions to make when investing in funds as if you were buying individual bonds. (See sidebar: *A Ton of Funds.*)

Once you have chosen which management company and family of funds to go with, you must then decide what sector of the bond market you'd like to be in. Bond funds run the whole gamut of bond sectors: Treasury funds, Ginnie Mae funds, investment-grade corporate bond funds, money market funds, and funds with combinations of all these bonds. Some funds are mixes of stocks and bonds.

Just like with individual bonds, different funds will have different amounts of credit risk depending on which sector of the bond market they are invested in. So Treasury bond funds will have much less credit risk than a high-yield bond fund, but at the same time will offer a lower yield than that of the more risky bond fund.

There is no finite maturity of most funds because the proceeds from securities in the fund that mature or are called are reinvested. However, the funds usually invest in one particular part of the yield curve. There are short-term, or money market, funds that invest in short-term securities (up to 90 days), intermediate funds that invest in intermediate securities (1 to 10 years), and long-term funds that invest in long-term securities (10 to 30 years).

As we discussed before, the longer the maturity, the more interest rate risk you are taking on. The price of the bonds in the fund, and therefore the NAV, will move up and down more sharply in response to a change in interest rates if the fund is invested in longer-term securities than in short-term securities. At the same time, the dividend payments will normally be higher in longer-term funds than in short-term funds.

If interest rates do fall, then the fund manager will probably have to reduce your dividend payments, although the NAV will rise because the price of the assets in the fund will have increased, thereby boosting your total return.

Finally, there are three types of bond funds: open-end bond funds, closed-end bond funds, and unit trusts.

OPEN-END FUNDS

There is a huge variety of open-end funds, or mutual funds, and there is usually something for everyone in the open-end arena.

With open-end funds there is a bond portfolio manager who purchases and sells bonds and there is an infinite amount of money that can be gathered in the fund under that manager. The more money invested in the fund, the more shares that are issued in the fund's name.

The price of a share in an open-end fund is calculated at the end of each day. This can create problems. For example, say you decide at mid-

A Ton of Funds

You would think that with so many bond funds available, both open-end and closed-end, it would be a fairly easy exercise to select two or three. However, the more choices there are, it seems the more they all blur together. So eliminate some of the unnecessary background noise. When I talk with investors about how they should select their bond funds, I give them the following checklist:

1. Decide if you need taxable or tax-free income.

2. Do you think interest rates are going up or down?

3. If you believe rates are moving up, select a short- to medium-term-duration fund. Lengthen the duration if you think rates are going lower.

4. Sift though the professional publications for the best returns, best managers, safest sectors, and sectors that are undervalued.

Stay with the consistent performers for income, and the zero-coupon and emerging market funds for the high-octane total return. The truly outstanding open-end funds seem to be the large ones: PIMCO, Loomis Sayles, Strong, and Vanguard.

day to buy into a particular bond mutual fund when the long-term 30-year Treasury bond is down two points. However, by the time the price of the fund is calculated at the end of the trading day, the market could have rallied to close down only one-half point on the day. The price at which you would buy the fund's shares is the closing price, not the cheaper midday price.

In open-end funds you are also at the mercy of other investors moving in and out of the fund. For example, in 1993 short-term rates in particular fell to historic lows of about 3% and people piled into bond funds because they didn't want to invest in money market funds and certificates of deposits. As a result, dividend payments from bond funds were reduced dramatically because the fund managers had to buy more bonds at lower rates than at the beginning of 1993.

The NAVs of the funds went up, creating capital gains for investors in the bond funds, but those same investors saw tremendous dilution as far as their dividend payments were concerned.

After the flurry of investors into these bond funds in search of higher yields, the bull market turned into the bear market of 1994.

Interest rates went up relentlessly month after month as the Federal Reserve increased interest rates six times during the year beginning at the end of January.

As a result, bond prices went down and you had a mass exodus from these bond funds. So bond fund investors had the worst of all possible worlds. Now the bond fund managers were forced to liquidate bonds at a breakneck speed in order to meet the redemptions of those same people who had piled into them in 1993 and were now pulling out at a similar rate.

The bond fund investor who stayed invested in the fund had a real roller coaster ride as the net asset value of the fund dropped like a rock. Eventually the dividend payments started moving up, but the investor had a terrible ride in order to make that transition to smoother sailing in 1995.

The hot money that went in and the scared money that just as quickly came out really hurt the open-end bond investor.

I said earlier in the chapter that if you only want to invest in Treasury securities, the ease with which you can buy them makes nonsense of paying a fund manager to do it.

However, one area where it might pay to have a fund manager is with zero-coupon Treasury securities in target term trusts, which we touched on in Chapter 4. In these funds, the manager buys a raft of zero-coupon Treasury securities that mature at various years.

The advantage of investing in such a fund over buying the bonds yourself is that such securities are less liquid than their regular coupon-paying counterparts. The fund manager can take advantage of economies of scale and buy many of these securities at a cheaper price than you could ever hope to get.

Investors typically use these target term trusts to make plays on interest rate moves. As I said in Chapter 4, the volatility of zero-coupon Treasury securities means their prices move about 20 to 25% more than comparable coupon Treasury securities' prices on any change in interest rates. If you think interest rates will fall, you can buy into these funds and if you are right, the NAV of the fund will rise accordingly.

The way investors "play" in zero-coupon Treasury open-end funds is by switching from a money market fund when bond prices are stable to long-term zero-coupon funds when bond prices are expected to rise.

CLOSED-END FUNDS

Like their open-end cousins, closed-end bond funds have a fund manager who buys and sells and sells and buys the securities within the fund. They also have no fixed maturity, but an average maturity.

However, the main difference between closed-end and open-end funds is that there is a fixed number of shares representing the closed-end fund. As such, the closed-end bond funds are listed on exchanges like the New York Stock Exchange (NYSE) and the American Stock Exchange (AMEX). You can trade the shares of these funds just as if you were trading a stock.

This is important because having a fixed number of shares means the shares can trade at a premium or a discount to the NAV.

Let's say you pay $5,000 for 500 shares of a closed-end fund. So is that what the assets within the fund are worth? Not necessarily. That's what you paid for the shares, but the fund could be trading at a discount to the NAV and the underlying securities in that fund are perhaps worth as much as $5,800.

Why can you buy the shares at such a discount? There are a number of possible reasons. It could be that the fund has been overlooked by the investment community, the fund wasn't promoted very well or very much, or perhaps a couple of big sellers just liquidated their positions in the fund, driving down the price.

It's very easy to trade closed-end funds compared with open-end funds, some of which, like the larger funds, require you to write a letter of your intent to sell, which takes time.

To sell a closed-end fund, all you have to do is call your broker or go online. If you wish to trade closed-end funds—to buy when they are at a discount and sell when they are at a premium—you would be wise to find out the trading volume of the fund first. Some funds have large trading volumes, others very little. If you're planning to take a small position in the fund and the trading volume is moderate, then chances are you're going to be able to get in and out whenever you want.

A large position in a less liquid fund, however, could create more difficulties.

Closed-end funds also suffer from hype so I would advise you not to buy them when they are first issued. Most closed-end funds are first issued at an average of $10 per share. But after the initial offering period, the brokerage firm that is the underwriter will normally stop supporting it and the price of the fund usually falls and starts to trade at a discount.

Much better to scan the pages of *Barron's* or the Sunday *New York Times* business section to find an appropriate fund that is selling at a discount to its NAV and hold the shares until the discount comes closer to parity with the NAV.

You can create a diversified portfolio of closed-end funds with the help of newsletters that exclusively follow them. Lengthy studies have been done on buying closed-end funds at a discount and holding them until the discount and NAV become closer aligned.

One of the truly great features about closed-end funds is that the professionals usually avoid them because of the relatively light trading volumes in them. A large institutional-sized order would totally disrupt prices. So for an individual investor, closed-end funds represent a playing field in which institutions normally don't dare tread.

Some informative closed-end websites include Site-by-Site (www.site-by-site.com) and Morningstar (www.morningstar.net).

We have seen trends for various types of closed-end funds come and go, whether municipal closed-end bond funds or high-yield closed-end bond funds. People who study closed-end funds closely and buy them at an extreme discount to their NAV can usually make a fair amount of money on these trades.

I think some of the closed-end funds suffered the same slings and arrows that were directed at the open-end funds about fund managers not sticking strictly to their investment criteria. But overall I think that they have a little bit less volatility than the open-end funds, plus you can buy them and sell them throughout the trading day whereas an open-end fund's NAV is only calculated at the end of each day.

UNIT TRUSTS

Unit trusts are a whole different kettle of fish and are often considered the nearest thing to making up a bond portfolio of your own. This is because, unlike the closed-end and open-end funds, they have a fixed maturity date.

Like the closed-end funds, a unit trust is made up of a variety of bonds that are pooled and sold to individuals in a fixed number of shares.

However, the bonds within the unit trusts don't change, and as the various bonds come due or are called by the issuer, you get a portion of the principal back. Unit trusts are basically unmanaged.

When the bonds in the unit trust have all been called or have matured, you have a choice of either putting your money back into a new unit trust or taking your money elsewhere. You do, of course, have the option of selling your shares in the trust, but to do so you have to call your broker to see whether there is a market for your shares. There is nowhere near the same active market for these trusts that there is for closed-end and open-end funds.

Drexel (these guys really had no shame) began offering high-yield unit trusts in 1982, but they stuffed them with the worst leftovers that didn't go into the client accounts. Needless to say there were a lot of losses and lawsuits.

Touted as the next best thing to having your own portfolio and because there is no turnover of bonds within the fund and investors are only charged a front-end fee, sales of unit trusts have been good and they've proved popular investment vehicles. Depending on the type of unit trust, whether it's full of municipal bonds or high-yield bonds, the fees run between 2% and 4.5%, and payment can be at the front end, at the back end, or over the life of the trust. Each is different.

THE PROS AND CONS

To summarize, here are tables of the pros and cons of open-end funds, closed-end funds, and unit trusts.

Open-End Funds

PROS	CONS
• Hugely diversified bond positions	• Danger of hot money flowing
• Professional management, research, and trading	• Can't lock in the return
• Ease of entry and exit	• Sometimes management strays from its discipline and gets into trouble with your money
• Track record	• Can only buy and sell at the closing day price
• Easy dividend reinvestment	• No finite maturity

Closed-End Funds

PROS	CONS
• Diversified bond portfolios	• No finite maturity
• Professional management, research, and trading	• Dividend subject to changes
• Can be traded all through the day on the exchange where it's listed	• Usually unsupported by Wall Street
• Track record	• Can't lock in the return
• Easy dividend reinvestment	• Less liquid than open-end funds
• Largely retail market	

Unit Investment Trusts

PROS	CONS
• Diversified bond portfolios	• High initial sales load that may be a maximum of 4.50%; this may wipe out a majority of the first year's income
• Unmanaged, therefore no annual fees	
• Fixed maturity	• Unmanaged, therefore, won't sell securities that are doing badly
• Totally retail product	
• Flow of money in and out of bond funds won't affect this investment	• No reinvestment
	• Lacks liquidity

PUTTING THE FUN BACK IN FUNDS

Picking the wrong fund can be anything but an enjoyable experience. Today, though, the investor is much better armed than before to make an informed choice.

If you haven't invested in bond funds before, finding out what is a good bond fund and what is a bad bond fund is relatively easy. Concurrent with the huge growth in the fund industry has been an equally impressive growth in the number of publications that cover it.

In the print media, *Forbes, Fortune, BusinessWeek,* and *Money* all do a fabulous quarterly review of stock and bond funds, picking out those funds that were hot and those that were not.

The reviews go through the funds' expense ratios, their volatilities, and whether they are load or no-load, even right down to giving you the toll-free number for the fund. These reviews are a great resource and you don't even have to pay a dime for them if you go to the library.

I would recommend *Money* for beginners in bond funds. *Money* spells things out in plainer English than the other publications and I think the recommendations it gives are geared more to the novice investor than those in other publications.

For more sophisticated investors, I would recommend the reviews in *Forbes* and *BusinessWeek*.

The financial website TheStreet.com offers good coverage of bonds and bond funds, and allows you to write in with any questions that you may have about the bond market.

Of course, Morningstar is the granddaddy of all sources on the fund industry. This Chicago-based independent investment information provider covers some 1,700 funds and, in my view, deserves its reputation as one of the best resources of the industry.

Through its publications and software, Morningstar has done a wonderful job of removing the mystique that used to surround the industry. Its close scrutiny has done much to eradicate the dubious and sometimes unscrupulous practices seen in the 1980s.

One of the major pieces of information now available to investors is when changes in personnel occur.

During the 1980s, people would buy a mutual fund based on its performance history. Much of the performance of a fund often comes down to who's running it, but in the 1980s many investors would buy a fund not knowing whether the portfolio manager who achieved these great past results was still there or had moved on.

Morningstar was a real instigator in telling people when there had been a change at the helm. Now it is an SEC regulation that once there has been a change of fund manager, the management company must publicly disclose this information.

Morningstar also now provides information to investors free over the Internet on its website at www.morningstar.net. There is also a premium membership for $99 per year, offering deeper analysis and e-mail alerts about goings-on in the industry.

PICKING THE WINNERS

Although all the information is readily available, it would be remiss of me not to at least pick out some funds that I think are at the top of their game and some I wouldn't waste my time on.

Information is time sensitive so no book can accurately select a top 10 bond fund list. But I can tell you that winning families of funds generally have winning progeny. As I said earlier, it is important that every quarter you read through the major personal finance magazines' top lists and cross-reference them with Morningstar.

Forbes has a Best Buy category list that accounts for low expenses and good performance. Sift through the list, find the fund that seems to fit your goals, then study the fund, its management style, portfolio composition, and past returns.

There is a ton of unit trusts for municipal bonds and they have proved extremely popular.

Tax rules for funds with municipal bonds are the same as if you owned the individual bonds. You don't have to pay federal income tax, and if you buy a unit trust that holds only bonds from your state where you reside, there are no state or local taxes either.

If the fund contains municipal bonds from outside your state, then you'd have to pay tax on that portion of the unit trust, but the brokerage will take care of that side of things for you.

Therefore, if you live in a high-tax state like California or New York, it's imperative to stick with unit trusts that buy municipal bonds within the state. Investors who have trouble here are those who live in small states such as Wyoming and Idaho, because a lack of large infrastructure projects means there are very few municipal bond issues to choose from.

For small investors ($1,000 to $50,000), I like the plain vanilla funds such as the Ginnie Mae funds and investment-grade corporate bond funds, which offer a way to purchase these securities at better prices than you could do on your own.

If you want to get more aggressive, many high-yield and emerging market bond funds can be useful. The sheer size of the open-end funds means that with over 200 bond issues in one fund, the fund manager can diversify across country and sector. This gives the investor a natural hedge against one part of the market crashing spectacularly.

These funds in the more risky part of the bond market also require a lot of analysis and you need to keep up to date with events. When you invest in a fund, the manager of the fund will take care of this for you.

In my opinion, the best management company of the lot is the Vanguard Group. Long known for its fee sensitivity, this family of no-load funds has bucked the industry trend by reducing management fees over the years, while still delivering excellent products. As such, Vanguard has built a reputation as being a low-cost provider of bond and index funds.

I personally own a Vanguard California tax-free money market fund. I use it as a slush account for short-term money as opposed to a long-term investment. To drive home the fact that Vanguard provides a great product at a low expense ratio, its Long-Term U.S. Treasury bond fund has well in excess of $1 billion and provides its services for a fee of only 0.01%. Very reasonable indeed.

The American Century Family's Target Maturity Funds are special, too. These no-load funds offer an aggressive investor a way to speculate in the bond market.

Northeast Investors always seems to come up on the mutual fund recommendation lists. Good management, good returns, and reasonable fees are the three main reasons.

The bond funds that consistently outperform the rest are usually found in the Vanguard family of funds including its bond index funds; PIMCO's Total Return Fund and other PIMCO bond funds; American Century; and Northeast Investors Trust Funds.

Of course, there are bad bond funds, too. Just like a cold slap on the face of reality, most investors don't know their bond fund stinks until it's too late. Sad but true.

In 1994 as interest rates rose and the derivatives debacle took down Kidder Peabody, bankrupted Orange County, and created hundreds of millions of dollars of corporate and hedge fund losses, unsuspecting bond fund investors suffered greatly.

Many of the fund managers who had invested in derivatives saw their NAVs plunge. We even saw some money market funds go below

$1.00 NAV per share and their management companies were forced to bail out investors. Piper Jaffrey got stung badly by meandering into inappropriate investments causing huge losses, which resulted in a number of lawsuits.

There's no insulation other than staying with the biggest and best family of funds, who will typically try to make amends if any of their rogue managers go over the edge.

CHAPTER 7

HOW TO FIND A BOND BARGAIN

As an individual investor, you will most likely have less money to invest than the institutions and that makes it more imperative that you get value for your money. In this chapter, I will first discuss the tools that Wall Street uses to find bargains in the bond market and, therefore, what Main Street needs to use to accomplish the same purpose. Then I will discuss a variety of situations that often cause these bargains to arise.

The starting point for finding a bargain in the bond market is the Treasury yield curve, which we first looked at in Chapter 2. Let's take a closer look at it.

MEASURING THE YIELD

To find whether a bond other than a Treasury security is worth the paper it's printed on, you must measure its yield against your baseline, the Treasury yield curve.

As I previously said, the Treasury yield curve is a graph that plots the interest rates for all Treasury securities, from the 3-month Treasury bills to the 30-year Treasury bonds. Since the U.S. government is perceived as being the ultimate creditor (it always pays on time and in full), then any other security from a municipal authority, corporation, or whomever is priced at a level over a Treasury security.

The following are some examples of what a Treasury yield curve may look like.

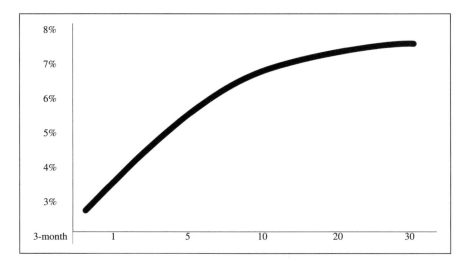

This is a positively sloped yield curve, indicating a good economy, little to no inflation, and a strong currency.

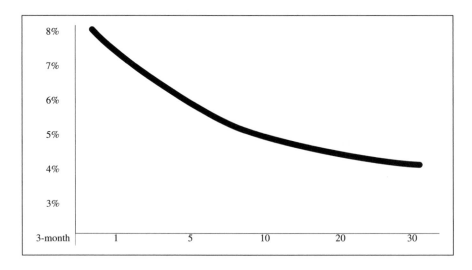

This is a negatively sloped yield curve, indicating inflation, a tight Federal Reserve monetary policy (interest rates are high), and probably a weak dollar.

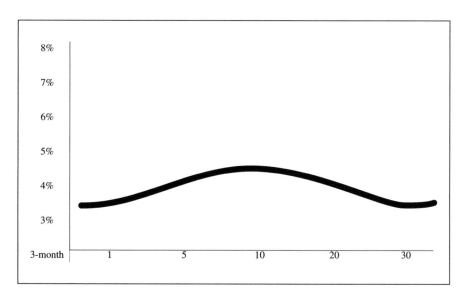

This is a humped yield curve, sometimes indicating a lukewarm economy that may heat up or slow down.

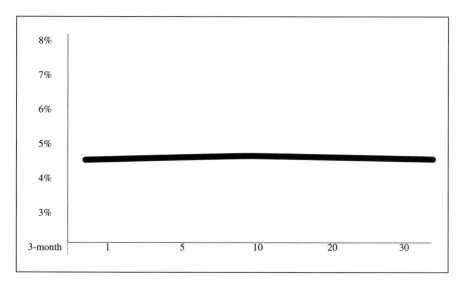

This flat yield curve is most terrifying of all. Why? Because it's anybody's guess whether it will turn to a positively sloped or a negatively sloped yield curve. It's not generally a harbinger of good things to come.

BUYING OFF THE CURVE

Let's say you're deranged enough to be interested in buying a bond from Cohen.com, and you see that a 10-year note from Cohen.com is priced at 200 basis points (1 basis point is 1/100th of a percentage point) above the rate for a 10-year Treasury note. In this way, you are being paid 200 basis points, or 2% more, because you are taking on extra risk by buying the Cohen.com note rather than the supersafe Treasury note.

Is this a reasonable payoff or not? I would love to be able to construct a table of what each spread, or difference, above Treasury securities you should expect for a particular rated bond of a particular maturity. Is an A-rated bond worth 50 or 100 basis points extra over a similarly maturing Treasury security? Is a BBB-rated bond worth 200 or 300 basis points more?

Unfortunately, it impossible to give hard-and-fast targets for spreads. There is a myriad of variables—from the general level of interest rates and the state of the world economy to the structure of the particular bond and what business the issuer is in—that would make giving such an exercise fairly meaningless.

Plus, to complicate matters further, the spreads are a dynamic target. Put simply, a corporate bond spread over the Treasury security will narrow or widen depending on the market's expectations of economic growth and the financial future of the company.

For example, spreads on investment-grade corporate bonds in 1997 were extremely narrow, between 35 and 80 basis points over Treasury securities. The reason for this was that the economy was on a roll with solid noninflationary growth. Then there arose the crisis in the markets in 1998 because of the near collapse of Long-Term Capital Management, which pushed the spreads on those same bonds out to between 100 and 200 basis points over Treasury securities.

Very basic benchmarks—and I stress the word *very* here—are 40 to 125 basis points over Treasury securities for an investment-grade bond; 150 to 200 basis points for bonds from companies on the cusp between investment grade and high yield; and 300 to 1,000 basis points for high-yield bonds. Obviously, at the higher end of the range you are buying something that may be unbelievably risky.

When looking at municipal bonds, the baseline to use is what percentage of Treasury securities the municipal bond is paying. Remember, municipal bonds are exempt from federal tax and sometimes state tax, too, so they yield less than, or below, Treasury securities. A municipal bond that is paying 100% of Treasury securities is an absolute steal, 80 to 100% is a really good buy, and 75 to 80% is normal. (You're not getting a bargain but something probably right on the market.)

With municipal bonds there is something called the "5% syndrome." This refers to the 5% yield barrier, below which both institutions and individual investors have a great resistance to purchasing 20- and 30-year tax-free municipal bonds.

The reason for this is simple: Why would anybody want to lock up an interest rate return for 30 years of less than 5% state- and federal-tax-exempt? I think the market has gotten this right, so beware of this barrier. If you are tempted to buy such a bond, then you will have to be a very agile investor because any hint of inflation will send the price of these low-yielding long-term bonds plummeting.

Having said that, you should not go to the other extreme either. In general I think that most people who have invested in the bond market themselves have tended to keep their money over the past decade in much too short-term debt, in certificates of deposit, commercial paper, or money markets.

The reason for this is that during the 1980s when interest rates rose to an extraordinarily high level, people presumed that interest rates would continue to go higher. As a result, these investors got into the habit of keeping their money in short-term securities.

In my opinion, if you are investing for income (just the interest payments) as opposed to total return, generally bond bargains in the corporate and tax-free market are not in the 20- to 30-year segment of the yield curve. Rather, the best buys are going to be found at the peak in the yield curve, the point where you get the most yield for the shortest maturity.

You can spot this peak by looking at a yield curve like the one here. The peak in this example is 10 years, where you will receive your highest yield for the least amount of interest rate risk. The risk versus reward of 50 basis points extra yield by extending your maturity 15 years just isn't worth it for an income investor.

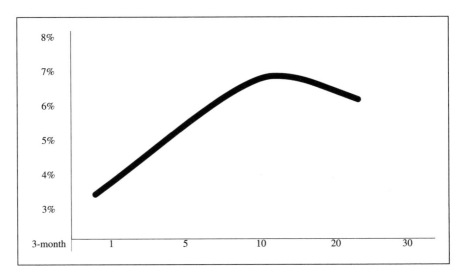

TELL ME THE (YIELD TO) WORST

In the late 1970s and early 1980s, most of the bonds that corporations and municipalities issued were noncallable, meaning that the issuer of the bond could not buy the bonds back from you before the stated maturity.

The reason they issued these noncallable, or *bullet,* bonds was that the U.S. was experiencing a climate of rising interest rates and terrible inflation. It had not occurred to these bond issuers that as the 1980s progressed, the situation would reverse and the 1990s would experience historically low rates coupled with low inflation.

The upshot of the change in direction of interest rates was the corporations and municipalities that had issued 20- and 30-year noncallable bonds at the time of high interest rates could not buy back these bonds and refund them at the much lower rates that were to come.

Just as homeowners who want to refinance high-interest-rate mortgages for lower ones, corporate America, states, and municipalities also want to be able to refinance their bonds and pay a lower coupon rate to bondholders if they can.

As conditions began changing in the mid-1980s, the corporations and municipalities realized that they had no escape hatch and they began to issue bonds with call features. For example, a bond with a 30-year maturity could be called after 10 years, and a bond with a 10-year maturity could be called after 5 years.

As discussed in the chapter on bond funds, I always recommend that you take a pessimistic approach to how much yield you will get when investing in bonds and funds of whatever type. This way you will avoid disappointments and sometimes be pleasantly surprised with a higher yield.

So when calculating your return on the bond investment, should you look at the current yield or the yield to maturity? (See Chapter 2.) Neither. Use the yield to worst call, which is the total return you will receive from the bond investment if the bond is called by the issuer at the least advantageous time for the investment.

Remember, the total return from your bond investment is dependent on what the issuer decides to do with its outstanding debt and the ups and downs of interest rates. A corporation is in the business of making money. If the company decides it is in its best interests to call the bond, then that is exactly what it will do. The investor's interest is diametrically opposed to the issuer's: You want to make money and it wants to save money.

Here's an example of the yield to worst call:

Waffles Incorporated has a bond with a 9% coupon due July 15, 2007. It is A-rated and has multiple call features starting in 2002.

If purchased on June 1, 2000, at a price of 105 ($1,050 per face value of $1,000), the yields are as follows:

Call Date	Call Price	Yield	Yield above Treasury
July 15, 2002	104.50	8.350%	2.617%
July 15, 2003	103	8.017%	2.210%
July 15, 2004	101.50	7.867%	1.997%
July 15, 2005	100	7.794%	1.907%
July 15, 2007	100	8.061%	2.140%

As you can see, the yield to first call is not the worst-case scenario, it is merely the first call date. The worst time for your bond to be called is on July 15, 2005, when it would yield only 7.794%.

Sophisticated bond software from a financial data supplier like Bloomberg gives bond managers the ability to look at the various call dates and prices in order to determine "what-if" scenarios for the various bonds in a portfolio.

If other similarly rated corporate bonds are yielding somewhere between 190 and 200 basis points over comparable maturing Treasury securities, then Waffles Inc. is right on the market.

Let's say this bond is also listed on the bond exchange and is quoted in *The Wall Street Journal.* The listing would look something like this:

Bonds	Cur Yld	Vol	Close	Net Chg.
Waffles Inc. 9% 07	8.6	10	105	+1

Now refer back to the yield to worst call chart and you will see that nowhere is there an 8.60% yield listed. So what good is the current yield when it doesn't compare to any of the call dates or maturity? The answer is it's no good. If anyone starts talking to you about current yield, don't listen.

Are you scratching your head, wondering about how to go about calculating the yield to worst call? I would advise you not to try doing it by hand. As most people don't have to do such complicated mathematical calculations on a daily basis, you will more than likely get it wrong.

Rather, I would buy a Hewlett-Packard calculator, a Monroe bond calculator, or a more pricey option such as a Bloomberg machine. Most online brokers have calculators built into their software and retail brokers have access to Bloomberg.

To sum up, focus on the yield to worst call for callable bonds and only look at the yield to maturity when considering noncallable bonds.

One final point on this: Although call dates give the issuer the right to call the bond, the issuer is not obligated to call the bond. If interest rates rise or the issuer gets into financial difficulties, it's unlikely that the corporation or municipality will buy back the bonds. There is a lot of uncertainty associated with callable bonds and you should be getting paid for it.

Now that you're armed with the yield curve and the yield to worst call measurement, let's go find some of those bond bargains.

SUPPLY AND DEMAND

Like all markets, the bond market is influenced by supply and demand. Too many bonds and not enough buyers may cause the price of bonds to fall and vice versa.

Historically, Treasury securities have not been hugely affected by supply and demand. From the early 1980s, the issuance of new Treasury securities at the periodic auctions never really seemed to depress prices to any great degree.

I can remember when the countries of the Middle East were a big influence in the auctions in the 1980s, but toward the end of that decade the question was whether the Japanese were going to be big buyers. There always seemed to be enough money sloshing around so that no matter how much debt the Treasury had to issue, it never really raised or lowered yields all that much.

Here we are in the new millennium and the amount of Treasury securities is falling as the government issues fewer and fewer bonds. As a result, the supply/demand issue may become more of a problem in the future. In Chapter 2 we discussed how some of the federal agencies are issuing humongous issues that may or may not become Treasury security surrogates, but only time will tell whether they can succeed in this.

New bond issues have a much greater influence on the corporate bond market, both the investment-grade and high-yield sectors. There is something called a forward calendar, which individual investors are not usually privy to. The forward calendar is put out by the institutions that underwrite the bonds to tell institutional investors about the new bonds that are about to come to market.

When interest rates are steady and low, many corporations rush to take advantage of the favorable conditions. As a result, the market can get really clogged up with too many new issues coming at once.

In 1997, the high-yield market was literally swamped with new issues. I was receiving up to eight prospectuses per day, and I'm only a small money manager. You can imagine how many of these prospectuses the big mutual fund managers like Vanguard were getting. This type of oversupply situation is often a good time to find cheap corporate bonds, as the glut of supply can put pressure on bond prices.

Conversely, bargains in the bond market also can be found when the forward calendar is sparse because a piece of bad news can send bond prices plummeting. (Of course, good news can cause bond prices to soar.) Similarly, when the market is taking a break for vacations, the lack of buyers and sellers in the market can mean a price move is exaggerated if a large player makes a move because there are so few other people around to take up the slack.

In the municipal bond market, the amount of new issues can affect the market quite dramatically. Supply affects the municipal bond market much, much more than most other bond sectors, principally because it is largely a retail product and foreigners, hedge funds, and corporations rarely buy municipal bonds.

There's a seasonality to new issues of municipal bonds. Generally, the first quarter of every year sees a drop in the amount of new issues because every authority that needs to issue bonds usually has done so by the end of the fourth quarter. As we move into the second and third quarters of the year, the refinancings and new issues of municipal bonds start to pick up.

However, over the past few years, the amount of municipal bond issuance has been drying up. We have seen the cities and states of the U.S. become a little more fiscally responsible, just like the federal government. Some types of municipal bond issues that used to be underwritten for certain services and projects are now being farmed out to private enterprise. Whether it's small stadiums or convention centers, many infrastructure projects are being privatized. As a result there aren't as many municipal bonds being issued anymore.

Also many brokerage firms have dropped out of underwriting municipal bonds, because there are fewer deals to be done and profit margins have eroded. So why stick around?

CRISIS? WHAT CRISIS?

Many investors have found that during times of economic or financial crisis, a look through the rubble can sometimes turn up a bargain. During such crises, the large institutions will often capitulate relatively early because they may have too much leverage and have to meet margin calls, their customers are in trouble, or their risk management programs just aren't working. The result is that they offload perfectly good bonds at perfectly reduced prices.

This happened in 1994 when some firms suffered because of problems with derivatives, to a lesser degree in 1995 when the municipal bond market was hit by the Orange County bankruptcy, and in 1998 when the Asian economic crisis and Russian default caused bond prices in the investment-grade and high-yield markets to fall considerably.

The latter occasion was not because the companies' financial wherewithal had really changed, but because the financial crisis caused liquidity in the market to dry up. (See sidebar: *Municipal Bomb.*)

There are times during financial crises when, as an individual investor, you will probably be most scared to step up to the plate and buy,

MUNICIPAL BOMB

The stage was set in December 1994. For several days the media was reporting on massive losses in Orange County's investment portfolio. The year had been a bloody one for bonds—a relentless bear market depressing bond prices, which increased yields, causing a derivative debacle. A few hedge funds like Askin Management, whose mortgage and derivative portfolio were supposed to be market neutral, crashed and burned. There was carnage everywhere.

One afternoon ABC news called me to videotape my comments on the tumult and carnage we were hearing about Orange County's highly leveraged investment portfolio. During the 10 to 15 minutes of tape I was asked the big question: "Would Orange County, whose losses were estimated to be $800 million to $1.5 billion, have to declare bankruptcy?" I answered, "Yes, I don't see any way around it." By late afternoon the county declared bankruptcy and there I was on ABC Nightly News with Peter Jennings! We had scooped everyone.

How could I have been so sure? Well, it was a calculated guess that was correct.

The real bargain play at that time wasn't munis at all—it was Treasuries. Yields peaked, there was a flight to quality between the Orange

but if you're brave enough, you can take advantage of a good buying opportunity.

I think crisis buyers have the tendency to buy Treasury securities because they're not sure what other bonds to buy. If you are looking to get into the market when it's at the bottom or you're seeking a fast way to increase your total return, then buying Treasury securities is a good way to go.

When a major shock hits the market, there is a flight to quality and you can get a good total return by buying long-term or intermediate-term Treasury securities or zero-coupon Treasury securities. If you are quick on your toes and buy these securities when the crisis first hits the headlines, you will see the prices of those securities rise significantly until the end of the crisis and the market readjusts itself.

If you miss the boat and don't get in at the beginning of the flight to quality, don't give up, because the structure of the Treasury market can sometimes throw up some bargains. As I said in Chapter 2, there are on-the-run Treasury securities and there are off-the-run Treasury securities. The on-the-run Treasury securities are the most recently auctioned, and as such are the most actively traded issues by the market. This liquidity premium means that the new issues generally yield less and cost more than the off-the-run issues, even though there is no credit difference between the two types.

County and Mexico crises, and Treasury prices flew while interest rates declined.

These meltdowns don't happen every year, but when they do, it's big.

This divergence between the two types of Treasury securities does not always occur during a crisis and it's impossible for me to say exactly how much the differential might be. However, it is not uncommon for there to be a 10- to 15-basis-point difference between the on- and off-the-run 30-year Treasury bonds. Basically you are buying the same security for about 15 basis points cheaper and this kind of differential in the normally staid Treasury market would constitute a good bargain.

Such a price difference between the two types of Treasury securities arose during the winter of 1998. The illiquidity in the market caused differences in yield to widen between 10 and 15 basis points. It was a fluke, but for knowledgeable investors it proved to be a profitable fluke. Earning 15 basis points more yield for an off-the-run U.S. Treasury bond is like buying Neiman Marcus merchandise at Wal-Mart prices.

Of course, the biggest bargains can be found if you are brave enough and decide to go down the food chain to the high-yield and emerging markets. When the rest of the bond market gets crushed, the emerging market and high-yield sectors as a whole bear the brunt of it, even though some particular companies may be doing fine in their business.

Hedge funds and leveraged money managers regularly trade both types of bonds, so when a crisis does hit the market, these players flee in droves. (Yes, institutional lemmings are alive and well.) During a crisis, anything goes, and this is why in 1999, when some of the Asian economies got back on their feet, we saw some total-return emerging-market bond mutual funds that had held onto their bonds rack up 30, 40, and even 50% returns.

SORTING THE WHEAT
FROM THE CHAFF

When the markets are down and out, it is often a good time to find a bargain in both individual bond issues and bond funds. Similarly, when one particular sector of the market gets crushed for whatever reason, that may present you with a good opportunity to find a gem amongst the rubble.

When one or two companies within a sector of the market encounter problems with making their earnings targets, it often causes the bonds of all the companies in the same business to fall, too, even though there may not be anything fundamentally wrong with them. In fact, ironically, these other companies may actually end up doing better at the expense of the companies in trouble.

These sympathy moves create good opportunities for an investor with the time and patience to sift through the various bond issues and separate the true bargains among the real losers. (See sidebar: *Sympathy Pains.*)

In this way, you can buy at a very cheap price a bond from a perfectly good company whose only fault was to be in a business with a bunch of losers. Eventually the market will correct itself and the price of your bond should rise to reflect the true fundamentals of the company.

In 1998, the U.S. experienced a massive amount of steel dumping from countries such as Russia, Japan, and the emerging markets. The countries in question were going to produce the steel no matter what and they needed to get it off their shores and onto ours.

The result was that many steel companies' bonds fell quite dramatically even though some of them had excess cash plus good interest coverage and EBITDA (earnings before interest, tax, depreciation, and amortization). Such sympathy moves have also affected the healthcare, high-tech, and telecommunication sectors at one time or another. All sectors can be vulnerable to this.

Sympathy moves also occur in the municipal bond market. For example, the Allegheny Health hospitals default was one of the largest defaults in recent memory and it caused a fall in the whole uninsured hospital sector of the municipal bond market, as many mutual funds and portfolio managers threw out the baby with the bath water.

The market didn't reach bargain basement levels, but there were nevertheless some good cheap bonds available.

So how do you know which are the good companies and which are the bad? Sometimes it's as simple as looking in your own backyard—the Peter Lynch investment approach to bond investing. Mr. Lynch (a former fund manager at Fidelity Magellan) advises you to buy stocks of companies you are familiar with.

By way of example, I have a number of clients who live in Las Vegas. These clients have watched the casino industry grow exponentially and seen companies such as Hilton and Circus Circus construct bigger and greater edifices to accommodate the legions of gamblers who descend on the city. Just by looking out the window, my clients could see which ones would succeed and which would not. Circus Circus is often packed to the gills and offers enough for the visitors to keep them coming back.

Another casino, Stratosphere, however, was a nonstarter. It is a space-needle-shaped tower located on the outer fringes of Las Vegas, well away from the main drag and the action. It had difficulty attracting the tourists and, unsurprisingly to anyone who lived in Las Vegas, eventually went bankrupt, taking bondholders down with it. Sometimes the obvious and simple investment ideas are the best.

A TRICKY BUSINESS

Many times when a bond is complicated, you are rewarded with a higher yield and a higher rate of return for buying it. Basically, the more words your broker has to use to explain the security, then the higher rate of return you should demand because it's not as simple or straightforward as buying a Treasury security or noncallable investment-grade bond.

Here's a question: Would you purchase a bond with a guaranteed loss? Most investors wouldn't, but I do it all the time for my clients and myself.

SYMPATHY PAINS

Just as a birthing mother has labor pains, sometimes those around her share the agony. And so it is in the bond market.

In June 1999, the entire healthcare sector appeared beyond resuscitation. The 1997 Balanced Budget Amendment cut Medicare payments, which in turn annihilated the bonds of hospitals, nursing care companies, and other healthcare providers.

For example, my clients owned Integrated Health Services (IHS) bonds, specifically the 9.50% high-yield bonds due September 15, 2007. This company is a subacute and postacute provider of services for nursing homes and rehabilitation centers. (I hope that when you read this, the present tense of the verb is still applicable.)

When the crisis in the healthcare sector hit, these bonds sank from 95 points ($950 face value) in January 1999 to 60 points by April and then recovered slightly to 70 points in June. By December the bonds were quoted at 7. In February 2000, the company filed for bankruptcy protection.

An agile trader who saw the disaster coming and (unlike me) didn't believe IHS management's claim that they had their costs under control in this new regulatory environment could have easily sold the bonds short (shorting is selling a security you don't actually own) and bought the bonds back when the price hit the

These bonds are called high-coupon *premium bonds*—investment-grade corporate, municipal, or high-yield bonds that were issued many years ago when interest rates were much higher and so now trade at a premium to their face value.

If you take the time to do the calculations, you may find that sometimes the overall return from a premium bond is higher than the return you would get from a comparable bond that is selling at par. Good-quality corporate and municipal premium bonds sometimes yield as much as 10 to 15 basis points higher than those that are selling at par. For no extra risk, I'd rather have the better yield.

There are tremendous tax advantages, too, if you buy taxable premium bonds outside of any tax-deferred accounts you may have. According to the IRS tax code, you have a one-time option to elect to amortize (gradually write off) the bond premium you have paid. This amortization can be a valuable adjustment against the interest income you receive from the bond. (This is done on Schedule A.) The IRS gives taxpayers few breaks in life, so you should take any that come your way. This seems so obvious that it is incredible that so few people take advantage of this. Lazy and/or inept accountants are the main reason.

Another advantage of high-coupon premium bonds regards the cash flow. High-coupon bonds generate more coupon cash flow than low-coupon bonds, and in an environment of rising interest rates you have the chance to reinvest more money in bonds that will be paying ever higher yields.

Let's take a hypothetical example. There is a 20-year corporate bond from ABC Corp., which was issued in 1987 at par ($1,000) with a 9% coupon. On June 1, 2000, the bond is trading above par because its coupon is so much higher than a similar bond would pay at today's much lower interest rates. As a result, it costs 110 or $1,100 per bond. (Always add a zero to the bond's price to arrive at its dollar price.)

bottom. In this way, the trader could have generated anywhere from 25 to 35 points (or $250 to $350) per bond.

Any individual investor with some spare cash at his disposal could have purchased almost any of the better-quality bonds in the sector like Tenet Health or Columbia/HCA. These issues were hammered in price but their survivability was never in question.

For myself, to be honest, I blew the chance to make money here. I couldn't do any of the above because I'm not allowed to short bonds on my clients' behalf and I had already used up my full allocation of this sector per account. And I couldn't sell any of the IHS bonds because they fell in such huge increments, from 95 to 85 and then in a blink of an eye to 65, so there was no way of getting out. Once they traded in single digits, there was liquidity. That's because the institutions that shorted bonds (borrowed bonds in the market and then sold them) were covering their shirts. What a disaster!

Now, if you buy 100,000 of such bonds, then it would cost you $110,000, but the amount of principal you would get back when it matures in 2007 would only be $100,000, so it looks like you are taking a $10,000 loss on the premium you paid.

Hmmm, at first glance this doesn't look like a good investment. However, a closer look at the math involved and comparing the ABC premium bond with a similar bond trading at par shows that buying the premium bond is not such a harebrained idea after all.

The following are the key details of the premium bond:

- ABC corporate bond issued June 1, 1987
- Noncallable
- 9% coupon
- Purchased on June 1, 2000
- 7 years until maturity due June 1, 2007

Here's the par bond:

- DEF corporate bond issued June 1, 1999
- Noncallable
- 6.90% coupon
- Purchased on June 1, 2000
- Maturing June 1, 2007

Now, let's take a look at the total return from the two investments. For ABC Corp.'s bond:

+$100,000 proceeds at maturity

+$63,000 coupon income (14 coupon payments)

-$110,000 less principal paid at maturity
_____

+$53,000 return

Remember, amortizing allows you an annual deduction on the bond premium. For the ABC bond, the $10,000 can be amortized over the 7 years until it matures. There are a ton of rules (no surprise there) that you must abide by and facts that you need to know. Your CPA will either do a straight-line or constant-yield amortization method. Amortizing the premium rather than capitalizing is an election. You can't legally opt for one way one year and the other the next. To do more research on the rules on premium bond amortization, pick up any tax guide by H&R Block or J.K. Lasser.

For DEF Corp.'s bond, total return is

+$100,000 proceeds at maturity

+$48,300 coupon income (14 coupon payments)

-$100,000 less principal paid at maturity

+$48,300 return

The high-coupon premium bond generates more cash flow and a higher yield to maturity even though you have a guaranteed loss of the premium paid if held to maturity. Certainly the differential isn't huge but I would rather have it than not.

To sum up: High-coupon premium bonds are a bargain because they generally yield more and have better cash flow. Also, a taxable bond (not municipal) premium may be used as a deduction.

Another type of complicated bond where you are paid a little more for your trouble is a *step-up bond*. A step-up bond is one that begins life paying a slightly higher yield than the going rate for short-term bonds, but after a certain number of years the bond "steps up" to pay a higher coupon. The issuer of the step-up bond, though, has the option to call the security fairly soon (perhaps after one year), usually at par.

Here's an example. The Federal Home Loan Bank (FHLB), a frequent issuer of such bonds together with other federal agencies, issues a step-up bond with a final maturity of 2003. The bond initially pays a coupon of 6.00% for the first year, slightly higher than the 5.75% coupon on a regular one-year, noncallable FHLB bond. If the bond is not called after the first year, it steps up to pay 6.375% in the second year and 6.50% in the final year.

If you take the time to look closely at these step-up bonds and try to determine where interest rates are headed, then these bonds can offer a nice bit of extra yield. You should buy these bonds with the idea that they will be called at the first opportunity.

For the issuer to call the bond, interest rates need to fall, because the issuer will want to take the opportunity to buy back the bond and issue another in its place at the lower rate.

If you think interest rates will fall significantly over the medium term, you would be wise not to buy these step-up bonds, but to try to lock in a high yield on a noncallable bond. Instead I suggest buying a longer-term bond of, say, 10 or 20 years.

Conversely, if you think interest rates are heading higher, I would advise you to hold off buying the bonds and instead put the money in short-term money market instruments so you can access your money quickly and buy the bonds issued at higher rates.

Basically, step-up bonds are for those times when you think interest rates are nearing a bottom, and may be in for a slight upward correction. If the time is right, it may be a good idea to spend a little time looking at these bonds.

Sinking fund bonds—securities where the issuer retires a certain percentage of the issue each year through the life of the bond—are complicated to analyze and often are priced very attractively.

There are many different types of sinking fund bonds—serial sinking fund bonds, funnel sinking fund bonds, consolidated sinking fund bonds—but basically the issuer creates a dedicated fund into which set sums are paid in and that fund must be used to periodically pay off a certain percentage of the outstanding issue.

One huge advantage of traditional sinking fund bonds is that you know when you'll get your money back, as opposed to regular callable bonds, whose call is at the discretion of the issuer. This is helpful when laddering your portfolio (we will discuss this in more detail in Chapter 10), a process whereby investors align their portfolios so that little pieces of it progressively mature and can be reinvested.

But the real beauty of sinking fund bonds is that they are complicated, and will often yield more because of it. Sinking fund bonds yield anywhere from 40 to over 100 basis points more than a comparably maturing nonsinking fund bond from the same company.

To work out the yield of sinking fund bonds, you have to calculate the yield of the average life, which is the yield to the date that the average dollar of principal is returned. If you buy the sinking fund bond at a discount to its face value, you have to include that gain as well.

Here's an example. There is a McDonald's sinking fund bond, AA-rated by Standard & Poor's, with a 7.23% coupon and a maturity of June 1, 2006. It's trading at 96.25 (or $962.50 per $1,000 face value). This gives an 8% yield to average life, which is a good 100 basis points higher than what you would get on a bond with a similar maturity and quality.

Although sinking fund bonds that are trading at par or at a premium are unlikely to give you such a large yield advantage, they can still be profitable investments. High-coupon sinking fund bonds often have an additional quirk. The first sink date may generate a negative return on that pro-rata portion being retired, but don't let that put you off. As long as the overall yield to the average life exceeds the yield to worst call and yield to maturity by a significant percentage, then the premium sinker is a good buy.

FEW AND FAR BETWEEN

When all is said and done, the market is a fairly efficient beast and bargains don't come along every day, week, or even month. But the market is by no means perfect, and because of this you can pick up some fairly good bargains if the circumstances are right and you take a little time and trouble to analyze the situation.

You generally get your best deals when everyone else is selling. It really goes back to the old stock market adage, "If they're yellin', you should be sellin'. If they're cryin', you should be buyin'."

CHAPTER 8

HOW TO BE A SAVVY BOND SHOPPER

By now you've hopefully gotten a reasonable understanding of bonds and you're ready to get out there and start buying a few. Take a deep breath and read this chapter very carefully. This will take you through the steps of actually buying the bonds and the pitfalls involved in buying bonds.

To be a savvy bond shopper, rule number one is, of course, not to get ripped off, which, unfortunately, is more likely to happen in the bond market than in the stock market.

You must understand that, despite the bond market being several times larger than the stock market, it's no friendlier to the individual investor for being so. The stock market is largely a listed market, meaning that there are a number of exchanges like the New York Stock Exchange where stocks are bought and sold. As a result, prices for the stocks are freely quoted and pricing is transparent.

The bond market, however, is a place dominated by the institutions and is, in reality, just a large over-the-counter market. There are some bonds that are listed on the exchanges, but this is a minuscule amount. Because most bonds are bought over the counter, all but the most liquid bonds, Treasury securities, will have several prices depending on from whom you are buying them. Much of the reason for this disparity is that the people involved in selling or buying a bond for you all need to get paid, and they do this by adding a markup or markdown to the bond's price.

136

The pricing of bonds is a complicated process so let's dissect how the price of bonds is related to you.

BID FAREWELL TO A DECENT ASKING PRICE

What you are shown when you are looking to buy or sell a bond is the *bid* (the price at which one is willing to buy a security) and the *ask* (the price at which one is willing to sell a security). The differential between the two is the *spread*. In bond-speak if you "hit the bid" you sell at the bid price, and if you "lift the offering" you buy at the ask price. You can bid for bonds at a specific price, making it clear that the price you are willing to pay is not necessarily the currently quoted higher ask price.

For example, say you're interested in buying or selling a bond from Cohen.com. You phone a broker and he tells you the bonds are 94 bid ($940 for a $1,000 face value) and 98 ask. That means that if you want to buy the bond, you will be charged 98 and if you want to sell it, the price you'll get is 94. See, it's easy to remember which is the buying price and which is the selling price. You pay the highest price and sell at the lowest price. Can you negotiate the price somewhere between the 94 bid and 98 ask? The answer is absolutely yes; the professionals do it on every transaction, sometimes unsuccessfully, other times at a price somewhere closer to the middle.

"Where's the commission?" I hear you ask. Well, the point is that the commission costs are hidden in the bid/ask price of the bond, which is why buying and selling bonds can be such a hit-or-miss venture; you just don't know how that particular price was arrived at. The market price for the bond is perhaps 95 bid/97 ask, but you don't know that because the broker is taking his cut.

At the time of writing this book, there is enormous pressure from the Securities and Exchange Commission and The Bond Market Association to make the prices when buying and selling bonds for retail investors more transparent. However, there are a lot of vested interests involved here, so I rather doubt that things are going to change in a revolutionary way. It will probably be in a more evolutionary way. Regulatory deadlines come and go but the market participants are moving ahead with online bond systems.

Hopefully, one day we will be able to see the posting of prices throughout the day like stock prices as opposed to just at the end of the day, but that's likely to still be some way off.

So now that you know what bond prices look like, let's get out there and buy some of them. There are two main avenues: using a broker and, the savior for the consumer in so many ways, using the Internet.

BROKERING A GOOD DEAL

It is easy to pontificate to bond investors about how you should shop around for bonds, but alas, due to the time and effort this involves, it is a case of easier said than done. But I do stress, if you've decided to go down the broker route, you have to shop around.

The bond market is a hierarchical place, with the large institutions at the top and the brokers at the bottom. Most people have a very negative opinion of the retail broker, which I'm sad to say is not all that undeserved. There's been a lot of publicity about how retail brokers, particularly those involved with bonds, have a nasty habit of not disclosing all of the relevant information about the investments they are selling to retail investors. They also have a few choice white lies that they use on retail investors to tempt them into buying a bond, of which I will go into more detail later.

Aside from the obvious fact that some brokers know more about bonds than others, one of the main reasons for shopping around is the issue of those hidden commissions and hence the different prices you will find for the same bond.

What happens after you contact a broker about a bond is that the broker goes to a liaison desk to find out what's available. The liaison desk then goes to the trading desk, which communicates back to the liaison desk what's available and what the markup or markdown is. The liaison desk in turn goes back to the broker, who then phones you back.

As you can see, a lot of people are involved and each is taking her nick out of the retail investor's price, adding onto the price when buying for you and taking away when selling for you. It's called the bond market food chain and everyone must be fed at your expense.

Not all full-service brokerage firms have liaison desks; sometimes the retail broker calls the trading desk directly. Find out how the firm operates and how many layers of people your broker must go through to execute a trade.

Now, is all this excessive? There are times when it is and times when it is not. The point is that every time you have intermediaries, you as a retail buyer or seller get a worse deal. With differences in price existing for the same bonds, I think it's crucial that you have a minimum of two brokerage firms that you do business with. I would prefer that people have three brokerage firms, but I have to be realistic. People don't shop around as much for bonds as they do for a television set, which I think is incredible given that they are investing so much more money.

If this chapter teaches you anything, it's that you need to take that extra step. As part of my fiduciary responsibilities when I manage money for my clients, I use about 14 different dealers for corporate bonds and maybe 10 to 12 for municipal bonds.

I also occasionally use third-party brokers to try to bid for bonds for me because sometimes they can get a better price from the dealers even if they charge me a small transaction fee. This is an important point, because many times an intermediary like a third-party broker will work harder for less money than a dealer whose brokerage has the bonds in inventory. Everybody should understand that institutional clients have favorite money managers just like retail brokers have favorite customers whom they deal with. Often there's a different price for different customers, even for institutional accounts.

Is there a way to give you better execution? If you decide to use a discount broker such as Charles Schwab, then it is unlikely to have a large inventory of various bonds. Therefore, the discount broker may have to

THE AMORALITY OF BOND BUYING

It would be hypocritical of me to stress the importance of shopping around when you buy bonds if I did not do so myself. Well, I do. I use numerous brokers as a way to comparison shop.

As in any other industry, there are people whom we enjoy conducting our daily business with more than others, and there are people who are perhaps not as warm and fuzzy as others, but nevertheless give you better service.

In my corral of brokers, there's one municipal bond person who isn't the warmest or fuzziest personality around, but always seems to get me some of the best municipal bond buys.

The offerings are generally small lots of between 10 and 55 bonds, which is a retail amount as opposed to an institutional amount, but the yields are always 10 to 15 basis points higher than those of any large comparable institutional offering. Consistently, I can get a small amount of high-yielding municipals for my clients.

How does this broker always seem to beat The Street?

First, he works at a small brokerage firm as opposed to a large, bureaucratically bloated Wall Street firm. As a result, this broker has to deal with numerous (maybe hundreds of) retail municipal bond investors, and because of limited capital, the broker

contact another dealer, who of course is charging the discount broker a markup or markdown. However, if you go through one of the larger houses, known as full-service brokerages, such as Merrill Lynch, Donaldson Lufkin & Jenrette, or Salomon Smith Barney, they keep their own inventories, so they might be able to get you a better price. (See sidebar: *The Amorality of Bond Buying.*)

Most retail investors, when they are buying municipal bonds, find that buying on the new issue market gives them a better shake. This is probably true because they know that at that minute when the new bond is priced, they are buying municipal bonds at exactly the same price as everyone else. Obviously there are underwriting fees and markups involved, but at least people know they're not getting scalped any more than the next guy, whether he is another individual investor or an institution.

However, institutions do enjoy economies of scale. I'm not buying bonds at the same price as Fidelity because a fund manager for Fidelity has billions under management and I have $80 million, so the big guys are always going to the favored client. (See sidebar: *Show Me the Municipal.*)

Buying new-issue corporate bonds is also advantageous. You have a prospectus and you don't have to put up with hearing little white bond lies from brokers about what's hot and what's not. The risks, facts, and what the proceeds from the bond sale will be used for are all spelled out in the bond prospectus.

Getting into new issues is not always easy because, the institutions being what they are, they get first bite at the cherry. You as a little guy are way, way down the list. However, if you use one of the bigger houses like Bear Stearns rather than a discount broker, then you are more likely to be able to get into a new issue because these houses often act as the underwriters of new issues.

TELL ME NO LIES

So we turn to those little white lies used to hype bonds to retail investors. There are a lot of bond lies around and I really have to blame this on the retail brokers. I've heard

carries little inventory. His clients' positions plus street offerings become the broker's inventory.

My suspicion is that the broker's customers are more trading oriented than buy-and-hold oriented. My second suspicion is that when I call the broker with a checklist of parameters of what I am looking to buy, the broker sifts through client positions. Then he calls the client with a pitch on why XYZ municipal bond (which incidentally is exactly within my parameters) should be sold and why another municipal bond should be purchased as a replacement. The broker may work to get the bond offerings on The Street, but that can't conceivably produce the bargains he regularly offers me.

This leads me to my third suspicion: that the broker is short-changing his clients when he sells those bonds to me. This process is called a "cross trade."

Now, while this doesn't necessarily mean that the broker's customer is selling at a loss, it does mean that the client is not getting the best execution. I do sometimes feel sympathy for the nameless, faceless customers who are selling their bonds below the market price while my clients benefit at their expense. However, I can't let my feelings get in the way of doing the best for clients, because if I don't buy these bargains, someone else will.

SHOW ME THE MUNICIPAL

As a baby boomer, I certainly didn't grow up with computers but I love and appreciate their benefits. In this book, I have referred to the benefits of owning a Bloomberg computer system, which gives me pricing, analytics, databases, models, and spreadsheets—whatever you want, it's got it. No self-respecting bond manager can be without this system.

One feature it has is the Bloomberg Pick List, which is a multidealer municipal bond offering list. I can sift through thousands of municipal bond offerings from hundreds of brokerage firms that have these positions in inventory. The custom screens allow me to pick my selections by maturity, state, size, coupon, rating, and whether they are insured or uninsured or subject to alternative minimum tax—you name it, and the system can sort it.

Bonds can be purchased either by e-mailing the broker over the Bloomberg (assuming the money manager has an existing account) and buying the bonds or, as I do 99.99% of the time, by calling the dealer and trying to negotiate a better price.

The point of this is that even with all the electronic bells, flat screens, and multimedia displays, as a fiduciary it's imperative that I try to buy bonds at the lowest possible price. I never accept the offering price as the

most of these little lies in my time and if you are unfortunate to hear any of them, I would advise you to hang up the phone on the spot.

One of the most popular fibs is a broker telling you that "I bought this bond for my mother" or "I bought these bonds for myself." What I tell retail investors is that if a broker tells you this, then ask him to either fax or post a copy of the confirmation slip to show that he really did buy the bonds for his mother or for himself.

As a money manager, I often tell my clients whether I bought the bonds myself, but I always offer to send them a confirmation to prove this. Of course, this is no guarantee that the investment will end up being a good deal, but it does show that you are putting your money where your mouth is, so it's easier for people to have more faith in you.

Another little trick that brokers use that is way, way overdone, but unfortunately is often successful, is quoting to you the yield to maturity as opposed to the yield to worst call. As I mentioned in the previous chapter, the yield to worst call is unequivocally the yield to use, not the yield to maturity (unless the bond is noncallable), not the current yield and not even the yield to first call.

Many times, particularly with high-coupon bonds, the yield to maturity is going to outstrip the yield to worst call by anywhere from 5 to 15 basis points. By jacking up the rate of return on a yield basis, the brokers are appealing to your greed and unsurprisingly find this often works.

One fib that has gotten some brokers into trouble in the past is the use of the phrase *government-guaranteed* when trying to sell an investment to a client. It sounds great, doesn't it? Buy a Treasury security and it's government-guaranteed, buy a more juicy collateralized mortgage obligation (CMO) and it's also government-guaranteed. If I didn't know any better, I know which one I would plump for. But look a little closer and this government guarantee is not strictly true.

In Chapter 4, we explained that a CMO is a derivative security that is backed with underlying mortgage pools as collateral. So while a CMO may contain federal

gospel, because often I can arrive at a marginally or even sometimes significantly better price. Other times the broker won't budge. If he's offering bonds I really want my clients to own, I'll be forced to "lift his offering" and buy at the ask price.

When I talk with the broker, I approach the bargaining in a few different ways:

1. I ask if there's any room. Can he narrow his profit from the price he purchased to the price he wants to sell?

2. I say I'm interested in a portion or all of his position, but at a different level (higher yield/lower price).

3. If the broker won't budge, I ask him to call me if the bonds cheapen up.

4. I tell the broker that I've seen a better offering and I'll buy his position if he matches the better price.

I may use one or any combination of the above. If none of these methods work, it's not beneath me to beg. After all, the worst he can do is say no.

agency bonds such as those from Freddie Mac and Fannie Mae, unfortunately they've been diced and sliced so many times that there is no way that the timing of interest and principal can be said to be "guaranteed" in any proper meaning of the word. In fact, they are hugely volatile, as

investors have found to their chagrin, and this has resulted in many complaints about the way that this truly awful product was sold to them.

Another little bond lie is a broker calling an investor like yourself
and saying, "I just got a great steal and I want to present this to you."

Now, for a start, great buys in the bond market are few and far
between. In any case, the dealers with whom you are doing the business
are usually the large brokerage firms, and what they are selling is what
they have in inventory. If it's such a great buy, why for goodness' sake
would they be getting rid of it?

As most large retail brokers are not selling anything other than the
widgets they have in inventory to sell that day, you are probably more likely
to get a steal from a third-party broker, who has the time to do the legwork
that you either are not able to do or can't be bothered with doing yourself.

Another question you should ask yourself when presented with a
steal by a broker is, why you? If it's such a great buy, why is he present-
ing it to you? Surely he has other, more important clients. This leads me
to the main point about doing business with a brokerage firm.

FIND OUT WHERE YOU STAND

If you do decide to go down the full-service brokerage route, you need to
become an important client. How do you become an important client?
Number one, you need to have a lot of money; and number two, you need
to do numerous transactions throughout the year.

Haven't you ever wondered how many clients your broker calls
before he rings you up? Where exactly are you placed on that list that the
broker has? Are you the first or are you the tenth person he calls?

This is really an important thing to ask your broker. How big a client
am I? After you've established your ranking, find out what the average
account size is and how can you move up on that list he has.

If you ever want to get a reasonable deal once in a while and reasonable service from a broker, you've got to be on the top 10 list. I think
in a very nonconfrontational way you need to talk to your broker about

this. You don't have to be golf buddies, but you need to be something more than just an account number with a few dollars in your account. Otherwise it is almost guaranteed that you will not be in the top 10 list of his clients. In fact, you will lucky to be somewhere above the bottom 10.

The first thing you should do is to arrange a face-to-face meeting with your broker. From this meeting, you need to establish the parameters of how you are going to operate with him; where you stand on his phone list; what you need to accomplish in terms of rate of return; and what kind of sector of the bond market you wish to focus on—municipal bonds, investment-grade bonds, or high-yield bonds.

With this established, you will be able to take your broker's calls with less trepidation and he should also get the idea that you are no soft sell.

When your broker phones, he will say something like, "I want to show you this bond," before launching into the pitch he was given by the manager in the morning meeting. These pitches are slick and well honed and need to be taken with a large grain of salt. The pitches I get sometimes send shivers down my spine, so goodness knows what the pitches they give retail clients are like.

After you've heard the pitch, get out your checklist of questions and go through them. Obviously, if he told you one of the bond lies I wouldn't even bother getting out the checklist; I'd just hang up. But assuming that you have a face-to-face meeting with your broker, he'll recognize that it's in his and your best interests to be upfront and straightforward in your bond dealings. So let's go through the questions you need to ask.

ASK A QUESTION, TELL ME NO LIES

- What type of bond is it?

A very basic question, but you need to make sure that the bond fits the parameters you set out during your meeting. If it doesn't, you should ask yourself why your broker is still trying to sell you something you've already said doesn't interest you.

- Is the bond callable or noncallable?

If the bond is callable, then you need to be wary of blanket statements by the broker about whether or not the bond will be called by the issuer. I've heard pitches by brokers claiming that the bond will be called early, giving me a fine rate of return, but nobody knows what the level of interest rates will be in 12 months' time. If the broker did, then he would be a very rich person and would not be spending his time trying to sell bonds to you, but rather lying on a private beach, looking at his private boat and preparing to fly off in his personal Lear jet.

- What's the yield to worst call?

As we said before, if the broker's talking about the yield to maturity on a callable bond, that's no good. You need to know the yield to worst call. With municipal bonds, there is something called municipal kickers. These are moderately high-coupon municipal bonds. The kicker is when the yield, which is perhaps 4.4% for the first 7 years, will kick up to maybe 4.7% in the twelfth year. However, no broker can tell you definitively where interest rates are going to be and whether those bonds are going to be called or not before the higher yield kicks in. So you need to stick to your yield to worst call calculations and ignore the sales pitch. Don't dream of a higher yield. If it happens, great, but if it doesn't, then you won't be too disappointed.

- What's the credit quality of the bond?

Again that phrase *government-guaranteed* might crop up. Not good enough, so hang up. If the broker doesn't use this, make sure the credit quality fits your parameters.

- If it's a corporate bond, is it on a watch list?

The ratings agencies periodically (or after a specific corporate event such as an acquisition) will investigate whether the company should keep its current rating. As a result, the agency will put the bond on a watch list for being either upgraded or downgraded in quality. This is important because the company in question may be A-rated, but if it's on a watch list to be downgraded, you could find yourself being sold a bond that won't fit your investment parameters in a month's time.

- Will the brokerage follow the company or municipality that issued the bond?

This is essential to know because the environment that the company or state operates in will change during the lifetime of the bond. You need to keep abreast of these developments, as they will impact the value of your investment, so you need to find out whether the brokerage has fixed-income analysts who issue good reports on the issuer of the bond. This is especially important if you're buying bonds of lesser quality. For example, it's easy to keep track of what AT&T is doing. But as for investing in smaller companies, information about them is not so widely disseminated by the mainstream press, and so it is imperative that your broker is prepared to phone you and tell you if something goes wrong with the company.

A brokerage that closely follows a company's earnings and earnings before interest, tax, depreciation, and amortization (EBITDA) will be giving you value for money. Since you're paying markups or markdowns, you should be getting something back in return. Also, companies and states don't operate in a vacuum; they are vulnerable to the swings of the economy as a whole, and so you should demand regular updates on the brokerage's view of the economy as a whole. A bank like Salomon Smith Barney regularly churns out very good research on how the various municipalities and the overall economy are performing.

- How wide or narrow is the bid/ask spread?

This is a key to being a savvy bond shopper. Try to arrive at a price somewhere between the bid and ask prices, whether you are buying or selling. In general, the differential between the two, the spread, can tell you much about the market's perception of the bond issuer. If the spread is wide, this indicates that the bond isn't particularly well traded and lacks market liquidity. The reverse is true of Treasury securities, which are easily sold and have narrow spreads. You should always ask the broker, if you bought the bond today and sold today, what would be the difference? If the broker doesn't know, then I would say don't do business with that broker anymore.

Finally, I would suggest that you bargain with your broker over the price of a bond. When he gives you a price, ask whether it is possible to take a sliver off that. Don't be afraid of haggling. Brokers are used to it and expect nothing less from investors who know their stuff. Brokers are in the business of making commissions, and they would much rather have a small commission than no commission at all. If you are assertive in bargaining over your bond price, the chances are that you'll be able to buy and sell at better levels than if you simply take what is handed to you.

HAIL THE ARRIVAL OF
THE INTERNET

Supporters of the little guy in the bond market have long called for more price transparency in the bond market. Now we have a powerful ally: the Internet.

The arrival of the Internet, as it is doing in so many other areas from buying stocks to buying books, is already revolutionizing the bond market. As this book is being written, online bond investing is still in its embryonic stages, but the changes are already being felt. I must say that in my 22-plus years in the business, the deals on the Internet are some of the best I have ever seen.

Will the Internet replace brokers and bond managers like myself? No, but it does offer you another option for investing, and the competition that online trading brings with it will inevitably lead to many changes for the better at the brokerage firms. They will have to offer good service and cut out the dubious selling practices, which can only be good news for the individual investor. Merely the threat of you moving onto the Internet for your needs should be enough for your brokerage to get the message: Get your act together or you won't see me for dust.

So what do the online brokers offer? Many things for less money. Essentially, the online brokers like E*Trade and DLJ Direct are cutting out the middleman. And as we said before, with so many people needing to get paid when you buy or sell a bond, the fewer people involved, the better.

Some of the trading platforms I've seen allow you, the individual investor, to not only bypass the retail broker but to also bypass the liaison desk.

How the platform works is that it allows you to directly access the inventories of many brokerage houses at once and see what each has on offer and for how much. For the first time in history, these platforms allow individual investors to go to multiple dealers, in one fell swoop helping you to become a savvy bond shopper with a minimum of fuss.

You can search the inventories by bond type (Treasury securities, municipal bonds, corporate bonds), by credit rating (A, BBB, high yield), by coupon (6.5 to 7%), by maturity (5, 10, 30 years), by industry (energy, gaming, steel), and, if you're looking for a particular bond issue, by CUSIP number (the number that each bond issue is assigned when it is first issued).

Not only that, the software includes calculators to determine essential aspects of the bond, like the yield to worst call, and it gives you all of the call dates, live quotes, and an ability to place limit orders. In essence, you have access to all the information and capabilities that until now the retail investor has either been denied or found difficult to obtain.

The software also allows you to build portfolios, such as a laddered portfolio, which we will deal with in Chapter 10.

Beware: Not all platforms are the same. Some offer live quotes for bond prices, others do not. Some allow you to access multiple dealer inventories, others do not, so all you are doing is bypassing the broker and merely seeing what one firm has on offer. That's not what you want; you want access to multiple dealer inventories.

In 1997, Clayton Christensen, an associate professor at Harvard Business School, published an important book, *The Innovators' Dilemma: When New Technologies Cause Great Firms to Fail* (Harvard Business School Press). Its theme is that technology is changing many large, successful bureaucratic companies by forcing them to make a choice. Faced with the new technology that is allowing new start-up firms to compete in their markets, they have a choice of either adopting the new technology and making it work, or ignoring it and continuing to do their business the traditional way and ultimately see that business cannibalized. Both choices are bad. In the case of brokerages, they must either adopt the technology and risk alienating some of their employees, or ignore it and find they have little business left.

Whatever the choice they make, it's a one-way street for you, the individual investor. You can't lose.

TRADING ONLINE

Such a glowing tribute to the Internet demands that I show you how to actually trade on the Internet. Here's a step-by-step guide using what I consider one of the best platforms.

Step 1: Check with *Barron's* and other financial publications that rate online brokerage firms and their online bond capabilities. Not all online brokerage firms sell bonds.

Step 2: Read the fine print or speak to a real person at the firm and find out whether its bond offerings are out of its inventory exclusively or it offers the multidealer platform we previously discussed. You'll want and need access to many dealers' inventories, as this allows you to comparison shop among hundreds of issues.

It appears that as online bond investing becomes more mainstream, different online brokerages will have access to different dealers, so don't assume every firm will be accessing the same dealers. Another way the online market may evolve is that a dealer may not offer the same bonds to different online brokerages. By this I mean that a dealer may offer online broker A its top 50 corporate bonds and broker B its next best 50 corporate bonds. As a result, it's probably advisable that you open at least two online accounts.

Step 3: Open your online account. Map out a specific strategy for your bond investing. Decide what type of bonds, or asset class, you wish to invest in: municipal, investment-grade corporate bonds, or perhaps zero-coupon Treasury securities for your IRA. (See Chapter 10 on how to manage your portfolio.)

Step 4: The menu will prompt you to give your investment parameters. Do you want investment-grade corporate bonds between 5 and 7 years in maturity? What level of coupons (for example, between 5 and 8%)? What rating of bonds (say, BBB+ to AA)? You set the parameters, and the software will do the search.

Step 5: After the search is completed, the software will tell you how many bonds fit your criteria. Brace yourself, because it can go into the hundreds!

Step 6: The list of candidates will appear on your screen. Some will be live offerings, those that are available now, while others will ask you to set the limit of your price and will try to complete it for you at the best price.

Step 7: Some firms will charge a flat fee for really small amounts of bonds (10 or fewer), but most will simply make a markup from the dealers, which will already be built into the price you are seeing on the screen.

Step 8: Point and click for your selection. Pay for the bond and get ready to start collecting your income.

Buying and selling bonds online is getting easy. Understand if your online broker charges a markup or acts as an agent and simply charges a fee. Look closely to see whether the offerings are "live" or whether you must place a "limit order." (See screens on pages 152–156.)

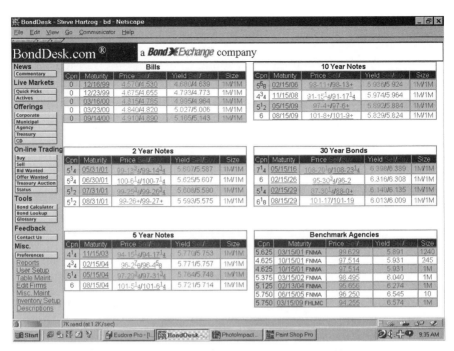

Look at the Treasury bond page to get a feel for the yield curve.

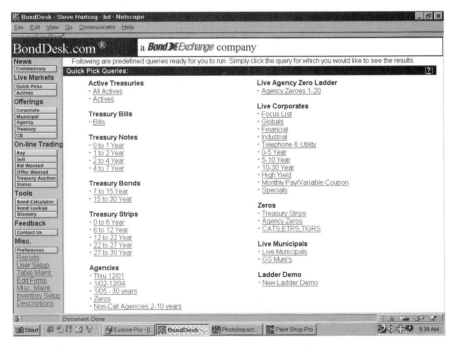

Which sector of the bond market are you interested in? Point and click onto it.

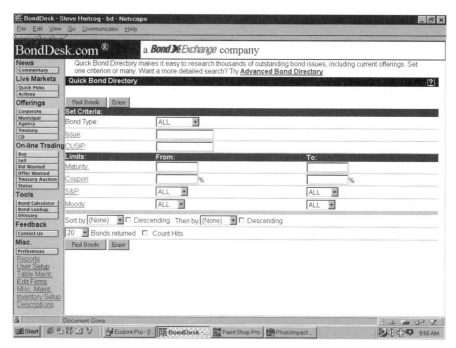

Define your bond search by sector, coupon, maturity, rating, or any combination.

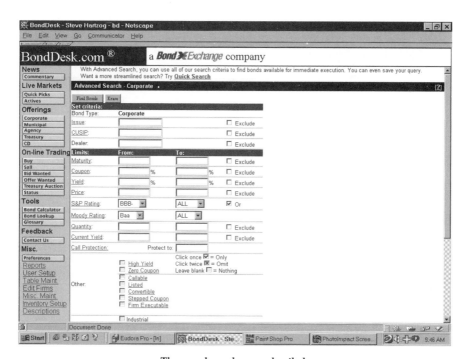

The search can be very detailed.

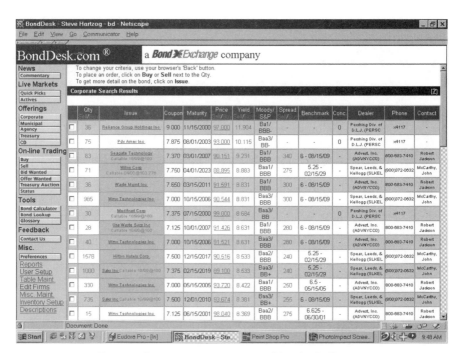

**Your search may extract zero to several hundred offerings;
some of the offerings are live markets, others are not.**

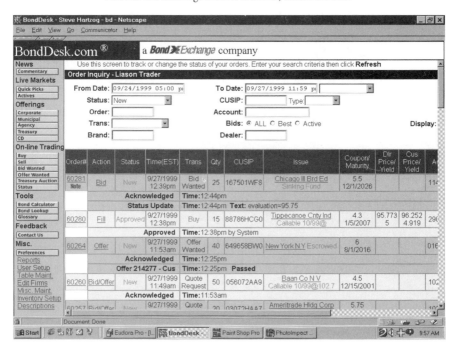

A screen tracks the status of your orders.

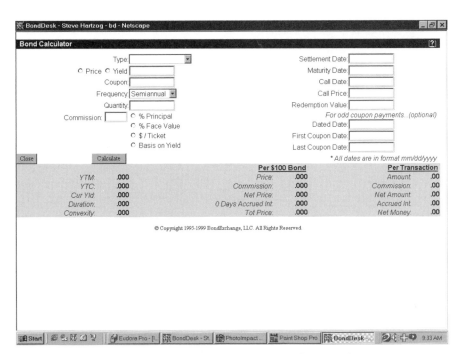

The bond calculator computes the important information for you.

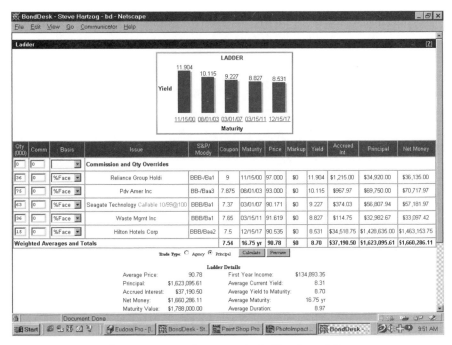

Investors can purchase an entire laddered portfolio.

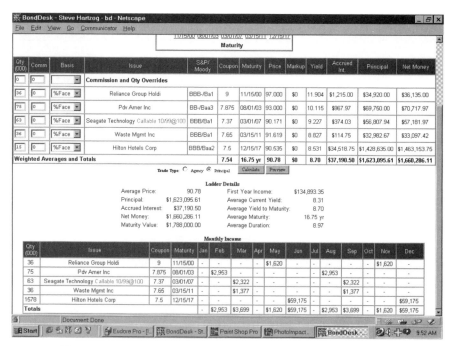

The bond screens will do all the necessary calculations including duration.
The handy monthly income grid allows you to know the coupon payments at a glance.

THE ROAD AHEAD

Whichever route you choose to go down—using a broker or the Internet—the next few years will offer you the chance to become a much savvier investor with less bother. The playing field, while still far from level, is at least not so inclined against the little guy. If you've been wary of buying bonds before, then surely now is the best time to at least take a peek at what is on offer. Go for it!

CHAPTER 9

ODDBALL BONDS: GETTING CREATIVE

The geeks on Wall Street forever spend their time devising new and complicated structures of bonds to hawk in the marketplace. While these esoteric bonds have until now largely been the prerogative of the institutions, I have decided to include a chapter on these bonds because what's considered an oddball bond today may very well be ordinary tomorrow.

Even if some of these bonds remain too complicated for the individual investor to understand, the manager of any bond fund you may be invested in certainly won't have any qualms about buying them. So at the very least, some of these bonds could end up as part of your fund.

The bonds that I will discuss in this chapter are all very different products, but they all share one main feature: They are, to varying degrees, complicated. As I explained in Chapter 7, the more words a broker needs to explain a bond to you, the more you should demand in terms of yield to compensate for this complexity.

However, there is a flip side to this. A bond's special feature may contain the seeds of its own destruction. Some of these bonds are so new and wacky that nobody really knows if they will behave quite as the nerds' mathematical models predict. Certainly the whiz kids on Wall Street are clever, but the market is a notoriously complex beast and has been a graveyard for much smarter men and women than those who currently spend their days hunkered over their computers on Wall Street.

So should you stay clear of these odd bonds? Not necessarily. Just be very careful and for the most part only invest money that you are willing to see go up in a puff of smoke.

I will go through these bonds in order of oddity, from interestingly structured bonds that have become almost commonplace to ones that are pretty far out there.

INFLATION-INDEXED BONDS

At the beginning of 1997, the government introduced *Treasury inflation protection securities (TIPS)* with 5-, 10-, and 30-year maturities. Although not a Wall Street invention, the Street has enthusiastically embraced TIPs.

The reasoning behind issuing bonds is that inflation erodes the value of fixed-income securities. Normally, bond yields are made up of two elements: the real rate and an inflation premium, which takes into account the expected level of inflation over the life of the bond. Should inflation rise, then the value of the bond falls and purchasing power erodes.

What these TIPS do is remove the inflation premium and hence the inflation risk that is present in normal Treasury securities. TIPS pay an underlying yield plus the rate of inflation, which is measured by the country's monthly consumer price index, so if inflation does rise above the expected level, then holders of regular Treasury securities will lose, while holders of TIPS will be protected.

The major problem with TIPS for people like you and me is that the adjustments made for inflation are added to the TIPS' principal amount and are payable at maturity. That means that the adjustments are taxed annually as interest, but you won't see any of the income until the TIPS matures. They are best for tax-deferred accounts.

The performance of TIPS has been uneven since they were first issued, mainly because the U.S. has been experiencing disinflation as opposed to inflation. (Disinflation occurs when price increases can't be passed on to consumers.) However, those who believe that inflation is dead are being so galactically naive that it doesn't bear thinking about. Inflation is dead until it isn't.

Inflation is like circus lions; you can tame them, make them jump through hoops, and even stick your head inside their mouths, but a lion is a feral beast. When you least expect it, it will bite your head off. Please, don't give me this nonsense about how we've entered a new paradigm and inflation is a thing of the past. Hubris, all of it.

There's also an interesting municipal variant of TIPS. The *municipal inflation-indexed securities,* or municipal CPIS, are municipal bonds that pay an underlying yield plus the All Urban Non-Seasonal Index of Consumer Prices—the regional version of the CPIS.

The difference from TIPS is that rather than the adjustment for the inflation being added to the principal, the semiannual coupons of the municipal CPIS are the sum of the normal fixed-rate coupon and a floating-rate coupon that is equal to the value of the inflation index. This means an investor does not have to wait until the maturity of the bond to reinvest the inflation adjustments.

Being a form of municipal bond, the municipal CPIS are also exempt from federal and sometimes state taxes.

TOP OF THE POPS

It was the English rock star David Bowie who was first to hit on the idea of selling an asset-backed security (ABS) tied to, or securitized by, future royalties from the sales of his recordings. In 1997, Mr. Bowie issued an ABS worth $55 million, which gave rise to the term *Bowie bonds.*

Since that seminal moment when rock music totally proved its distaste for the capitalist system was nothing more than youthful extravagance, those legendary heavy metal rockers Iron Maiden and the King of Soul himself, James Brown, have followed Mr. Bowie's lead. The advantage for the singing and dancing issuers is that they receive in one big swoop money that they might have had to wait for many years to get. And let's face it, these guys need the money to spend now, since their bank accounts are probably down to the last million dollars or so.

Alas, like much in the music industry, these bonds have been subject to a lot of hype. The number of issues has not exploded like many people predicted they would and other than the cachet factor of owning something that is at best tenuously related to a rock legend, there is unlikely to be any reason for you to rush out and buy them.

One of the reasons why there have not been more Bowie bonds is that when Mr. Bowie first issued his bonds, the financial markets were stable and yields on normal Treasury securities were falling to all-time lows. As a result, investors were thrashing around for new and exciting investment opportunities, and Mr. Bowie seized his chance. However, since then the bond market has been afflicted with the Asian economic crisis and near collapse of the Long-Term Capital Management hedge fund, and people are less sanguine about where they put their money.

In addition to there not being very many of these bonds, investors will find they are not terribly large issues compared with the more traditional ABSs backed by credit card or auto payments. The latter are often in excess of $1 billion, while the rockers normally keep their issues to under $50 million. After all, how much money do they need? As a result, the Bowie bonds make up only a tiny fraction of the overall ABS market, which is worth some $700 billion.

This small size means these securities are also very illiquid, so should you decide to sell the bond before it matures, it's unlikely that you will do so without a great deal of difficulty.

If you decide to get into the royalty bond market, you'd be best to stick with a dead rocker or at the very least one who is so far out of the public realm that his or her less savory antics can't upset the flow of royalties. Just think about what would have happened to an ABS from Michael Jackson after he was accused of sexually molesting a minor. Enough said.

'TIL DEATH US DO PART

This section is a little macabre, but I want to spotlight a rather good bond feature that has crept into the market over the years and is really beginning to take off. These bonds have an option embedded in them called a *death put*. In previous chapters, I explained that a "put" option is one that allows the bondholder to put, or sell, back the bonds to the bond issuer at a certain time and at a certain level; in this case it's when the bondholder shuffles off this mortal coil.

The idea is actually not really a new one. Until 1971, the federal government issued flower bonds, which were Treasury securities that you could buy at a price below par ($1,000 face value) because they had lower-than-normal coupons.

What these flower bonds allowed the executor of your will to do upon your death was to sell back these securities at par to pay your federal estate taxes, even if the maturity date of the security was still some way off.

Although the government has gotten out of this part of the death business, the private sector, perhaps sensing the demand from baby boomers, has introduced both corporate and agency bonds with these death puts.

One of the main advantages of these bonds is that your heirs will be protected from a rise in interest rates. Although for the past 20 years or so interest rates have fallen and the prices of bonds risen, this bull run in the bond market is likely to prove as mortal as we are ourselves. Therefore, when interest rates do start to rise again and the prices of bonds fall, if you own these bonds your heirs will still be able to put back the bonds at par even if they are trading below that level at the time of your demise.

There are only two certainties in life: death and taxes. So when we do go to a better place, the ready cash that will be available to our heirs if they decide to put back the bonds to the issuer will come in mighty handy if they have to pay estate taxes. Also, your heirs will be protected from having to sell the bonds if the market is in a terrible state. I've had a few bad experiences of having to liquidate a late client's bond investments into a poor market when good bids were all but impossible to find and mark-downs ran as high as four points ($40 per $1,000 face value) per bond.

These death put bonds are reasonably liquid and as they increase in popularity so will their liquidity.

The federal agency Freddie Mac has gotten in on the act and issued several securities with death puts in 1999. Perhaps realizing death is no easy sell with investors, Freddie Mac has decided to call these issues "estate notes."

The estate notes, underwritten by LaSalle National Bank, are tar-geted at the retail investor and allow the estate of the bondholder to sell the bond at par, with no markdown, before the security matures. Alterna-tively, the estate can elect to hold onto the bond and keep earning the interest.

These estate notes were issued in May 1999 and each issue is worth a total of $20 million. The notes are noncallable for one year and pay interest monthly. One of the issues matures in May 5, 2009 (10-year maturity), and has a 6.70% coupon, while the other has a slightly longer maturity date of May 5, 2014 (15 years), and so has a higher coupon of 6.90%. The minimum investment for both issues is $1,000.

An example of a corporate issue with a death put—and one I have owned for my clients—was issued by AES, a New York Stock Exchange–listed electric power company. The bonds have an 8% coupon and will mature on December 31, 2008. The company is rated just below investment grade at BB and has $200 million of these bonds outstanding.

As far as oddball bonds go, these death put bonds are an interesting option for some investors, and they are now being issued by some very creditworthy institutions and corporations.

Some words of caution: If you decide to invest in these bonds, read the prospectus very carefully because not all death put bonds are the same. For example, some of these bonds can't be put back to the issuer under any circumstances during the first year after issuance. There are annual redemption limits per owner and maximum limits the issuer will allow to be put back yearly.

A SMOKING GUN

No matter whether you are selling tobacco or actually trying to stop it from being sold, this weed means big money.

New York City, never a place to shy away from trying to make a buck from whatever the source, has decided to sell about $2.5 billion worth of bonds backed by the payments it expects to get over the coming years from the $200 billion-plus federal tobacco settlement. These *tobacco bonds* are basically another form of an ABS—bonds that are normally backed by payments from credit cards as well as auto and home equity loans.

The lawyers involved in the cases against the tobacco companies are expected to follow suit (no pun intended) and have said that they intend to issue ABSs tied to their not inconsiderable payments from the tobacco suits. This was hardly surprising since these parasites want to get their hands on the money now, no doubt to donate to the various cancer charities whose noble cause they have taken up and pursued so vigorously.

These tobacco bonds, however, look a little premature. Nothing that involves the tobacco industry can be said to be a sure thing, other than that you are more likely to die early if you smoke. Prudential Securities, a major underwriter of bonds, has criticized such issues—and as a result has been shut out of helping to underwrite New York's issue—arguing that tobacco litigation payments are too uncertain to realistically be used as security for such bonds.

No doubt these issues will have juicy yields, but be very careful before you delve into this moral and financial minefield. After all, if one or two tobacco companies go bankrupt, your interest payments will go up in smoke.

JUNO WHERE INTEREST RATES ARE GOING?

Although not strictly an oddball bond, the *Rydex Juno bond fund* is still a bit strange and not a little risky.

If you are bearish on bonds and think interest rates are set to rise and bond prices to fall, then the Rydex Juno no-load fund could be for you. This is because the Rydex Juno fund moves in the opposite way as the bond market—bond prices fall, the fund goes up, and vice versa.

In this way, the Rydex Juno fund is a good way to hedge your other bond portfolio against a sudden swing in the market or to park some funds if your crystal ball tells you that we're in for a protracted rise in interest rates. So if the prices of your bond holdings are falling, then at least you're making money from this fund.

How does it work? The fund makes money when long-term interest rates are rising by selling short Treasury securities, selling short Treasury bond futures, and buying put options on these contracts.

Does it work? Absolutely. For example, from January 1, 1999, to December 1999, interest rates went up relentlessly and bond prices went down, but the Rydex Juno fund had a positive rate of return because as interest rates went up the price of Rydex Juno rose.

Before you bet your house on a rise in interest rates, it is worth remembering that nobody, and I mean absolutely nobody, knows where interest rates will be in 12 months. Better men and women than you or I have been wrong in this regard. This fund provides you with a hedge against a move in interest rates, not something you'd want to stake your future on.

Also the Rydex Juno bond fund is not for small fries, but for investors with a minimum of $25,000 to invest.

NOT AN INVESTMENT TRUST
TO TRUST

The following is one of the oddest investment vehicles I've seen, odd because I can't understand why anyone in his right mind would want to invest in it. These investments are unit investment trusts (covered in Chapter 6) that consist of closed-bond funds rather than the usual variety of individual bonds with specific call dates, maturities, and locked-in yields.

Stay away from this critter because it has the worst of all possible features.

First of all, unit investment trusts are normally unmanaged investments. You buy them and the bonds contained in the unit investment trust are either called or mature and are not replaced. Therefore, you are not charged an annual management fee.

The closed-end bond funds, however, are actively managed and so you are charged management fees, thus negating the key advantage of the unit investment trust. As with most unit investment trusts, you must pay a maximum 4.50% sales load, and on top of that there are the closed-end fund management fees. All this is undoubtedly good for the institutions that sell these things, but for the investor the word *fleeced* immediately springs to mind.

Another counterproductive feature of these closed-end unit investment trusts is that the only price available to you is the closing day's price. One of the great features of buying closed-end funds is that they trade on the stock exchanges and their prices are quoted on an intraday basis. So if you see a closed-end fund trading at a juicy discount to the net asset value, you can snap it up. However, you can only buy or sell unit investment trusts at the day's closing price, by which time the attractive discount may have gone out the window.

The creators of these oddball closed-end unit investment trusts took two perfectly good financial products—traditional unit investment trusts and closed-end bond funds—and combined them into one perfectly awful concoction.

The sellers of these investments will argue that because each of these trusts are made up of municipal bonds or high-yield investments with 15 to 35 funds in each, this gives the investor tremendous diversification. True, but there is such a thing as too much diversification. Any good traditional unit investment trust or closed-end fund is diversified enough and much cheaper.

All in all, you would be far better off consulting *Forbes, Barron's, Money,* or Morningstar on the best closed-end bond funds and then going out and buying them yourself, either online or through a broker.

ALL AT SEA

We talked in Chapter 8 about how some brokers like to tempt bond investors into buying some awful investments by using the term *government-guaranteed*. Well, there actually is a small niche in the market that offers bonds with a juicier yield than Treasury securities but whose principal and interest payments are guaranteed by the federal government. These bonds are called *ship-financing bonds.*

In the 1950s, the Maritime Administration set up a program to guarantee bonds sold by shipbuilders and shipowners as a way to help the nation's ship business by allowing these parties to borrow cheaply from the market.

The program has ebbed and flowed since then. The oil crisis in the 1970s increased the number of bonds issued as the domestic shipbuilding industry became a federal priority. But with oil prices falling in the 1980s during a time of rising interest rates, the industry and the bonds were hit hard.

The shipbuilding industry rebounded during the 1990s, though, as the economy improved and the Clinton administration extended the financing initiative to foreign shipbuilders with operations in the U.S. The result is that the amount of such ship-financed bonds outstanding at the turn of the millennium was around $3 billion.

Despite their government guarantee, these bonds generally yield about one percentage point above Treasury securities with a similar maturity. That means that while a Treasury note with a 10-year maturity offers you a coupon of 6.0%, a 10-year ship-financing bond could have a coupon of as much as 7.0%, which is a good return considering you're not taking on any extra risk.

However, most shipbuilding bonds are sinking fund bonds (see Chapter 8), which means that they are complicated to analyze and, because of that, you deserve to get a comparatively high yield for your trouble.

Another problem is that the bonds are scarce, so it's hard to get your hands on them. Also, they are not very liquid, so they are definitely a buy-

and-hold proposition because it's difficult to actively trade them. Treasury securities, on the other hand, are the most liquid bonds around.

Companies that have issued such ship-financing bonds include Empresa Energetica Corinto, Astro Offshore Corporation, and Petrodrill Offshore.

BONDS WITH CATASTROPHIC CONSEQUENCES

Most individual investors won't have heard of *catastrophe bonds* and are unlikely to be buying them soon, but the market for these debt instruments has grown since 1997 when the first bond of this type was issued. As a result, many portfolio managers, and perhaps one who manages your bond fund, hold them in their portfolios.

With an increasing number of people living in areas prone to catastrophes such as hurricanes and earthquakes, insurers are feeling the heat from claims. Therefore, by issuing catastrophe bonds, these insurers can protect themselves against the most expensive disasters.

A typical catastrophe bond works by the insurer setting up a subsidiary to act as the reinsurer. The subsidiary issues the catastrophe bonds in the capital markets and, using this as collateral, provides a reinsurance policy to the insurer. The reinsurance policy will have a predefined loss limit, above which the reinsurer provides the coverage in the amount of the bond issuance. This loss limit, which functions like a deductible, is known as the *attachment point*. Should there be an event causing losses in excess of the attachment point, proceeds that would otherwise go to the bondholders are used to pay the claims.

In essence, what the buyer of the catastrophe bond is doing is taking the extra yield over Treasury securities (perhaps some 400 to 600 basis points above Treasury securities) in return for betting that some sort of catastrophe won't happen. If there is a cataclysm of mythical proportions, the buyer may not get the interest or principal back on the investment.

Not only is the market for these bonds getting larger but the ratings for them are getting higher, too. The first catastrophe bonds were all high-yield bonds, but lately the rating agencies have been giving these bonds investment-grade ratings. The reason for this is that the storm-modeling technology is getting so much more sophisticated.

My problem with these bonds is that trying to model the likelihood of acts of God occurring seems to me slightly foolhardy, since by their very nature they are unpredictable. For example, Tokyo, based on historical models, should have been devastated by an earthquake sometime in the early 1990s, but, as we know, the Japanese capital is still standing. In fact, the operator of Tokyo Disneyland, Oriental Land Company issued about $200 million of catastrophe bonds to insure against the risk of an earthquake in 1998. Unless you feel particularly blessed, I would leave these bonds to the professionals. (See sidebar: *How Odd Is Odd?*)

BONDING WITH THE INTERNET

Most Internet companies have turned to the stock market for financing rather than the bond market, unsurprisingly, given that the companies have little to no earnings to pay any interest to investors. But happily for those of you who want to get into the Internet sector but don't like the risk involved, there is now a bond whose return is based on a basket of stocks.

The investment bank Salomon Smith Barney was the first issuer of these *Internet bonds* in 1999. The bonds, or callable equity-linked notes, as Salomon likes to term them, are basically securities whose value is linked to *TheStreet.com Internet Index* of 20 stocks. The safety of the security is that it protects your investment by limiting the downside risk, but needless to say it also limits the chances of making a killing.

The notes have a face value of $10 each, pay no interest, have a maturity of 7 years, and are callable after 3 years. What Salomon pays at maturity, or when the notes are called, is the $10 principal per note, plus or minus what the Internet index has risen or fallen per year within the limits.

No matter how far the index may have fallen, Salomon promises to pay a minimum of $9 per note, therefore limiting your downside risk to 10% of the initial investment. On the flip side, Salomon will pay a maximum of $25 per note, or 25% per year. This means that if Salomon decides to call the notes after 5 years, your maximum return would be $125 per note (there being no compounding of interest).

Sounds great. Yes, but only as long as you intend to hold them to maturity or when they are called. If Internet stocks start dropping (which they have a nasty habit of doing from time to time), then there is absolutely no way you will find a buyer for these bonds if you want to get out. Second, the Internet sector is changing fast and we're likely in for a massive period of consolidation, so you'll have to rely on the index changing quickly to adequately reflect the sector as a whole.

Although the Salomon issue was the first, as long as the obsession with the Internet continues there are likely to be many more of these Internet bonds, or variants of them, to come. Wherever there's a cent to be made, Wall Street won't be far behind.

HOW ODD IS ODD?

Although I have never purchased any oddball bonds, there seems to be no limit to new ideas.

Take for instance the large and growing populations that are subject to catastrophic disasters: hurricanes, earthquakes, tornadoes. These events are killers of people and destroyers of property, which creates huge losses for property and casualty insurance companies. So earthquake, hurricane, and windstorm bonds seem perfectly logical. But what about bonds that insure for a certain amount of snowfall at a ski resort? Sounds wacky? Well, in the summer of 1999 a large French bank, Societe Generale, created a bond that limited a Japanese ski resort's financial risk if the snow levels didn't exceed a specific predetermined amount. It sounded like a joke, but it wasn't.

Wall Street brain power has created bonds for corporations that need to be shielded from pollution liability, too. The theme continues to repeat itself—insurance companies want to "offload" potential liability to bond holders.

Hmm. I wonder if anyone would issue some bonds for my firm, Envision Capital Management in Los Angeles, California (1-800-400-0989), in case any of my client portfolios lose value or clients die? Don't laugh—there seems to be a bond for every circumstance.

TURBO-CHARGED CDs

Staying with the stock theme, there are certificates of deposit (CDs) and bonds based on the Standard & Poor's 500 Index of stocks. These aren't pure fixed-income plays, but rather derivative plays, a word that strikes terror into the heart of most investors. The mainstream media likes to portray them as the greatest threat to mankind since global warming.

Bonds tied to the S&P 500, though, can be a good way to hedge against a massive fall in the stock market, because like the Internet bonds, there is a limit to your downside risk. For example, if you are feeling a bit worried that the stock market has risen too far and too fast and is due for a significant decline, you could buy the callable S&P 500 Linked CD issued by LaSalle Bank. This little number has a maturity of 5 years, is callable after the first year, is insured by FDIC, and even has a death put.

Now if your instincts were right and the stock market did take a tumble, the original capital that you invested would remain intact. What if the stock market rises? Well, because the principal is guaranteed, the CD would rise in value but only as a percentage of the rise in the S&P 500. So with these CDs you are protected on the downside, but your upside is limited in order to pay for that protection.

CDs and bonds linked to an underlying index aren't new and the number of these types of securities is growing. So if this quasi fixed-income equity derivative entices you, read the fine print and do some comparison shopping because some issues will be more attractive than others.

A PENSION IS OBLIGATORY

It was only a matter of time before the cities and municipalities would get the stock market bug. Watching private pension funds rake in the cash and plow it into the soaring stock market must have been galling for those cities and municipalities with weak economies and increasing pension obligations. Of course, public pension funds have long invested in the stock market, but the fundamental problems associated with the pay-as-you-go pension system mean the public pension funds need to generate big returns to keep up with the demands of an aging population.

What the cities and municipalities, together with Wall Street, have come up with are *pension-obligation bonds,* the proceeds from which will be immediately invested into the stock market to take advantage of the potential huge returns.

The economics behind such bonds is simple. By issuing bonds with, say, a 6.50% coupon (the coupons are higher than those of normal municipal bonds because they are not federal-tax-exempt), as long as the returns from the stock market are in excess of 6.50%, then the city or municipality will make a profit.

Also, because the pension-obligation bonds are generally long-term securities—20 or 30 years—the cities and municipalities reckon they will be safe from the short- and medium-term downward corrections that the stock market experiences from time to time.

The simple concept behind these bonds and the potential rewards from the surging stock market means that the market for these bonds has grown from one deal in 1991 to 28 in 1998. These aren't small issues either. Some of them are over $1 billion in size.

So what is the future for these bonds? Well, the stock market was on a tear during the 1990s so the credit rating agencies are treating these debt instruments kindly. However, as I noted in Chapter 5, the rating agencies are notoriously reactive. So if—more likely, when—the stock market does start to shift in the other direction, I wouldn't bet the house on those agencies being ahead of the curve and letting you know that the situation for these bonds has become dicey. By the time the rating agencies do, it will probably be too late and you will have difficulty selling these bonds.

NO ROAD BLOCKS AHEAD

Another newly minted municipal bond issue is something called a *Garvee bond.* These bonds are named after Jane Garvey, who was the head of the Federal Highway Administration, and the different spelling is a somewhat tortured acronym for grant revenue anticipation vehicles.

For anyone driving in areas where highway bumps, buckles, and awful surfaces are common, it seems like it takes forever for repairs to be done—and you aren't wrong. It does take forever. Although the Federal Highway Administration parcels out $25 billion to states annually for road repairs, large projects take an eternity to complete.

The money that the federal government provides comes from a federal gas tax of 18 cents per gallon. However, many states want their portion of this money immediately rather than have it dribble at the pace that it actually comes to them.

To remedy this state of affairs, some states are issuing bonds backed by these federal highway funds. I think this is a smart idea, mainly because it doesn't involve raising any new taxes.

Where's the catch? Well, if for some reason the Federal Highway Administration cuts back on the funding, then those Garvee bonds that are uninsured might hit a pothole. However, overall I believe that these bonds will increase in popularity.

BEING ODD IS NOT ALL BAD

To sum up this bond chapter on oddball investments, I would say that you should expect these products to arrive on the investment shelves in ever increasing numbers. New investment vehicles are the lifeblood of the brokerage industry.

However, sometimes something rare and beautiful happens: The aims of the brokerage industry and the investor are aligned, making some of these oddball bonds a good buy. Alas, many others won't add any value to your portfolio, so pick and choose wisely. Wise investing is not about following fads.

CHAPTER 10

MANAGING YOUR BOND PORTFOLIO

So here we are at the grand finale—putting into practice everything you've learned so far about how to manage your bond portfolio.

In the previous chapters, I have discussed among other things interest rate risk, credit risk, the types of bonds available, how to buy them, and how not to get ripped off.

But before you plunge in and start buying bonds willy-nilly, I think it's necessary to take a step back and pose an important question. Managing your bond portfolio properly has as much to do with knowing yourself as with knowing the various bond products, interest rate risk, and the other concepts of the bond market.

So at this point I want you to pause and ask yourself this question: "What kind of an investor am I?"

I INVEST, THEREFORE I AM

Now this isn't a test. Everyone is different and therefore this book is being read by people with very different ideas of what they want to get out of their money.

So what kind of an investor are you? Are you an income investor, who doesn't much care about capital gains and just wants to hold the bonds to maturity and clip the coupons to live on or reinvest? Or are you a total-return investor, who is not satisfied with just the income from the coupons, but also wants to make money from the appreciation in the bond's price? In the latter case, you are betting that interest rates will decline and you can sell the bonds or a portion of those bonds some time down the road at a higher price and generate capital gains as well as income.

When deciding what kind of an investor you are, I think it's imperative to understand clearly what kind of risk you can take.

An investor must decide through a process of elimination the risk versus the reward that he is willing and able to accept.

A professional, whether he is a money manager or a portfolio manager, has investment parameters regarding risk versus reward that he must adhere to. However, as an individual investor, it's your money and you're ultimately going to have to live through any trials and tribulations that the bond market is going to throw at you. Like death and taxes, that's one thing I can assure you will happen: You will have good times and bad times with your investments.

To measure the amount of risk you are willing to accept, I use something I call a "stomach barometer." I believe your stomach is one of the best indicators of how much risk you are able to take. If you are a semi-wealthy or a very high net worth investor, you probably already know what you can live through. You've probably been through the good and bad times in the equity market and perhaps the good and bad times in the bond market, too. And you no doubt remember those times when you were sick to the bottom of your stomach when things were going badly. That's your stomach barometer warning you that you've taken on too much risk and no amount of antacid will neutralize this problem.

Then there is the opposite situation when you have no problem eating, but you grimace slightly when you see the measly rate of return you are getting on your investments. Perhaps in this case you are not taking enough risk.

We all want to make as high a rate of return as possible on all of our investments. But one thing is for certain: Each asset class we have gone over in the previous chapters has its pros and cons, from too low yielding to too unpredictable and volatile, so you need to let your stomach rather than your wallet be your guide.

If you can't take the heat when things go wrong—and things will go wrong no matter what kind of investment you're in or what kind of investor you are—then the rate of return or money that you are going to generate from that particular investment just won't be worth it. That's what we call blood money. No matter how much it is, it's just not worth the pain.

First and foremost, when you are starting to manage your own portfolio, you must understand what kind of investor you really are. And the number one indicator to measure what kind of investor you are is the stomach barometer.

TAKE CONTROL OF THE BUYING PROCESS

Throughout this book I've been rather hard on the retail brokers, and I wouldn't blame you for thinking, this woman's convinced that the whole brokerage industry is riddled with avaricious charlatans whose only function is to screw the small guy, regardless of the consequences.

Actually, I don't think that. A majority of brokers are dedicated to selling fixed-income securities in an honest and honorable way to the general public, and others at the very worst just do it because retail selling goes with the territory.

However, I do know that ultimately a broker's job is to sell products and in the process encourage you to part with as much money as possible.

Now if you are unlucky enough to encounter a money-fleecing robot dressed up as a broker, it's imperative that you understand exactly how he's programmed and trained to overcome your objections and fears about investing in the bond market.

Many brokers have to cold call retail investors. Some brokers have detailed scripts that they either read off or refer to, while others, after years of sales meetings, simply have excellent selling skills and don't have to bother with these scripts.

The cold caller's first goal is to keep you on the phone and qualify you as a lead. Here are a few questions that he might ask you:

- Are you a conservative or an aggressive investor?
- Do you invest for income or for growth?
- How much money do you have at hand to invest?
- How much do you invest on average? $10,000? $20,000?
- What was your most recent purchase?

An individual investor might think that by telling the broker that he isn't interested in buying anything, the broker will just end the call. Not at all. The likeliest response from the broker will be, "That's good, because I'm not selling anything. This is just a call to introduce myself in the event that I find something that coincides with your investment profile."

One of the secrets to selling financial products is to create a sense of urgency to the situation. The broker will also try to pinpoint the exact objections to a particular bond or fixed-income product that the customer may have. For each problem a customer may have with a product, the broker is armed with slick rebuttals and responses that are peppered with leading questions that will elicit "yes" responses from you.

Here's how a typical cold call might go:

Caller:	Hello, I'm Joe Schmoe from Bond Brokers Inc.
Target:	Yes.
Caller:	Are you a fixed-income investor looking for a 6% tax-free yield with little risk?
Target:	Well, hmmm, that sounds good.
Caller:	Have you purchased municipal bonds before?
Target:	Well, yes, I have.
Caller:	Then you are aware that a 6% tax-free yield for people in high tax brackets is a good yield.

Target: Well, sure.

Caller: When you buy munis, how much do you usually buy? $20,000 or $25,000?

Target: Usually $25,000.

Caller: We are underwriting a new municipal bond issue, 6% due in 10 years. Is this something that might interest you?

Target: Maybe, but how safe is it?

Caller: Oh very safe, although it's not rated because the issue is small and the issuer didn't want to pay the rating agencies.

Target: I'd have to check with my wife.

Caller: Your wife wouldn't prevent you from increasing your tax-free income, would she?

Target: I don't know, I guess not. But I'm afraid interest rates might rise and now might not be a good time to buy.

Caller: Well, most of our high net worth, smart money accounts are snapping these up and they won't be around in the secondary market.

Target: I'm unsure.

Caller: We're positioning our wealthiest, high net worth clients with these munis and we'd like to position you with them.

Target: I don't know.

Caller: So how would you like your account to read? Joint Tenant or a Living Trust?

If you think I made this up, I didn't. I got this verbal selling script directly from a broker who actually uses these questions, rebuttals, and the nice assumptive close.

The subtlety used by brokers can be that of a butcher or a trained surgeon, but the point is that the only real urgency in the bond market is that of people trying to sell these financial products. The bond market is not like the stock market, where Internet initial public offerings shoot up (or down) 20 to 50 points within minutes of the shares starting to trade. For the bond market, it's only during those moments when some major financial crisis or other defining external event occurs that a sense of urgency is injected into the market.

Therefore, it's essential that you take control of the bond-buying process. Seek out alternatives and comparison shop. Don't be intimidated and harried into buying something that you haven't thought through. You should be asking the questions, not the other way around.

Refer to the checklist we went through in Chapter 8. Your talking points need to be precise and direct, and you must have a good idea of what you want from credit quality, the amount of money you want to spend, the duration, and of course, the yield to worst call.

Do be open-minded when the broker tells you about a new issue or an interesting opportunity, because the ideas may actually fit your investment parameters. Remember, always quantify the risk by thinking about how this investment will sit with your stomach.

CONSTRUCTING THE RIGHT PORTFOLIO FOR YOU

Okay, so you now have an inkling of what kind of investor you are and you are confident that you can control the buying process. It's time to make your bond portfolio reflect that.

The previous chapters described the various concepts of the bond market such as credit risk and interest rate risk, and it is these that help you construct a bond portfolio that will accurately reflect what kind of bond investor you are.

Let's look again at some of these concepts.

Volatility and Duration

Volatility, probably more than anything else, is tied to that stomach barometer I talked about above. If you have a bond portfolio whose value is moving anywhere between 5 and 8% up or down, how would your stomach feel? Would you be able to sleep at night knowing that by the time you wake up in the morning your bond investments may be worth 8% less than the night before?

To measure volatility, professionals use a gauge called duration. Duration is a measure of the sensitivity of a bond, fund, or portfolio's price to a change in interest rates. It is a concept that is very important to consider when you are constructing your portfolio.

Calculating the duration of a bond can be done on all bond calculators, but it is a long and arduous process to do by hand. The online brokerages, on the other hand, will tell you the duration of each bond you click on, and if you are using a discount or a full-service broker, you should ask the person you are dealing with what the duration is of the particular bond.

Apart from zero-coupon bonds, where the duration is the same as the maturity, the duration of a bond will be less than the final maturity. For example, a 30-year zero-coupon Treasury bond has duration of 30 years, but a 15-year bond with coupons may have duration of only 10 years. If you have a bond with a maturity of 15 years and the duration is 10 years, this means that if interest rates go up one percentage point, or 100 basis points, then the bond will fall 10% in value. Conversely, if interest rates decline by one percentage point, then the value of the bond will rise 10%. The longer the duration, the more sensitive your bonds will be to fluctuations in the market. If, for example, the Federal Reserve increases interest rates 25 basis points, long-term zero-coupon bond prices will react much more violently than long-term Treasury bonds paying coupon income. By the same token, 5-year Treasuries will have much smaller price movements than 10-year paper.

Duration quantifies how sensitive your bond portfolio is to interest rate gyrations and therefore indicates price volatility.

An individual investor who is going for very large total returns on his investments (income and capital gains) would have a very long duration on his portfolio of bonds. He wants the value of his portfolio to be the most sensitive to interest rate moves.

If your portfolio of bonds has a long duration, your stomach must be lined with cast iron. What you are looking for is volatility in the price of the bonds. You want to buy the bonds when conditions are very volatile and sell when that volatility has calmed down and bond prices are headed up.

You don't have to focus a lot on duration, but it is part of knowing what kind of investor you are so an understanding of it will help you invest accordingly. Here are two guidelines to keep in mind:

- To increase the duration of your portfolio, load up bonds such as long-term zero-coupon Treasury securities.

- To shorten your maturity, buy regular coupon-bearing short-term securities.

Credit Risk

No one wants to own a stock or a bond of a company that goes belly up, but how damaging would it be to you if it did? After all, even the Roman Empire fell, so you have to consider the worst-possible-case scenario. If there is just no way you could tolerate a bankruptcy, then you should stick to Treasury securities, federal agency securities, or very high-grade municipal bonds. Moving further down the credit chain, you could buy high-grade corporate bonds like AT&T or Ford Motor, or if you're feeling downright frisky you could go all the way down to high-yielding bonds of cab companies in Indonesia.

It's the old Goldilocks and the three bears scenario: finding the porridge whose temperature is oh so right. Work out how much risk of a default you are willing to put up with and buy those corresponding bonds.

A HISTORICAL PERSPECTIVE

Throughout this book I have often referred to the horrendous bond bear market of 1994 and the steep declines in the corporate bond market in the winter of 1998 when the hedge fund Long-Term Capital Management got itself into all sorts of financial difficulty and had to be bailed out.

The reason why I have referred to these two time periods so frequently is that although we invest for the future, we can only understand those investments by studying the past.

As a professional portfolio manager, I think it's mandatory that fundamental analysis should play a very large part when you are studying companies and their individual bond issues.

The first question you should ask yourself: Where are interest rates going? If you reflect for a moment on the past two decades, you will see just how important a question this is.

In October 1981, Treasury securities were yielding 15%, the discount rate—the rate that the Federal Reserve lends to banks—was 14%, the federal funds rate was 22%, and the inflation as measured by the consumer price index was 14.6%. Basically it was a time of high inflation and high interest rates.

By the end of 1998, the situation had reversed. The inflation rate stood at just over 1.0% and the yield on the 30-year Treasury bond was below 5.0%, a huge move.

The driver of this whole disinflationary environment that began in 1981 was the Fed, which ultimately allowed interest rates to decline but nevertheless kept a tight rein on inflation. This decline in inflation over the past 20 years has been the catalyst for the decline in bond yields with bond prices catapulting higher.

So with one eye on the past and one eye on the current situation, you have to ask yourself where you think interest rates are going as you are constructing your portfolio.

With so many big-time economists around, you might wonder: What's the use of insignificant me predicting where interest rates are going? Well, most economists have been utterly wrong with their predictions about interest rates in recent years. Of course, just because they've been wrong doesn't mean you will be right, but you should bear in mind that if you do some background work and make an educated guess, then at the very worst you can be only as wrong as many of the professionals.

Keeping your eye on the economic ball is essential when you consider how the economy affects all bonds. For example, let's say you hold bonds from Ford Motor Co. or General Motors Acceptance Corp. The behavior of these corporate bonds is directly tied to whether consumers are flush with cash and auto loans are low.

In addition to the fundamental research available to you from banks and brokerages, keep a firm eye on the Treasury yield curve, which I have discussed in depth in previous chapters.

If all this sounds a bit cumbersome and time consuming, then that is probably because it is, I'm afraid. Managing your own portfolio is not easy, but then again what in life is? I will say, however, that portfolio management does get easier with time and a little practice.

DEVELOPING AN INVESTMENT THEME

After you have answered the question about interest rates, it's then time to establish a theme for your portfolio.

These themes can be anything and everything you want. For example, one of the themes I've seen professional investors follow is buying taxable bonds, which include investment-grade and high-yield bonds. An overriding reason to purchase taxable bonds may be as simple as needing the highest taxable income to live on because you are in a low tax bracket.

Perhaps a part of your theme is establishing not what you do want in the portfolio, but what you don't want. For example, you may not want to buy any bonds of basic industry companies because you think the U.S. economy is set to slow and the cyclical sectors, such as steel, are on their way down.

You may also not want any commodity-based companies such as oil, fertilizer, or chemicals in the portfolio, because these companies are also too open to adverse effects from a slowing economy.

Perhaps one of the themes that you want to follow is buying the bonds of companies that are generating nice cash flows, because regardless of whether the bond issue is investment-grade or high-yield, these cash flows go straight to the bottom line.

You may also decide to invest only in investment-grade companies whose managements are targeting earnings growth of 10 to 15% per annum. As a bondholder in a company such as this, if the earnings do actually materialize, then there would be plenty of interest coverage and the chances are that the company's bonds will be upgraded along the way.

Another theme for your portfolio could be good diversification, which is never a bad idea. The portfolio could be diversified and sprinkled with as many industry groups as possible, but not the dicier ones such as the newly started telecom companies. Excessive concentration on a few particular industries may work in the short run, but you are operating on borrowed time. Diversification will limit your downside to a specific segment of the economy. (See sidebar: *Excessive Concentration.*)

Developing a theme for your portfolio helps you map out a strategy to manage your portfolio properly. Your theme doesn't need to be complicated; it can be very simple.

CHOOSING AN INVESTMENT STRATEGY

After you've decided what kind of investor you are, determined where you think interest rates are going, and developed a theme of what to put in your portfolio, you need a strategy.

I'm going to assume that you will follow what is referred to as a "passive strategy," which is essentially a buy-and-hold strategy. The opposite of that would be an "active strategy," which involves constantly buying and selling securities in the hope of creating capital gains. That kind of strategy is much more speculative and relies on market timing. One of the biggest problems with such an active approach for an individual investor is not just that market timing is an inherently difficult thing to do, but you will also end up giving away a lot of money in commissions. A small investor buying and selling small lots of bonds

EXCESSIVE CONCENTRATION

Once upon a time, the telecommunications industry was a fairly simple, lumbering business dominated by the old monopolies. Then along came deregulation, followed closely by new technology such as the Internet, greater bandwidth, and mobile phones. Mergers and acquisitions are now almost a weekly occurrence as the industry repositions itself for the brave new world of communications.

Now one thing I've learned over my career is that you should learn to accept what you don't understand and live with it. The telecom industry has been moving and shaking so rapidly since the late 1990s that I have found it virtually impossible to keep up with all the changes happening.

Consequently my clients don't have many of these bonds in their portfolios, and of course I've missed the huge run-ups in the prices of the bonds of telecom companies like Global Crossing. But at the same time I also avoided the collapse in the bonds of the satellite phone company Iridium.

I know that many portfolio managers have huge concentrations of telecom bonds in their portfolios because they are looking for large total returns. Good for them! But because I just don't have the time to devote myself to the subject, I can't be sure that I will always choose the Global Crossings and not the Iridiums.

on a regular basis is a godsend to brokers, who can make a hefty amount of commission from such a person.

Of course, a passive strategy does not bind you to holding all the bonds to maturity. Something may go wrong with one of your investments and you will want to liquidate your position. Or maybe you have chosen well and there has been a nice run-up in one of the bonds that you own and you'd like to cash in while the going is good. But in general you are buying the bonds in the hope of generating your coupon income and getting your principal back at the end.

I believe that if you are managing your own portfolio, then this passive strategy is the better way to go. Following a buy-and-hold philosophy means that when interest rates go up and the price of bonds go down, you won't immediately panic because you know that you can hang on to the bond until it comes due. During the life of the bond, prices may recover, meaning that you won't have had to sell your bonds during that horrible time when they are declining or when they are in the process of recovering. You can wait out the turbulence for each and every bond until the maturity or until it is called.

One strategy some investors follow is called the "barbell strategy." This strategy involves putting half your portfolio in short-term bonds (say, 1 to 5 years) and the other half in long-term bonds (say, 20 to 30 years). Professionals frequently use this strategy when they think interest rates will decline, thereby creating capital appreciation in the bonds maturing in 20 to 30 years. This is a total return approach but does have its drawbacks, though. Consider the scenario of falling short-term rates and rising long-term rates. If you'd followed a barbell strategy here, the duration of your short-term bonds would be so short that any rise in the price of them would be muted, whereas the price of the long-term end of the barbell would drop precipitously. Heads you lose, tails you lose.

Instead, an allocation of between 2 and 2.5% in these telecom bonds suited my clients' portfolios just fine. I haven't benefited from the huge run-up in some parts of the telecom sector, but at the same time I wasn't exposed to a degree that would make my lack of knowledge of the industry a liability.

You don't have to be an expert on everything.

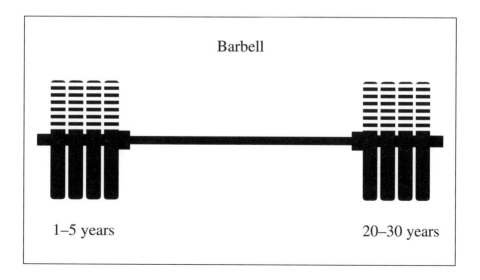

Barbell

1–5 years   20–30 years

A barbell strategy works well if rates stay relatively calm for a period of time. This strategy may also appeal to a total return investor, because if the bond market rallies and prices move up, this will generate large gains from the appreciation of the 20- to 30-year bonds.

A much safer and more common strategy to adopt is laddering your portfolio. There is a whole host of information on this strategy and most consumer financial publications such as *Money* magazine and *The Wall Street Journal* have written about laddering portfolios.

To understand the concept of a laddered portfolio, just visualize a ladder and imagine that each rung of the ladder represents a year when some of the bonds in your portfolio will mature. When the bonds come due on one of these ladder rungs, you will replace those bonds with another issue that has a longer maturity which will be at a higher or lower yield depending on the level of interest rates.

There are various sizes of ladders: stepladders, medium-sized ladders, and ladders that go all the way from the ground up to the roof of your house. Just as there are different sizes of ladders, you have to decide just how long a laddered portfolio you want to construct.

If you are a retired person and you know that you can't comfortably live through bond market volatility, you may just want a short stepladder going from 1 to 5 years. If you're a baby boomer and you know that you're going to retire in 10 to 15 years, then you may want to start your ladder not on rung one or two, but perhaps on year five going out an extra 10 to 15 years. Therefore, as your income starts waning and you get closer and closer to retirement, then your income stream from your bond ladder starts to crank up.

A long-term bond ladder would really be for an individual who has decided to construct a portfolio from which he wants a large total return. A very long or high ladder would mean that you are making a bet on interest rates and are going for the highest yield and the most market volatility.

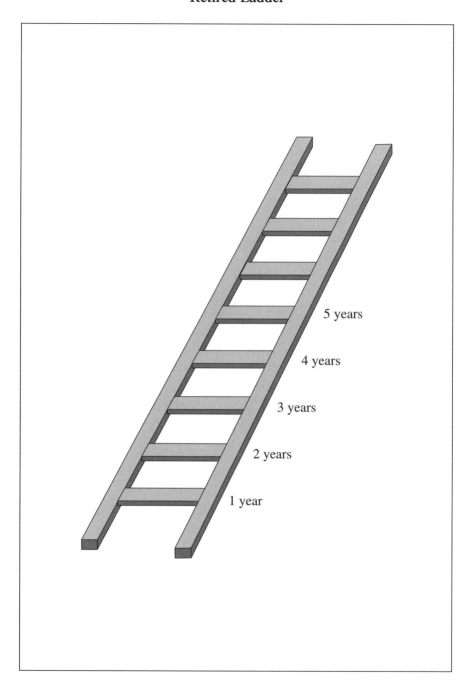

Boomer Ladder

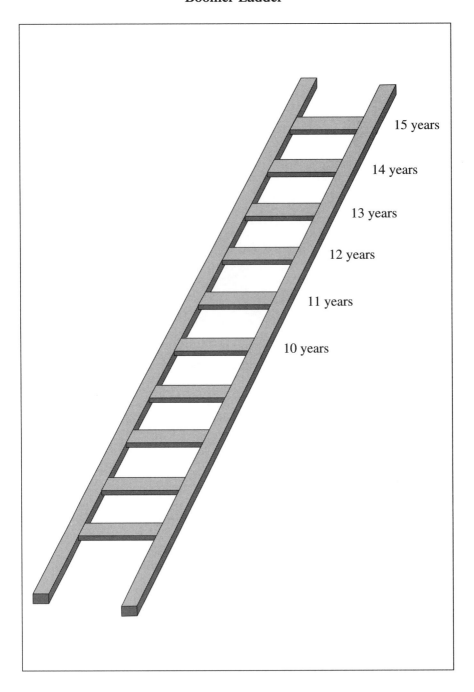

15 years

14 years

13 years

12 years

11 years

10 years

Go-for-the-Gusto Ladder

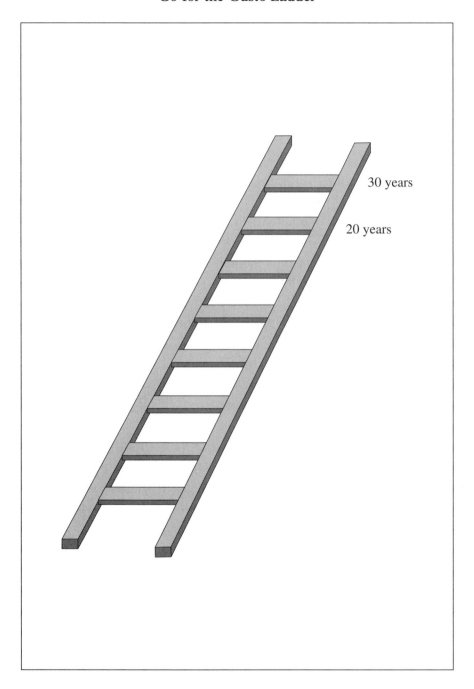

30 years

20 years

Most people with laddered portfolios have ladders that go out anywhere from 10 to 15 years. When I am managing my laddered portfolios, I normally have something coming due about every year and a half to two years.

Admittedly, it's not quite as easy as it sounds to pick out exact maturity dates because it depends on what bonds are available at the time when you need to fill in your ladder rung. Also, if you have a lot of callable bonds in your portfolio—which is likely because there are a lot of callable municipal bonds, corporate bonds, and government agency bonds out there—then you won't exactly know when those bonds are going to be called so you have to make an educated guess.

We talked earlier in the chapter about the concept of duration. Don't assume each rung of the ladder is going to have the same duration. This is only possible if you buy all noncallable bonds or bonds with all the same coupons and maturity, which would not serve a ladder's purpose. The calculation you need to make for a laddered portfolio is the average-weighted duration. This doesn't have to be exactly precise (is the portfolio 3.25 years or 3.15 years in duration?), but you do need to know whether the duration is closer to 3 years than 4 years. The calculators you find in the online brokerages will provide you with this information.

The weighting is important if your bond positions are not all equally distributed. For example, one bond issue may represent 2% of your portfolio and another, 3.5%.

Finally, a laddered portfolio allows you to incorporate that most attractive feature of bonds: receiving money at exactly the time you need it. If, for example, you have children who you hope will one day attend college, then you can plan for this by buying bonds that will mature at the time you need this money.

Predictable Ladder

(My ladder doesn't have total predictable annual maturities
because many bonds have multiple call dates.
But I do post the final maturity dates.)

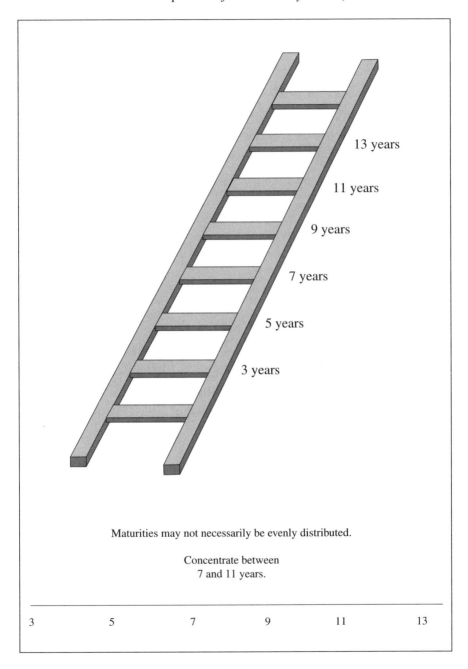

Maturities may not necessarily be evenly distributed.

Concentrate between
7 and 11 years.

| 3 | 5 | 7 | 9 | 11 | 13 |

THE GANG OF FOUR

In general, I think there are four different types of investors. You must determine which profile you most closely match at this point in time.

First, there is the *risk-averse investor.* This investor is probably retired, in a middle to high tax bracket, and an income investor, meaning he invests in bonds to live off the income. To pinpoint exactly when the bonds will come due, he will try to buy bonds with few call features.

A risk-averse investor who is managing his own portfolio will undoubtedly have a short- to intermediate-term laddered portfolio with a short duration.

Such an investor will want to avoid the swings and roundabouts of the bond market and so will need to manage his credit risk carefully. As a result, he'll probably have a mixture of some municipal bonds, some investment-grade bonds, and some Treasury securities in his portfolio.

The second type of investor is the *quantifiable-risk investor.* This would likely be a semiretired worker in a medium to high tax bracket. I think that this investor will have some tax-free bonds (but they will be going out a little longer in duration than the risk-averse investor's) and maybe some zero-coupon tax-free bonds also.

This investor would also want to sprinkle his portfolio with a little bit of higher-yielding bonds to capture a higher rate of return. He will suffer some degradation in the value of his portfolio if interest rates go up, but he won't get killed, and he'll enjoy a higher return if interest rates go his way.

Next there is the *average investor.* The average investor is a combination of the above and is probably like most of us. An average investor wants to go for a little bit of total return, but most of the portfolio is just for income.

He would probably buy some investment-grade corporate bonds, some municipal bonds, and some high-yield bonds, and would not be concentrated in any one particular segment of the credit chain.

Finally, there is the *total return investor,* the go-for-the-gusto guy who needs to keep his Alka-Seltzer® nearby. He is perhaps a seasoned equity market investor or speculator, and he is looking for a significantly higher rate of return than what the bond market can generate safely and effectively. He is willing to take some risks and will buy long-term zero-coupon bonds and perhaps invest in that Rydex Juno fund that we talked about in the previous chapter. When interest rates start going up, he will have no qualms about popping $25,000 or so into that particular fund to offset the fall in his portfolio.

Both the average investor and the go-for-broke investor need to monitor their bond ratings like a hawk in order to manage the portfolio well. However, because healthy, well-run companies don't go broke overnight, the average investor has more leeway here. But just as with stocks, the companies' quarterly earnings reports must be monitored.

MONITORING THE COMPANIES

Getting to the heart of how well a corporation is doing, you must look at the quarterly earnings reports. In the old days, investors would have to wait and read about these reports in *The Wall Street Journal* or business section of the local newspaper. Now the Internet allows investors to see the information at the same time as the largest institutions.

Websites are also popping up that allow you to enter the once off-limits analysts' quarterly conference call. Yes, the unwashed masses are now allowed to hear what the company has to tell all those "experts." Lord only knows why we weren't allowed to hear before what should be public information, but I think this is really another example of how the financial world is becoming less opaque. Some sites archive the calls while others are real time.

The websites also offer earnings trackers, financial analysis, and access to databases that cover thousands of companies.

Here are just a few of the good financial news sites:

BestCalls	www.bestcalls.com
Street Fusion	www.streetfusion.com
Broadcast.com	www.broadcast.com

TheStreet.com	www.thestreet.com
CBSMarketWatch	www.cbsmarketwatch.com
The Motley Fool	www.fool.com
The Fly on the Wall	www.theflyonthewall.com
Vcall	www.vcall.com
CNBC.com	www.cnbc.com

If you invest in high-yield or corporate bonds on the cusp of high-yield and investment grade, then staying on top of the earnings, news, litigation, and any management changes is critical. Because moves in the markets are faster and more furious than ever, you can't rely on reading the news in tomorrow's newspaper. By then it's already yesterday's news, which the market has absorbed, responded to, and moved past.

DEVISING AND FOLLOWING A STRATEGY

After some thought and reflection on what kind of investor you are and the direction of interest rates, developing a theme and following a strategy is much easier than it sounds. The professionals use a very simple approach that works well no matter what sector of the economy is going great guns. This also assumes tiptoeing beyond Treasuries. The strategy is buying bonds in various industry groups in order to diversify risk and concentration.

Just as with stocks, various corporate debt reacts differently to swings in interest rates. For example, financial companies like banks (Bank of America, Bank One, Chase Manhattan, Citigroup) are negatively impacted by rising interest rates. Corporations, builders, and entrepreneurs are less likely to borrow and expand their business as the cost of borrowing increases. The same is true of brokerage firms (DLJ, Merrill Lynch, Bear Stearns). As rates rise, usually corporate and municipal bond underwriting come to a screeching halt. The cost of capital becomes too expensive and the return on the capital declines, which squeezes profit margins. Therefore the brokerages suffer profit erosion, too.

So rather than relying on three or four sectors of the economy to do well, the professionals invest in dozens of industry groups. The groups run the gamut from autos, financial services, phone companies, home builders, retailers, textiles, lumber, oil, and gas to the small sectors like bus companies, fitness centers, and firms that sell fertilizer.

I think you are best served by staying with the better known industry groups and sprinkling your portfolio with the smaller sectors. Mind you, small sector does not mean small or illiquid issues. It simply means the industry sector may not have yet consolidated or there are only a few major players with publicly traded bonds.

Take a look at the corporate bond mutual fund listings Morningstar compiles and rates. Each one-page synopsis lists the fund's major holdings. You'll see that no one issue or industry group represents an overwhelmingly large percentage of the portfolio. (If it does, the manager is making a concentrated bet with his clients' money.) You'll detect the industry group each manager favors and also spot those that are totally absent from the portfolio. It's true you are looking at old news regarding the portfolio holdings, but Morningstar's display, on just a few pages, allows you to visualize how the pros logically build their portfolios. And, it will reinforce the fact that you can do the same.

So devise and implement a bond strategy like the pros. Invest in various industry groups that will move when industrial America is doing well. Also, invest in companies that will flourish when the consumer is spending. Don't forget issues that chug along (like those of food companies, pharmaceutical firms, and healthcare facilities) no matter what the economic horizon has in store.

MANAGING A LADDER

The whole idea of constructing a bond ladder is that the ladder or maturities on each rung need little management. It's the credit quality of each corporate issue—including profitability and interest coverage—that requires monitoring.

The laddered approach is not as rigid as it visually appears. It is simply a framework that helps you space out your portfolios and consciously think about what the maturity (taking into consideration duration) of a new purchase does to your overall portfolio.

One great flexible quality a ladder provides is that when a bond matures, say three years from now, and your interest rate outlook has changed from cautious to bullish, you can skip rungs, double up on some, or mentally insert rungs.

Investors change their minds all the time. If for some reason we move into an inflationary environment that looks long lasting, you may decide to sell some or all of your bonds maturing in 10 to 15 years in order to avoid price erosion.

I've lived through many bull and bear markets in bondland. This simple, low-tech, understandable, laddered approach works well for the average income-seeking investor.

GENTLEMEN, START YOUR ENGINES

If you've read most of these chapters, you probably aren't a beginner in the bond market. The whole idea is to be a smarter investor and a savvier shopper. The model portfolios that follow take into consideration all the elements we've discussed. If you have an existing bond portfolio, then dissect your industry sectors and know your duration. Do you have a strategy or theme for your portfolio? Are your bond maturities a mishmash? Or can you start creating a laddered approach?

In other words: Build a bond portfolio framework and use it as your investment infrastructure.

My model portfolios aren't perfect. By the time you study them, it's possible some of the issues may have been upgraded or downgraded. It's possible some of the high-yield bonds may have fallen on hard times. But barring a bond market cataclysm, due to diversity and allocation, the portfolios won't get totally pummeled or annihilated. It's not a science with strict formulas and rules. Besides, investing should be fun and rewarding.

MODEL INVESTORS

Risk-Averse Investors

The typical risk-averse investor is probably retired and in a middle to high tax bracket. He may have such an aversion to risk that many of his municipal bonds aren't even from his own state. An exception to this are municipal bonds issued by Puerto Rico, Guam, U.S. Virgin Islands, and American Samoa, which are double tax-exempt (federal and state) so they can be bought by an investor in any state to generate tax-free income no matter where one lives.

The risk-averse investor is probably sensitive to tax consequences so he needs to be cautious when buying municipals; it makes sense to purchase bonds at par or a premium, but less sense to buy municipal bonds at a discount to face value. The reason for this is that the yield to worst call or yield to maturity on a low-coupon, market discount bond won't be totally tax-free. The difference between the purchase price and par is ordinary income, not tax-free income. (See pages 199–201 for Risk Averse portfolio and detail.)

The risk-averse investor's tax-deferred IRA, Keogh, or pension will consist of the best-quality corporate bonds and some zero-coupon Treasury securities. (See pages 202–203 for Risk Averse, Tax-Deferred portfolio and detail.)

Quantifiable Risk Takers

The portfolio of the quantifiable risk taker is overwhelmingly on the safe side, but does contain a smattering of high-yield bonds. The municipal bonds are investment grade and the corporate bonds are on the cusp of investment grade. The corporate names are readily identifiable, thereby allowing the investor to follow all the current news and financial information.

The zero-coupon municipal bonds provide a locked-in bullet payment because this investor doesn't need the income to live on yet. This investor usually shoots for a specific overall taxable portfolio yield of around 7 to 8%. (See pages 204–213 for Quantifiable Risk Taker and Tax-Deferred portfolios and details.)

Average Investors

The average investor wants an above-average return and is willing to take a modicum of risk for it. The average investor also uses his bond portfolio as the anchor for his other investments. He most likely has stocks, stock mutual funds, maybe equities managed by professionals, and, if he's very sophisticated, perhaps a hedge fund or two. He needs the assurance that his bond money will be there for the future. (See pages 214–218 for Average Investor portfolio and detail.)

Go-for-Broke Total-Return Investors

The go-for-broke total-return investor is a smart, well-seasoned, sophisticated investor who has plenty of bond market experience. He selects moments in time to place leveraged bond market bets using the repo market. The bet is that interest rates will fall and the price of his bonds will rise. The time frame may be short-term or even run to years. (I know an investor who has held on to the same long-term leveraged Treasury bond position since 1987. Now there's a person who laughs at danger.)

Sometimes this investor will use the maximum leverage available and his portfolio is not diversified because he has conviction about what he is betting on. He may also have some high-yield corporate bonds for the income stream and to speculate on credit rating upgrades. (See pages 219–226 for Total-Return Investor portfolio and detail.)

These model portfolios are subject to extreme changes in price, yield, and credit quality. The bond issues are not meant as recommendations.

Risk Averse
January 5, 2000

Trade Date	Quantity	Security	Unit Cost	Total Cost	Market Price	Value	Pct. Assets	Yield to Worst
CORPORATE BONDS								
01-05-00	25,000	Republic Bank New York *Noncallable* 8.875 % Due 02-15-01	101.90	25,475	101.90	25,475	8.4	7.05
01-05-00	25,000	General Motors Accept Corp *Noncallable* 9.000 % Due 10-15-02	103.75	25,937	103.75	25,937	8.5	7.47
		Accrued Interest				1,363	0.4	
				51,412		52,775	17.3	
		Average Weighted Yield	7.28 %					
MUNICIPAL BONDS								
01-05-00	25,000	Hempfield Pa Sch Dist Lancaster Cnty *Prfd 6.100 % Due 08-15-02	103.55	25,887	103.55	25,888	8.5	4.64
01-05-00	25,000	Eagle County Colorado School Dist 5.750 % Due 02-01-03	102.91	25,727	102.91	25,728	8.4	4.67
01-05-00	25,000	Pennsylvania State Hghr Edl 100% Esc US Govt 6.100 % Due 01-01-04	104.72	26,180	104.72	26,179	8.6	4.79
01-05-00	25,000	Northwest Subn Mun Jt Action *Noncallable*	105.78	26,445	105.78	26,445	8.7	5.00
01-05-00	25,000	San Antonio Tex Wtr Rev 6.400 % Due 05-15-06	105.70	26,425	105.70	26,424	8.7	4.63
01-05-00	25,000	Rhinelander Wis Sxh Dist G/O 5.00 % Due 03-01-07	99.16	24,790	99.16	24,790	8.1	5.14
		Accrued Interest				2,155	0.7	
				155,455		157,612	51.7	
		Average Weighted Yield	4.85 %					
GOVERNMENT BONDS								
01-05-00	25,000	US Treasury 7.250 % Due 05-15-04	102.78	25,695	102.78	25,695	8.4	6.50
01-05-00	25,000	US Treasury 7.000 % Due 07-15-06	102.00	25,500	102.00	25,500	8.4	6.62
		Accrued Interest				1,078	0.4	
				51,195		52,273	17.2	
		Average Weighted Yield	6.59 %					
CASH AND EQUIVALENTS								
			CASH	41,937		41,937	13.8	
				41,937		41,937	13.8	
TOTAL PORTFOLIO				300,000		304,598	100.0	

Average Weighted Duration 2.64   (Common Stock, GNMAs & Cash are weighted at 0 years)

CORPORATE BONDS

Republic Bank New York
8.875% due 2-15-01, noncallable
Rated A by S&P, A2 by Moody's
Business: merged with HSBC holdings,
   international banking and financial services
Issue size: $100 million

General Motors Acceptance Corp.
9% due 10-15-02, step-up bonds, noncallable
Rated A by S&P, A2 by Moody's
Business: Finance arm for General Motors
Issue size: $300 million

MUNICIPAL BONDS

Hempfield, PA, School District
6.10% due 8-15-02, escrowed to maturity (ETM), general obligation bonds
Rated AAA by S&P, Aaa by Moody's
Collateral: U.S. government securities
Issue size: $38 million; maturity size: $2.7 million

Eagle County, Colorado, School District
5.75% due 2-1-03, general obligation bonds, callable
Rated AAA by S&P, AAA by Moody's
FGIC-insured
Issue size: $20.4 million; maturity size: $2.5 million

Pennsylvania State Higher Education Facilities
6.10% due 1-1-04, revenue bonds
Escrowed to maturity with U.S. government securities
Rated AAA by Moody's
Issue size: $21.7 million; maturity size: $850,000

Northwest Municipal Joint Water Agency, Illinois Water Supply
6.25% due 5-1-05, noncallable, revenue bonds
Rated AAA by S&P, Aaa by Moody's
MBIA-insured
Issue size: $165 million

San Antonio, Texas, Water Revenue
6.40% due 5-15-06, prerefunded 5-15-02 @ 102, revenue bonds
Rated AAA by S&P
Collateral: state and local government securities
FGIC-insured
Issue size: $635 million

Rhinelander, Wisconsin, School District
5% due 3-1-07, callable, general obligation bonds
Rated Aaa by Moody's
FSA-insured
Issue size: $6.3 million; maturity size: $605,000

Risk Averse, Tax-Deferred
January 5, 2000

Trade Date	Quantity	Security	Unit Cost	Total Cost	Market Price	Value	Pct. Assets	Yield to Worst
CORPORATE BONDS								
01-05-00	50,000	AT&T Corp	100.01	50,007	100.01	50,007	12.3	7.81
		8.200 % Due 02-15-05						
01-05-00	50,000	Merrill Lynch & Co	93.00	46,500	93.00	46,500	11.4	7.57
		Noncallable						
		6.000 % Due 07-15-05						
01-05-00	50,000	Southwn Bell Tel	89.50	44,750	89.50	44,750	11.0	7.47
		5.375 % Due 06-01-06						
01-05-00	50,000	Atlantic Richfield	101.70	50,850	101.70	50,850	12.5	7.55
		Noncallable						
		7.870 % Due 02-13-07						
		Accrued Interest				4,817	1.2	
				192,107		196,925	48.5	
		Average Weighted Yield	7.62 %					
GOVERNMENT BONDS								
01-05-00	50,000	US Treasury	105.43	52,715	105.43	52,715	13.0	6.65
		7.625 % Due 02-15-07						
		Accrued Interest				1,483	0.4	
				52,715		54,198	13.3	
		Average Weighted Yield	6.69 %					
ZERO COUPONS								
01-05-00	50,000	US Treas Sec Stripped	73.00	36,500	73.00	36,500	9.0	6.70
		0.000 % Due 10-15-04						
01-05-00	50,000	US Treas Sec Stripped	55.00	27,500	55.00	27,500	6.8	6.87
		0.000 % Due 11-15-08						
		Accrued Interest				0	0.0	
				64,000		64,000	15.8	
CASH AND EQUIVALENTS								
			CASH	91,177		91,177	22.4	
				91,177		91,177	22.4	
TOTAL PORTFOLIO				400,000		406,300	100.0	

Average Weighted Duration 2.29   (Common Stock, GNMAs & Cash are weighted at 0 years)

CORPORATE BONDS

AT&T Corp.
8.20% due 2-15-05, callable
Rated AA– by S&P, A1 by Moody's
Business: Telecommunication services, phone, cellular, and video
Issue size: $100 million

Merrill Lynch & Co.
6% due 7-15-05, noncallable
Rated AA– by S&P, Aa3 Moody's
Business: Financial services, brokerage, investment banking,
    banking, lending
Issue size: $500 million

Southwestern Bell Telephone
5.375% due 6-1-06
Rated AA by S&P, Aa3 by Moody's
Business: Telecommunications, long-distance and local, Internet access,
    and messaging; a competitor of AT&T in certain businesses but one
    of the few AA-rated companies around
Issue size: $150 million

Atlantic Richfield
7.87% due 2-13-07, noncallable, medium-term notes
Rated A by S&P, A2 by Moody's
Business: Integrated oil company
Issue size: $10 million

Quantifiable Risk Taker
January 5, 2000

Trade Date	Quantity	Security	Unit Cost	Total Cost	Market Price	Value	Pct. Assets	Yield to Worst
CORPORATE BONDS								
01-05-00	10,000	Musicland Group Inc Sr Sub Nt 9.000 % Due 06-15-03	97.00	9,700	97.00	9,700	1.5	10.05
01-05-00	10,000	Nortek Inc 9.875 % Due 03-01-04	98.50	9,850	98.50	9,850	1.5	10.32
01-05-00	10,000	Flemings Companies Inc 10.500 % Due 12-01-04	91.75	9,175	91.75	9,175	1.4	12.81
01-05-00	10,000	K-III Communications Corp *Noncallable* 8.500 % Due 02-01-06	98.50	9,850	98.50	9,850	1.5	8.82
01-05-00	15,000	Occidental Petroleum *Noncallable* 7.650 % Due 02-15-06	99.54	14,931	99.54	14,931	2.3	7.74
01-05-00	15,000	Michaels Stores Inc 10.875 % Due 06-15-06	106.00	15,900	106.00	15,900	2.4	9.60
01-05-00	15,000	Lehman Bros Hldgs Inc *Noncallable* 8.500 % Due 05-01-07	102.59	15,388	102.59	15,389	2.3	8.02
01-05-00	15,000	American Finl Group Inc Ohio *Noncallable* 7.125 % Due 12-15-07	91.79	13,768	91.79	13,768	2.1	8.57
01-05-00	20,000	Time Warner Entmt Co L P *Noncallable* 7.250 % Due 09-01-08	97.50	19,500	97.50	19,500	3.0	7.65
01-05-00	10,000	AES Corp 8.000 % Due 12-31-08	92.50	9,250	92.50	9,250	1.4	9.34
01-05-00	10,000	AMC Entmt Inc 9.500 % Due 03-15-09	89.00	8,900	89.00	8,900	1.4	11.46
01-05-00	10,000	Seagram Joseph E & Sons Inc *Noncallable* 8.875 % Due 09-15-11	106.03	10,603	106.03	10,603	1.6	8.07
01-05-00	10,000	K-Mart Corp *Noncallable* 8.850 % Due 12-15-11	93.44	9,344	93.44	9,344	1.4	9.79
01-05-00	10,000	Westinghouse Elec Corp-Deb *Noncallable* 8.625 % Due 08-01-12	105.41	10,541	105.41	10,541	1.6	7.94
		Accrued Interest				3,161	0.5	
				166,701		169,862	25.8	
		Average Weighted Yield	9.05 %					
MUNICIPAL BONDS								
01-05-00	40,000	Gregg Cnty Tex *Noncallable* 0.000 % Due 03-01-05	76.63	30,652	76.63	30,652	4.7	5.23
01-05-00	25,000	Lynn Mass Wtr & Swer FGIC Insd 6.125 % Due 06-01-05	104.45	26,112	104.45	26,113	4.0	4.93

Trade Date	Quantity	Security	Unit Cost	Total Cost	Market Price	Value	Pct. Assets	Yield to Worst
01-05-00	25,000	Kokomo Center Ind Sch Bldg 6.750 % Due 07-15-05	108.57	27,142	108.57	27,143	4.1	4.96
01-05-00	25,000	Philadelphia Pa Sch Dist Ser A 5.650 % Due 07-01-06	103.85	25,962	103.85	25,962	4.0	4.79
01-05-00	35,000	Port Everglades Au Fl Port Imp 7.500 % Due 11-01-06	110.43	38,650	110.43	38,651	5.9	5.10
01-05-00	75,000	Seattle Wash *Noncallable* 0.000 % Due 12-15-06	69.85	52,387	69.85	52,387	8.0	5.23
01-05-00	25,000	Nevada St RFDG-B 6.400 % Due 04-01-07	104.09	26,022	104.09	26,022	4.0	4.87
01-05-00	20,000	North Cent Tex Health Fac Dev *Noncallable* 5.500 % Due 04-01-07	101.66	20,332	101.66	20,333	3.1	5.22
01-05-00	35,000	Houston Tex Indpt Sch Dist *Noncallable* 0.000 % Due 08-15-07	67.22	23,529	67.22	23,529	3.6	5.29
01-05-00	25,000	Los Angeles Cnty Calif Pub Wks 5.100 % Due 12-01-08	100.71	25,177	100.71	25,177	3.8	5.00
01-05-00	25,000	Suffolk Cnty NY G/O Ser A *Noncallable* 5.250 % Due 08-01-09	100.22	25,055	100.22	25,055	3.8	5.22
01-05-00	25,000	Nevada St G/O RFDG Colo River 6.500 % Due 10-01-09	105.24	26,310	105.24	26,310	4.0	4.78
01-05-00	25,000	Austin Tex Pub Impt 6.125 % Due 09-01-10	103.67	25,917	103.67	25,917	3.9	4.64
01-05-00	30,000	King & Snohomish Cntys Wash Sch Prfnd 6.600 % Due 12-01-10	105.21	31,563	105.21	31,562	4.8	4.66
01-05-00	25,000	Forsyth Cnty Ga Sch Dist 6.700 % Due 07-01-12	111.26	27,815	111.26	27,815	4.2	5.05
		Accrued Interest				3,968	0.6	
				432,629		436,597	66.4	
		Average Weighted Yield	5.04 %					

CASH AND EQUIVALENTS

			CASH	50,670		50,670	7.7	
				50,670		50,670	7.7	

TOTAL PORTFOLIO

				650,000		657,129	100.0	

Average Weighted Duration 4.35   (Common Stock, GNMAs & Cash are weighted at 0 years)

CORPORATE BONDS

MUSICLAND GROUP SR., SUB NOTES
9% due 6-15-03, callable, poison put @101%
Rated B– by S&P, B3 by Moody's
Business: Retail music, home entertainment stores
Issue size: $110 million

Nortek Inc.
9.875% due 3-1-04, callable
Rated B– by S&P, B3 by Moody's
Business: Manufactures and sells all types of building
    and remodeling products like ventilating products,
    air conditioning and heating systems
Issue size: $218 million

Flemings Companies Inc.
10.50% due 12-01-04, callable
Rated B+ by S&P, B3 by Moody's
Business: Distributes food to supermarkets
    on a wholesale basis
Issue size: $250 million

K-III Communications
8.50% due 2-1-06, callable
Rated BB– by S&P, Ba3 by Moody's
Business: Specialty magazine publishing
Issue size: $300 million

Occidental Petroleum
7.65% due 2-15-06, noncallable
Rated BBB by S&P, Baa3 by Moody's
Business: Integrated oil company
Issue size: $450 million

Michaels Stores Inc.
10.875% due 6-15-06, callable
Rated BB– by S&P, Ba2 by Moody's
Business: Retail arts and crafts stores
Issue size: $125 million

Lehman Brothers Holdings
8.50% due 5-1-07, noncallable
Rated A by S&P, Baa1 by Moody's
Business: Financial services, brokerage,
    investment banking
Issue size: $250 million

American Financial Group
7.125% due 12-15-07, noncallable
Rated BBB+ by S&P, Baa2 by Moody's
Business: Provides all types of insurance products
Issue size: $100 million

Time Warner Entertainment Co.
7.25% due 9-1-08, noncallable
Rated BBB– by S&P, Baa3 by Moody's
Business: Multimedia entertainment company
Issue size: $600 million

AES Corp.
8.00% due 12-31-08, callable, death put
Rated B+ by S&P, Ba3 Moody's
Business: Electrical generation company
    with global facilities
Issue size: $375 million

AMC Entertainment Inc.
9.50% due 3-15-09, callable
Rated B by S&P, B2 by Moody's
Business: U.S. theater owners
Issue size: $198 million

Joseph Seagram & Sons Inc.
8.875% due 9-15-11, noncallable
Rated BBB– by S&P, Baa3 by Moody's
Business: Spirits and wine business and entertainment industry
Issue size: $225 million

K-Mart Corp.
8.85% due 12-15-11, noncallable
Rated BB+ by S&P, Ba1 by Moody's
Business: Discount retail business ranges from
    clothes to small appliances
Issue size: $22 million

Westinghouse Electric
8.625% due 8-1-12, noncallable
Rated BBB– by S&P, Baa3 by Moody's
Business: Multimedia, television, radio,
    outdoor advertising
Issue size: $275 million

MUNICIPAL BONDS

Gregg County, Tex., capital appreciation-ref
0% due 3-1-05, noncallable, general obligation
Rated AAA by S&P, Aaa by Moody's
AMBAC-insured
Issue size: $17.6 million; maturity size: $657,000

Lynn, Mass., Water & Sewer Community
6.125% due 6-1-05, revenue bonds, callable
Rated AAA by S&P, Aa by Moody's
FGIC-insured
Issue size: $28.4 million; maturity size: $3.5 million

Kokomo Center, Ind., School Building Corp.
6.75% due 7-15-05, sinking fund, revenue bonds
Rated AAA by S&P, Aaa by Moody's
AMBAC-insured
Issue size: $28 million; maturity size: $1.56 million

Philadelphia, Pa., School District, Ser A
5.65% due 7-1-06, prerefunded 7-1-04 @ 100.50, general obligation bond
Rated AAA by S&P, Aaa by Moody's
MBIA-insured
Issue size: $160 million; maturity size: $12.8 million

Port Everglades Authority, Fla.
7.50% due 11-1-06 (ETM), revenue bonds, sinkable and callable
Rated AAA by S&P, Aaa by Moody's
Collateral: U.S. government securities
Issue size: $104.1 million; maturity size: $17.27 million

Seattle, Wash., Deferred Interest Series E
0% due 12-15-06, noncallable, general obligation
Rated AA+ by S&P, Aa1 by Moody's
Issue size: $13 million; maturity size: $1.1 million

Nevada State RFDG Series B
6.4% due 4-1-07, callable, general obligation
Rated AA by S&P, Aa2 by Moody's
Issue size: $33 million; maturity size: $3.6 million

North Central Tex., Health Facilities, Hospital-Zale Lipshy University Project
5.50% due 4-1-07, noncallable, revenue bonds
Rated AAA by S&P, Aaa by Moody's
FSA-insured
Issue size: $52.11 million; maturity size: $2.275 million

Houston, Tex., Independent School District
0% due 8-15-07, noncallable, general obligation
Rated AAA by S&P, Aaa by Moody's
AMBAC-insured
Issue size: $190 million; maturity size: $5.533 million

Los Angeles County, Calif., Public Works, Multiple Capital Facilities
5.1% due 12-1-08, callable, revenue bonds
Rated AAA by S&P, Aaa by Moody's
AMBAC-insured
Issue size: $115.68 million; maturity size: $2.55 million

Suffolk County, N.Y., Series A
4.5% due 8-1-09, noncallable, general obligation
Rated AAA by S&P, Aaa by Moody's
FGIC-insured
Issue size: $49.41 million; maturity size: $1.255 million

Nevada State, Colorado River Commn-Hoover
6.5% due 10-1-09, callable, general obligation
Rated AA by S&P, Aa2 by Moody's
Issue size: $72.31 million; maturity size: $3.93 million

Austin, Tex., Public Improvement
6.125% due 9-1-10, callable, prefunded 9-1-02 @ 100, general obligation
Rated AAA by S&P, Aaa by Moody's
Issue size: $52.49 million; maturity size: $5 million

King & Snohomish Counties, Wash., School District
6.6% due 12-1-10, callable, prefunded 12-1-02 @ 100, general obligation
Rated AAA by S&P, Aaa by Moody's
FGIC-insured
Issue size: $16.15 million; maturity size: $1.23 million

Forsyth County, Ga., School District
6.7% due 7-1-12, sinking fund, general obligation
Rated AA– by S&P, Aa3 by Moody's
Issue size: $19.6 million; maturity size: $6.6 million

Quantifiable Risk Taker—Limited Diversification
Tax-Deferred Account
January 5, 2000

Trade Date	Quantity	Security	Unit Cost	Total Cost	Market Price	Value	Pct. Assets	Yield to Worst
CORPORATE BONDS								
01-05-00	50,000	American Express Cr 6.250 % Due 08-10-05	98.50	49,250	98.50	49,250	7.5	7.64
01-05-00	50,000	Ford Motor Co *Noncallable* 8.875 % Due 04-01-06	106.00	53,000	106.00	53,000	8.1	7.64
01-05-00	15,000	Michaels Stores Inc 10.875 % Due 06-15-06	106.00	15,900	106.00	15,900	2.4	9.60
01-05-00	10,000	Ameriking Inc Sr Note 10.750 % Due 12-01-06	92.00	9,200	92.00	9,200	1.4	12.51
01-05-00	65,000	Worldcom Inc 7.750 % Due 04-01-07	101.25	65,812	101.25	65,812	10.0	7.52
01-05-00	20,000	Sinclair Broadcast Group Inc 9.000 % Due 07-15-07	93.75	18,750	93.75	18,750	2.9	10.21
01-05-00	20,000	Chattem Inc 8.875 % Due 04-01-08	91.75	18,350	91.75	18,350	2.8	10.38
01-05-00	50,000	Nextel Intl Inc 0% to 4-15-03 12.125 % Due 04-15-08	57.00	28,500	57.00	28,500	4.3	15.77
01-05-00	25,000	AMC Entmt Inc 9.500 % Due 03-15-09	89.00	22,250	89.00	22,250	3.4	11.46
01-05-00	50,000	Tele-Commun Inc *Noncallable* 7.875 % Due 08-01-13	101.25	50,625	101.25	50,625	7.7	7.72
		Accrued Interest				7,648	1.2	
				331,637		339,286	51.6	
		Average Weighted Yield	8.93 %					
ZERO COUPONS								
01-05-00	100,000	US Treas Sec Stripped 0.000 % Due 11-15-05	68.00	68,000	68.00	68,000	10.3	6.70
01-05-00	100,000	US Treas Sec Stripped 0.000 % Due 08-15-07	60.25	20,250	60.25	60,250	9.2	6.78
01-05-00	200,000	US Treas Sec Stripped 0.000 % Due 05-15-09	53.25	106,500	53.25	106,500	16.2	6.86
		Accrued Interest				0	0.0	
				234,750		234,750	35.7	
CASH AND EQUIVALENTS								
			CASH	83,612		83,612	12.7	
				83,612		83,612	12.7	
TOTAL PORTFOLIO				650,000		657,648	100.0	

Average Weighted Duration 2.16   (Common Stock, GNMAs & Cash are weighted at 0 years)

211

CORPORATE BONDS

American Express
6.25% due 8-10-05, callable
Rated A+ by S&P, Aa3 by Moody's
Business: Credit card, travel-related, financial advisory, and
     international banking services
Issue size: $100 million

Ford Motor Co.
8.875% due 4-1-06, noncallable
Rated A by S&P, A1 by Moody's
Business: Automobiles and light trucks
Issue size: $250 million

Michaels Stores Inc.
10.875% due 6-15-06, callable
Rated BB– by S&P, Ba2 by Moody's
Business: Retail arts and crafts stores
Issue size: $125 million

Ameriking Inc.   **(No Publicly Traded Stock)**
10.75% due 12-1-06, callable, poison put @ 101%
Rated B– by S&P, B3 by Moody's
Business: Aquires, develops, and operates
     Burger King restaurants
Issue size: $100 million

MCI Worldcom
7.75% due 4-1-07, callable
Rated A– by S&P, A3 by Moody's
Business: Telephone—long distance
Issue size: $1.1 billion

Sinclair Broadcast Group
9% due 7-15-07, callable, poison put @101%
Rated B by S&P, B2 by Moody's
Business: Owns and provides programming for television
  and radio across the United States
Issue size: $200 million

Chattem Inc.
8.875% due 4-1-08, callable, poison put @ 101%
Rated B– by S&P, B2 by Moody's
Business: Cosmetics and toiletries
Issue size: $274.75 million

Nextel International Inc.
0% to 4-15-03, 12.125% due 4-15-08, callable, poison put @ 101%
Rated B– by S&P, Caa1 by Moody's
Business: Wireless equipment
Issue size: $729.67 million

AMC Entertainment Inc.
9.50% due 3-15-09, callable
Rated B by S&P, B2 by Moody's
Business: U.S. theater owners
Issue size: $198 million

Tele-Communications Inc.
7.875% due 8-1-13, noncallable, poison put @ 100%
Rated AA– by S&P, A2 by Moody's
Business: Cable TV
Issue size: $550 million

Average Investor
January 5, 2000

Trade Date	Quantity	Security	Unit Cost	Total Cost	Market Price	Value	Pct. Assets	Yield to Worst
COMMON STOCK								
01-05-00	1,000	Blackrock Advantage Term Trust	9.12	9,120	9.12	9,125	1.8	
01-05-00	500	Independence Square Income	14.75	7,375	14.75	7,375	1.5	
01-05-00	1,000	Morgan Stanley Dean Witter	14.75	14,750	14.75	14,750	2.9	
01-05-00	500	Putnam Master Inter Income Tr	6.12	3,060	6.12	3,062	0.6	
				34,305		34,312	6.8	
CORPORATE BONDS								
01-05-00	15,000	Gulf Canada Resources Ltd 9.250 % Due 01-15-04	101.00	15,150	101.00	15,150	3.0	8.70
01-05-00	15,000	Chattem Inc Sr Sub Nts-Ser B 12.750 % Due 06-15-04	106.75	16,012	106.75	16,012	3.2	8.72
01-05-00	20,000	Occidental Petroleum *Noncallable* 7.650 % Due 02-15-06	99.54	19,908	99.54	19,908	3.9	7.74
01-05-00	30,000	Bankers Trust New York Corp 7.125 % Due 03-15-06	96.96	29,088	96.96	29,089	5.7	7.75
01-05-00	20,000	Dow Chemical Co Debs-Reg *Noncallable* 8.625 % Due 04-01-06	105.44	21,088	105.44	21,089	4.2	7.51
01-05-00	10,000	Burlington Northern Railroad 9.250 % Due 10-01-06	107.69	10,769	107.69	10,769	2.1	7.76
01-05-00	20,000	Lehman Bros Hldgs Inc *Noncallable* 8.500 % Due 05-01-07	102.59	20,518	102.59	20,519	4.0	8.02
01-05-00	20,000	Sinclair Broadcast Group Inc 9.000 % Due 07-15-07	93.75	18,750	93.75	18,750	3.7	10.21
01-05-00	25,000	American Finl Group Inc Ohio *Noncallable* 7.125 % Due 12-15-07	91.79	22,947	91.79	22,947	4.5	8.57
01-05-00	20,000	Time Warner Entmt Co L P *Noncallable* 7.250 % Due 09-01-08	97.50	19,500	97.50	19,500	3.8	7.65
01-05-00	15,000	Household Finance Corp 6.500 % Due 11-15-08	92.43	13,864	92.43	13,865	2.7	7.69
01-05-00	15,000	AES Corp 8.000 % Due 12-31-08	92.50	13,875	92.50	13,875	2.7	9.34

Trade Date	Quantity	Security	Unit Cost	Total Cost	Market Price	Value	Pct. Assets	Yield to Worst
01-05-00	15,000	Seagram Joseph E & Sons Inc *Noncallable* 8.875 % Due 09-15-11	106.03	15,904	106.03	15,904	3.1	8.07
01-05-00	15,000	K-Mart Corp *Noncallable* 8.850 % Due 12-15-11	93.44	14,016	93.44	14,016	2.8	9.79
01-05-00	20,000	Westinghouse Elec Corp-Deb *Noncallable* 8.625 % Due 08-01-12	105.41	21,082	105.41	21,082	4.2	7.94
		Accrued Interest				5,823	1.1	
				272,473		278,297	54.9	
		Average Weighted Yield	8.30 %					

MUNICIPAL BONDS

Trade Date	Quantity	Security	Unit Cost	Total Cost	Market Price	Value	Pct. Assets	Yield to Worst
01-05-00	25,000	Los Angeles Calif Dept Wtr & Power 5.400 % Due 09-01-06	102.09	25,522	102.09	25,523	5.0	4.97
01-05-00	15,000	California St G/O RFDG *Noncallable* 5.000 % Due 10-01-07	100.44	15,066	100.44	15,066	4.0	4.93
01-05-00	15,000	California St Dept Wtr Res *Noncallable* 6.000 % Due 12-01-08	107.19	16,078	107.19	16,079	3.2	4.99
01-05-00	20,000	Puerto Rico Comwlth G/O 5.750 % Due 07-01-09	102.50	20,500	102.50	20,501	4.0	5.24
01-05-00	25,000	California St G/O *Noncallable* 6.600 % Due 02-01-10	111.67	27,917	111.67	27,918	5.5	5.10
		Accrued Interest				1,464	0.3	
				105,084		106,552	21.0	
		Average Weighted Yield	5.10 %					

CASH AND EQUIVALENTS

Trade Date	Quantity	Security	Unit Cost	Total Cost	Market Price	Value	Pct. Assets	Yield to Worst
			CASH	88,137		88,137	17.4	
				88,137		88,137	17.4	

| **TOTAL PORTFOLIO** | | | | 500,000 | | 507,298 | 100.0 | |

Average Weighted Duration 3.47   (Common Stock, GNMAs & Cash are weighted at 0 years)

CORPORATE BONDS

Gulf Canada Resources Ltd.
9.25% due 1-15-04, callable
Rated BB– by S&P, Ba2 by Moody's
Business: Oil exploration and production
Issue size: $300 million

Chattem Inc.
12.75% due 6-15-04, callable, poison put @ 101%
Rated B– by S&P, B2 by Moody's
Business: Cosmetics and toiletries
Issue size: $75 million

Occidental Petroleum
7.65% due 2-15-06, noncallable
Rated BBB by S&P, Baa3 by Moody's
Business: Integrated oil company
Issue size: $450 million

Bankers Trust New York
7.125% due 3-15-06
Rated A+ by S&P, A2 by Moody's
Business: Money center banks
Issue size: $150 million

Dow Chemical
8.625% due 4-1-06, noncallable
Rated A by S&P, A1 by Moody's
Business: Manufactures and sells chemicals, plastic materials,
     agricultural and consumer products
Issue size: $200 million

Burlington Northern Railroad
9.25% due 10-1-06, nonredeemable
Rated BBB+ by S&P, A3 by Moody's
Business: Operates a railroad system in the United States and Canada
Issue size: $275 million

Lehman Brothers Holdings
8.50% due 5-1-07, noncallable
Rated A by S&P, Baa1 by Moody's
Business: Financial services, brokerage, investment banking
Issue size: $250 million

Sinclair Broadcast Group
9% due 7-15-07, callable, poison put @101%
Rated B by S&P, B2 by Moody's
Business: Owns and provides programming for television
    and radio across the United States
Issue size: $200 million

American Financial Group
7.125% due 12-15-07, noncallable
Rated BBB+ by S&P, Baa2 by Moody's
Business: Provides all types of insurance products
Issue size: $100 million

Time Warner Entertainment Co.
7.25% due 9-1-08, noncallable
Rated BBB– by S&P, Baa3 by Moody's
Business: Multimedia entertainment company
Issue size: $600 million

Household Finance Corp.
6.50% due 11-15-08
Rated A by S&P, A2 by Moody's
Busness: Finance—consumer loans
Issue size: $1 billion

AES Corp.
8.00% due 12-31-08, callable, death put
Rated B+ by S&P, Ba3 Moody's
Business: Electrical generation company with global facilities
Issue size: $375 million

Joseph Seagram & Sons Inc.
8.875% due 9-15-11, noncallable
Rated BBB– by S&P, Baa3 by Moody's
Business: Spirits and wine business and entertainment industry
Issue size: $225 million

K-Mart Corp.
8.85% due 12-15-11, noncallable
Rated BB+ by S&P, Ba1 by Moody's
Business: Discount retail business ranges from clothes to small appliances
Issue size: $22 million

Westinghouse Electric
8.625% due 8-1-12, noncallable
Rated BBB– by S&P, Baa3 by Moody's
Business: Multimedia, television, radio, outdoor advertising
Issue size: $275 million

MUNICIPAL BONDS

Los Angeles, Calif., Dept. of Water & Power
5.4% due 9-1-06, callable, revenue bonds
Rated A+ by S&P, Aa3 by Moody's
Issue size: $579.465 million; maturity size: $20.01 million

California State G/O
5% due 10-1-07, noncallable, general obligation
Rated AA– by S&P, Aa3 by Moody's
Issue size: $850 million; maturity size: $76.46 million

California State Department of Water Resources
Central Valley Project
6% due 12-1-08, noncallable, revenue bonds
Rated AA by S&P, Aa2 by Moody's
Issue size: $266.63 million; maturity size: $14 million

Puerto Rico Commonwealth
5.75% due 7-1-09, callable, general obligation
Rated AAA by S&P, Aaa by Moody's
MBIA-insured
Issue size: $538.995 million; maturity size: $28.75 million

California State G/O
6.6% due 2-1-10, noncallable, general obligation
Rated AA– by S&P, Aa3 by Moody's
Issue size: $1.256 billion; maturity size: $62.8 million

Total-Return Investor
January 5, 2000

Trade Date	Quantity	Security	Unit Cost	Total Cost	Market Price	Value	Pct. Assets	Yield to Worst
COMMON STOCK								
01-05-00	1,000	Dreyfus Strategic Governments Income Fund	7.75	7,750	7.75	7,750	1.1	
01-05-00	2,000	Emerging Markets Income Fund	11.75	23,500	11.75	23,500	3.5	
01-05-00	2,000	Global High Income	11.50	23,000	11.50	23,000	3.4	
				54,250		54,250	8.0	
CORPORATE BONDS								
01-05-00	5,000	Wickes Lumber Company 11.625 % Due 12-15-03	85.25	4,262	85.25	4,262	0.6	16.89
01-05-00	10,000	K-Mart Corp Lease Ctf Yld to Average Life 6.000 % Due 01-01-04	84.68	8,468	84.68	8,468	1.3	10.83
01-05-00	10,000	Gulf Canada Resources Ltd 9.250 % Due 01-15-04	101.00	10,100	101.00	10,100	1.5	8.70
01-05-00	15,000	Nortek Inc 9.875 % Due 03-01-04	98.50	14,775	98.50	14,775	2.2	10.32
01-05-00	10,000	Dairy Mart Convenience Stores 10.250 % Due 03-15-04	82.00	8,200	82.00	8,200	1.2	16.33
01-05-00	10,000	Archibald Candy Corp 10.250 % Due 07-01-04	96.50	9,650	96.50	9,650	1.4	11.26
01-05-00	10,000	Leslies Poolmart Inc 10.375 % Due 07-15-04	85.00	8,500	85.00	8,500	1.3	15.06
01-05-00	10,000	Hollywood Entertainment Corp 10.625 % Due 08-15-04	92.50	9,250	92.50	9,250	1.4	12.82
01-05-00	10,000	Nextel Communications Inc 9.750 % Due 08-15-04	103.00	10,300	103.00	10,300	1.5	8.17
01-05-00	10,000	Flemings Companies Inc 10.500 % Due 12-01-04	91.75	9,175	91.75	9,175	1.4	12.81
01-05-00	10,000	WCI Steel Inc 10.000 % Due 12-01-04	101.50	10,150	101.50	10,150	1.5	9.60
01-05-00	10,000	Packaged Ice Inc 9.750 % Due 02-01-05	91.50	9,150	91.50	9,150	1.4	12.03
01-05-00	10,000	Coinmach Corp 11.750 % Due 11-15-05	103.00	10,300	103.00	10,300	1.5	11.03
01-05-00	15,000	K-III Communications Corp 8.500 % Due 02-01-06	98.50	14,775	98.50	14,775	2.2	8.82

Trade Date	Quantity	Security	Unit Cost	Total Cost	Market Price	Value	Pct. Assets	Yield to Worst
01-05-00	20,000	Occidental Petroleum *Noncallable* 7.650 % Due 02-15-06	99.54	19,908	99.54	19,908	2.9	7.74
01-05-00	15,000	Michaels Stores Inc 10.875 % Due 06-15-06	106.00	15,900	106.00	15,900	2.4	9.60
01-05-00	5,000	Iron Mountain Inc 10.125 % Due 10-01-06	101.75	5,087	101.75	5,087	0.8	9.65
01-05-00	10,000	Kaiser Aluminum & Chem Corp 10.875 % Due 10-15-06	100.25	10,025	100.25	10,025	1.5	10.80
01-05-00	10,000	Motors & Gears Inc 10.750 % Due 11-15-06	99.25	9,925	99.25	9,925	1.5	10.90
01-05-00	10,000	Ameriking Inc Sr Note 10.750 % Due 12-01-06	92.00	9,200	92.00	9,200	1.4	12.51
01-05-00	5,000	Central Tractor Farm & Country 10.625 % Due 04-01-07	92.00	4,600	92.00	4,600	0.7	12.32
01-05-00	10,000	Lehman Bros Hldgs Inc *Noncallable* 8.500 % Due 05-01-07	102.59	10,259	102.59	10,259	1.5	8.02
01-05-00	10,000	Sinclair Broadcast Group Inc 9.000 % Due 07-15-07	93.75	9,375	93.75	9,375	1.4	10.21
01-05-00	10,000	Bally Total Fitness Hldgs Corp 9.875 % Due 10-15-07	97.00	9,700	97.00	9,700	1.4	10.44
01-05-00	10,000	Big 5 Corp 10.875 % Due 11-15-07	98.50	9,850	98.50	9,850	1.5	11.16
01-05-00	10,000	Engle Homes Inc 9.250 % Due 02-01-08	90.00	9,000	90.00	9,000	1.3	11.16
01-05-90	15,000	Mastec Inc 7.750 % Due 02-01-08	94.00	14,100	94.00	14,100	2.1	8.80
01-05-00	10,000	Musicland Group Inc 9.875 % Due 03-15-08	92.50	9,250	92.50	9,250	1.4	11.30
01-05-00	15,000	AES Corp 8.000 % Due 12-31-08	92.50	13,875	92.50	13,875	2.1	9.34
01-05-00	10,000	AMC Entmt Inc 9.500 % Due 03-15-09	89.00	8,900	89.00	8,800	1.3	11.46
01-05-00	20,000	Seagram Joseph E & Sons Inc *Noncallable* 8.875 % Due 09-15-11	106.03	21,206	106.04	21,206	3.1	8.07
		Accrued Interest				8,293	1.2	
				327,216		335,509	49.7	
		Average Weighted Yield	10.37 %					

220

Total-Return Investor (continued)
January 5, 2000

Trade Date	Quantity	Security	Unit Cost	Total Cost	Market Price	Value	Pct. Assets	Yield to Worst
GOVERNMENT BONDS								
01-05-00	2,000,000	US Treasury 5.250 % Due 11-15-28	81.58	1,631,600	81.58	1,631,600	241.7	6.70
		Accrued Interest				14,583	2.2	
				1,631,600		1,646,183	243.9	
		Average Weighted Yield	6.71 %					
ZERO COUPONS								
01-05-00	1,000,000	US Treas Sec Stripped 0.000 % Due 02-15-29	15.00	150,000	15.00	150,000	22.2	6.63
		Accrued Interest				0	0.0	
				150,000		150,000	22.2	
CASH AND EQUIVALENTS								
						-1,447,753.85		
						-1,447,753.85		

Trade Date 01-05-00

$2,000,000   U.S. Treasury 5.25 % due 11-15-28
duration 13.612 years
price 81.58, 6.70% YTM

Principal	1,631,600.00
Accrued	16,153.85
Total	1,647,753.85
Deposit 10%	200,000.00
Debit balance	1,447,753.85

Financed at approximately 50 basis points above Federal Funds

Average Weighted Duration 9.13   (Common Stock, GNMAs & Cash are weighted at 0 years)

CORPORATE BONDS

Wickes Inc.
11.625% due 12-15-03, callable, poison put @ 101%
Rated CCC+ by S&P, Caa1 by Moody's
Business: Retail building products
Issue size: $100 million

K-Mart Corp.
6% due 1-1-08, sinking fund, lease certificates
Rated BB+ by S&P, Ba3 by Moody's
Business: Discount retail business ranges from clothes to small appliances
Issue size: $49.296 million

Gulf Canada Resources Ltd.
9.25% due 1-15-04, callable
Rated BB– by S&P, Ba2 by Moody's
Business: Oil exploration and production
Issue size: $300 million

Nortek Inc.
9.875% due 3-1-04, callable
Rated B– by S&P, B3 by Moody's
Business: Manufactures and sells all types of building and
    remodeling products like ventilating products, air conditioning
    and heating systems
Issue size: $218 million

Dairy Mart Convenience Stores
10.25% due 3-15-04, callable, poison put @ 101%
Rated B by S&P, B3 by Moody's
Business: Retail convenience stores
Issue size: $75 million

Archibald Candy Corp.   **(No Publicly Traded Stock)**
10.25% due 7-1-04, callable, poison put @ 101%
Rated B by S&P, B2 by Moody's
Business: Food retail
Issue size: $100 million

Leslie's Poolmart   **(No Publicly Traded Stock)**
10.375% due 7-15-04, callable, poison put @ 101%
Rated B+ by S&P, NA by Moody's
Business: Full-service specialty retailer of swimming pool supplies
    and related products
Issue size: $90 million

Hollywood Entertainment
10.625% due 8-15-04, callable, poison put @ 101%
Rated B– by S&P, B3 by Moody's
Business: Retail—video rental
Issue size: $200 million

Nextel Communications
9.75% due 8-15-04, callable, poison put @ 101%
Rated B– by S&P, B2 by Moody's
Business: Wireless equipment
Issue size: $1.126 billion

Flemings Companies Inc.
10.50% due 12-01-04, callable
Rated B+ by S&P, B3 by Moody's
Business: Distributes food to supermarkets on a wholesale basis
Issue size: $250 million

WCI Steel Inc.   **(No Publicly Traded Stock)**
10% due 12-1-04, callable, poison put @ 101%
Rated B+ by S&P, B2 by Moody's
Business: Produces flat-rolled steel with an emphasis on custom carbon,
    alloy, and electrical steel products
Issue size: $300 million

Packaged Ice Inc.
9.75% due 2-1-05, callable, poison put @ 101%
Rated B by S&P, B3 by Moody's
Business: Manufactures and distributes packaged ice
Issue size: $270 million

Coinmach Corporation
11.75% due 11-15-05, callable, poison put @ 101%
Rated B+ by S&P, B2 by Moody's
Business: Supplies outsourced laundry equipment services for multifamily
   housing properties
Issue size: $296.655 million

K-III Communications
8.50% due 2-1-06, callable
Rated BB– by S&P, Ba3 by Moody's
Business: Specialty magazine publishing
Issue size: $300 million

Occidental Petroleum
7.65% due 2-15-06, noncallable
Rated BBB by S&P, Baa3 by Moody's
Business: Integrated oil company
Issue size: $450 million

Michaels Stores Inc.
10.875% due 6-15-06, callable
Rated BB– by S&P, Ba2 by Moody's
Business: Retail arts and crafts stores
Issue size: $125 million

Iron Mountain Inc.
10.125% due 10-1-06, callable, poison put @ 101%
Rated B– by S&P, B2 by Moody's
Business: Commercial services
Issue size: $165 million

Kaiser Aluminum & Chemical
10.875% due 10-15-06, callable
Rated B by S&P, B1 by Moody's
Business: Produces alumina, primary aluminum, and fabricated aluminum products
Issue size: $175 million

Motors and Gears Inc.   (No Publicly Traded Stock)
10.75% due 11-15-06, callable, poison put @ 101%
Rated B by S&P, B3 by Moody's
Business: Miscellaneous electric products
Issue size: $270 million

Ameriking Inc.   (No Publicly Traded Stock)
10.75% due 12-1-06, callable, poison put @ 101%
Rated B– by S&P, B3 by Moody's
Business: Aquires, develops, and operates Burger King restaurants
Issue size: $100 million

Central Tractor   (No Publicly Traded Stock)
10.625% due 4-1-07, callable, poison put @ 101%
Rated B by S&P, B2 by Moody's
Business: Retail gardening products
Issue size: $105 million

Lehman Brothers Holdings
8.50% due 5-1-07, noncallable
Rated A by S&P, Baa1 by Moody's
Business: Financial services, brokerage, investment banking
Issue size: $250 million

Sinclair Broadcast Group
9% due 7-15-07, callable, poison put 101%
Rated B by S&P, B2 by Moody's
Business: Owns and provides programming for television
    and radio across the United States
Issue size: $200 million

Bally Total Fitness Holdings
9.875% due 10-15-07, callable, poison put @ 101%
Rated B– by S&P, B3 by Moody's
Business: Fitness centers
Issue size: $299.749 million

Big 5 Corporation   (No Publicly Traded Stock)
10.875% due 11-15-07, callable, poison put @ 101%
Rated B– by S&P, B2 by Moody's
Business: Retail sporting goods
Issue size: $131 million

Engle Homes Inc.
9.25% due 2-1-08, callable, poison put @ 101%
Rated B by S&P, B1 by Moody's
Business: Residential and commercial builder
Issue size: $249.67 million

Mastec Inc.
7.75% due 2-1-08, callable, poison put @ 101%
Rated BB– by S&P, Ba3 by Moody's
Business: Designs, builds, installs, and maintains telecom
    equipment and services
Issue size: $200 million

Musicland Group Sr., Sub Notes
9.875% due 3-15-08, callable, poison put @ 101%
Rated B– by S&P, B3 by Moody's
Business: Retail music, home entertainment stores
Issue size: $150 million

AES Corp.
8.00% due 12-31-08, callable, death put
Rated B+ by S&P, Ba3 Moody's
Business: Electrical generation company with global facilities
Issue size: $375 million

AMC Entertainment Inc.
9.50% due 3-15-09, callable
Rated B by S&P, B2 by Moody's
Business: U.S. theater owners
Issue size: $198 million

Joseph Seagram & Sons Inc.
8.875% due 9-15-11, noncallable
Rated BBB– by S&P, Baa3 by Moody's
Business: Spirits and wine business and entertainment industry
Issue size: $225 million

FOR SMALL INVESTORS ONLY

These are the best of times for you. As a small investor with $100,000 or less to invest in bonds, the mutual funds will serve your needs.

If you are in a medium to high tax bracket, you must consult your accountant to determine whether you need all tax-free income or taxable income sprinkled with tax-free income.

Then consult the publications mentioned in Chapter 6 on bond funds and decide how to allocate your $100,000. I think investing in three to five funds is the absolute maximum number. Buy the no-loads that Morningstar, *Forbes,* and *Money* list as their best buys. Make certain that each fund is different from the others in terms of management style, duration, and composition. To own four long-term New York municipal bond funds isn't diversified as far as I'm concerned. Owning a New York tax-free money fund plus short-duration and long-duration New York funds provides a diversified portfolio in my opinion.

If you want taxable money managed by the bond market guru, then invest through a discount broker in PIMCO's Total Return Fund managed by Bill Gross. Most bond professionals believe Bill Gross is the best manager money can buy. However, there's one drawback: PIMCO's Total Return Fund is one of the largest bond funds around and even though his track record is smokin', if investors leave en masse his returns will suffer, too. Having said that, here's what two open-end bond fund model portfolios might look like.

High Tax-Bracket Investor, $100,000 portfolio, all tax-exempt

$35,000 Vanguard Insured Long-Term Tax-Exempt Fund

1. No load

2. Management fee .21%

3. 13 years' average maturity

4. 8.2 years' duration

$60,000 Vanguard Intermediate Tax-Exempt Fund

1. No load
2. Management fee .21%
3. 6.9 years' average maturity
4. 5.3 years' duration

$5,000 Vanguard Short-Term Tax-Free Money Market Fund

1. No load
2. Management fee .20%
3. 40 days' average maturity

All information is subject to change. For investors living in states with high state income tax, like New York, California, and Massachusetts, Vanguard has state-specific funds.

Medium Tax-Bracket Investor, $100,000 portfolio, taxable and tax-exempt with some risk

$50,000 PIMCO Total Return Institutional (must be purchased at a discount brokerage firm; otherwise $5,000,000 minimum)

1. No load
2. Management fee .43%
3. 7.71 years' average maturity
4. 4.61 years' duration

$35,000 Vanguard Intermediate Tax-Exempt Fund

1. No load
2. Management fee .21%

   3. 6.9 years' average maturity

   4. 5.3 years' duration

$10,000 PIMCO High Yield Institutional (must be purchased at a discount brokerage firm)

   1. No load

   2. Management fee .50%

   3. 7.08 years' average maturity

   4. 4.55 years' duration

   5. BB weighted average credit quality

$5,000 American Century Target 2020 (for periodic bets on interest rate decline)

   1. No load

   2. Management fee .60%

   3. 21.01 years' average maturity

   4. 20.99 years' average duration

A FEW WORDS TO CONCLUDE

Most people don't think of the bond market as exciting, but I do. However, I think more and more people are coming over to my side of the fence. The Internet is changing every aspect of the bond market, whether it is access to information, conference calls, bond pricing, or executing trades. This is good news for the individual investor.

At the time this book was written there were almost weekly announcements of more bond information becoming available to everyone over the Internet. For example, the National Association of Securities Dealers (NASD) plans to begin distributing corporate bond prices by spring of 2000 over the Internet. Its website, www.investinginbonds.com, will carry price information from large brokers on corporate bonds bought and sold on a single day.

The future is already present. Some of the outstanding features the Internet will provide you are new issue road shows and the ability to download a prospectus, view the new transaction in detail, and e-mail the underwriter your questions on the new issue. You also have free access to Fitch, Moody's, and Standard & Poor's research. Institutions already can do all of the above; now you're next.

The veil of secrecy over the bond market is slipping and I believe these changes are just the beginning of a process that is empowering the individual investor. It only remains for me to say, "Good luck. Let's show those institutions that whatever they can do, we can do just as well if not better."

INDEX

A

American Century
Target 2020, 229
Target Maturity Funds, 113
Annualized return, calculation of, 60
Ask
bid/ask spread, 147–48
meaning of, 137
Asset-backed bonds, 72–73
operation of, 72–73
Attachment point, catastrophe bonds, 167
Auctions, Treasury securities, 23–24
Average investor
bond portfolio for, 214–19
profile of, 192, 198

B

Back-end load, 98
Barbell strategy, 185–86
Bargaining, with brokers, 148
Benchmark index, rating bonds, 85
Benchmark issues, Fannie Mae, 29
Bid
bid/ask spread, 147–48
meaning of, 137

Bloomberg, 122, 123
Bond Exchange, 149
Bond funds
advantages of, 101–2
closed-end bond funds, 95, 106–8
for high tax-bracket investors, 227–28
versus individual bonds, 100–102
information sources on, 110–13
for medium tax-bracket investors,
228–29
net asset value (NAV), 95
open-end bond funds, 95, 103–6
prospectus, examination of, 101
recommended funds, 113
Rydex Juno bond fund, 163–64
structure of, 94
total return, 97
unit trusts, 108–10
yield of, 95–97
Bond futures, 75–78
risk factors, 78
for Treasury securities, 77–78
Bond portfolio
for average investors, 214–19
barbell strategy, 185–86
buy-and-hold strategy, 183–85
and credit risk, 180
diversification, 183